COME AWAY WITH ME

COME AWAY WITH ME

EDITED BY SARAH MACDONALD

BANTAM BOOKS

SYDNEY • AUCKLAND • TORONTO • NEW YORK • LONDON

COME AWAY WITH ME
A BANTAM BOOK

First published in Australia and New Zealand in 2004
by Bantam

National Library of Australia
Cataloguing-in-Publication Entry

Come away with me.

ISBN 1 86325 457 9.

1. Voyages and travels. 2. Australians – Travel.
I. Macdonald, Sarah.

910.4

Transworld Publishers,
a division of Random House Australia Pty Ltd
20 Alfred Street, Milsons Point, NSW 2061
http://www.randomhouse.com.au

Random House New Zealand Limited
18 Poland Road, Glenfield, Auckland

Transworld Publishers,
a division of The Random House Group Ltd
61-63 Uxbridge Road, London W5 5SA

Random House Inc
1745 Broadway, New York, New York 10036

Cover design by Christabella Designs
Cover image courtesy of Photolibrary.com
Internal design and maps by Darian Causby/Highway 51 Design Works
Internal images from clipart.com
Typeset by Midland Typesetters, Maryborough, Victoria
Printed and bound by Griffin Press, Netley, South Australia

10 9 8 7 6 5 4 3 2 1

Contents

Introduction • vii

IRRIS MAKLER
From Russia with Love, Sweat and Steam • 1

CHRISTOPHER KREMMER
The Global Empire of the Heart • 31

NIKKI GEMMELL
Disneyland Paris: A Notebook • 63

NICK EARLS
A Battle with the English Equipment • 89

TONY DAVIS
Exactly as I Remember • 111

CAROLINE OVERINGTON
Be it Ever so Humble . . . • 131

PETER MOORE
Same Same but Different • 157

ANNETTE SHUN WAH
China Ghosts • 185

TIM ELLIOTT
Sri Lanka • 215

SARAH MACDONALD
Country of Love • 245

About the Authors • 271

Introduction

DOWN A dirt road on the north coast of New South Wales is a place of childhood perfection. I won't tell you where it is, for I still occasionally visit and love it with a possessive ferocity. Lakes of warm water are fringed by grey eucalypts and hairy melaleuca; paths through pockets of temperate rainforest lead to white sand pummelled by wild waves; dirt roads echo with the songs of children. It's a place where it always seems sunny by day and moonlit by night. A place where I will always feel safe and loved.

Every time I walk along a beach, I am transported back to this place and to a time when life was simple and uncluttered. It's as if each wave washes away another layer of hardened adulthood. If I walk for long enough, the years fall onto the sand and I can almost look down to see skinny, scabby, 10-year-old knees.

We all carry within us every travel experience, right back to our first family holiday. So, most travel tales reveal as much about the writer and the life they have lived as about the place they are set. *Come Away With Me* is a collection of journeys to ten very different places, captured by the hearts and minds of ten different writers. Vietnam is seen through the eyes of Peter Moore, a bloke who always seems to attract good luck and then rides it with such serene engagement and good humour that he cannot help but go far and have fun. Nick Earls finds London triggers a wider trip around the extraordinary planet that is his mind. It's a tour of a universe of emotion, including pain, regret, embarrassment, fatigue, loss and obsessive thoughts about Kmart sex. Only Nikki Gemmell could possibly find that Dumbo, Tinkerbell and Mickey Mouse trigger the musings of Leo Tolstoy and Denise Levertov, while teaching her that the joy of a place can be in appreciating the passion it instills in others. I find at this time in my life I cannot clearly relive the many places I have been. Utterly absorbed in new motherhood, I find it impossible to transport myself out of the country of love, bewilderment and frustration I've discovered, but realised I can never conquer.

When anyone travels, they are, to some degree, transported beyond the routines and rituals of everyday existence. As Irris Makler says in her story about Russian steam, sweat and love, the traveller is 'fresh minted with each exchange'. This means we mutate in order to absorb more of a new place. For Irris this means getting nude and letting two strangers beat her – nearly giving her a heart attack. In Christopher Kremmer's fictional journey through Portugal, the characters dye their hair when they cross a border. This adoption of a new identity liberates one of them enough to embrace the risks of doomed love but it cannot withstand the threats brought about by the proximity and constancy of companionship with friends. Christopher's story will bring back horror moments for many travellers when they recognise those fractious alliances that form on the road. Weeks of waiting in Sri Lanka transform Tim Elliott's desire for adventure into a risky search for knowledge.

A stranger in a strange land spends much time and energy trying to come to some sort of understanding about that land. Yet this is always a slippery goal. Preconceptions are often shattered; Tim will never look at a monk in the same way again and finds the more he learns the less he knows. Landing in a place you've long dreamed of visiting can destroy fantasies. Annette Shun Wah cannot begin to discover her China until she exorcises the ghost of the country that haunts her heart – a ghost created by her father's story of a place that that cannot exist today. She then battles to understand a land that is a part of her in the way that an appendix is part of a body. Tony Davis searches for the 'real' Japan; a Japan as he needs it to be and, of course, can find only fleetingly. He comes to understand that memory can be the only preservation of place.

Much of the understanding a traveller gains about another land comes by living the little intimacies of life and adopting the etiquette of a culture. In her story Caroline Overington takes on the pleasure of parading around in her underwear in high-rise New York and then learns to squelch through the flooded, goblin-infested corridors of her underground flat. Intimacy can come in the new tastes, sounds and smells of a place and the fleeting but sometimes acutely enlightening connections we make with others along the road.

In reality, travel can make a person feel elated, enraptured and fulfilled. It can also bring up feelings of anxiety, loneliness and isolation. Yet every journey offers a pathway to understanding that is always (even if only in retrospect) worth making. Sharing the stories of others is a less rigorous (but hopefully as rewarding) process. While you will take journeys through emotions, thoughts and feelings in this book, you will also meet the man who is fleecing Donald Trump, discover the danger of the South-Asian dinner party, learn what Marlon Brando really meant when he talked about 'the horror' in Vietnam and find a new use for kitchen implements.

If Nick Earls is right and ideas travel better than we do, then you've picked the right way to travel!

Enjoy as you come away with us.

Sarah Macdonald

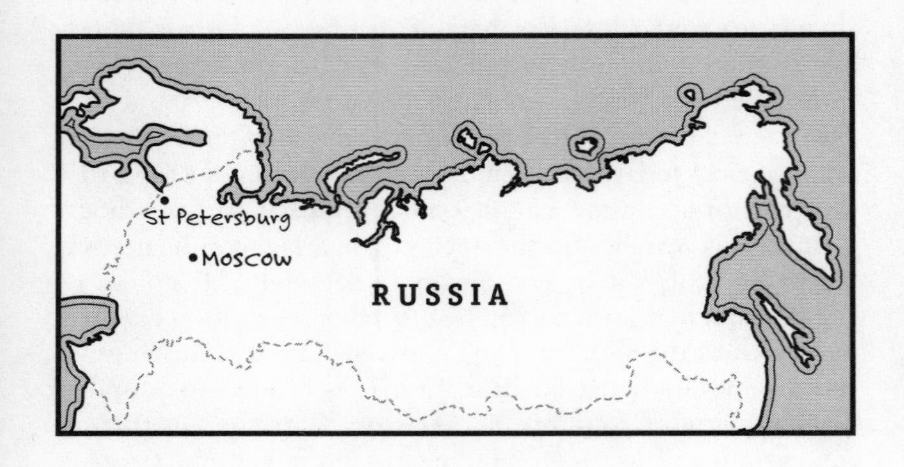
St Petersburg
Moscow
RUSSIA

From Russia with Love, Sweat and Steam

IRRIS MAKLER

STEAM

THWICK, THWACK

The first time I hear the unmistakable sound of birch twigs hitting bare skin – once heard, never forgotten – one woman is standing over another and whacking her repeatedly. She traces the shape of the prone woman's body with two bunches of twigs, making a sound like a rattlesnake; there's an audible frisson before she whacks her again.

Thwick, thwack

The birch comes down. The beating goes on. The woman holds a bunch of twigs in each hand. She raises them above her head, crossing them over theatrically, and lowers them to hit her friend again. It is like watching some strange version of flamenco, performed nude, in clouds of steam.

The women are partially obscured by vapour, but I can see that the one lying down is slender and the one doing the whacking is solid and determined and putting all her energy into the task, despite the fact that it is more than 45 degrees Celsius in here and we are all slick with sweat.

The other thing I can see, as I perch carefully on superheated slats of wood, is that although both women are naked, they are wearing pointed woollen caps on their heads. They look like goblins. Goblins trying their hands at S and M.

'Didn't you bring a hat?' The whacker turns to me, shocked. She pauses with the bunches of twigs above her head like castanets. I almost expect her to throw back her head and let out a Spanish wail before she launches into the next round. 'If you don't cover your hair it will dry out,' is the last sentence she throws my way. The steam billows behind her and she holds her pose for 10 seconds more, concentrating, before returning to her task.

I am naked, and have never felt more so – *imagine, coming to a sauna without a hat!*

The two women – whacker and whackee – aren't as shocked at this social solecism as they could be, because they've already had to help me earlier with bathhouse etiquette: I am plainly a foreigner on her first visit to Moscow's oldest and most famous steam bath, Sandunovski's Banya.

Sandunovski's has been a public bath since 1790. It's a Moscow institution in the heart of the city, only 15 minutes' walk from the Kremlin. That's in summer. In winter, everything takes more time. The snow sits heavily on the city. You can't rush through the slippery white streets, as the risk of falling is too great.

It's winter when I set out on my first visit, so I catch the Metro, the underground train system that is one of the jewels of Moscow and possibly the most beautiful underground rail network anywhere in the world. All the station names are written in Russian, so, like a small child on her first day alone on public transport, I count them out to make sure I get off at the right stop. My destination is Kuznesty Most station, a confection of grey, pink and white marble. On the long escalator ride up to the surface, I pull on my gloves, taking care not to drop the map that an American friend has drawn on the back of an envelope for me, with the street names written in Russian and English.

The area immediately outside the station is grimy and dark. Broken pavements poke through grey snow, and crowded stalls sell pirated CDs and fried sausages and hamburgers – or 'gamburgers', as the Russians call them, since they have no letter for H. (This can lead to misunderstandings. There is the popular children's book *Garry Potter* and the evil totalitarian leader Adolf Gitler.)

But once I struggle out of the station area, hoping I've taken the right turn, Romantic Russia reasserts itself. Snow is falling on wide, grand streets where graceful buildings are painted in pastel colours, their curlicues and gargoyles picked out in darker shades. The windows and fretwork are individually lit, lending the street the feel of a stage set. It's so cold it hurts to breathe.

The snow swirls past signs in Cyrillic, a magical script still mysterious to me, with letters like Christmas decorations. I look up and slowly read out loud, one letter at a time, till I finally make out the name of the street. 'Ulitsa Neglinnaya,' I recite triumphantly.

The area has remained unchanged since it was built hundreds of years ago, when Russia was a confident kingdom and no one dreamt that Communism would take over this sleepy white land and turn it Red. Three streets away there is still a statue of Lenin, striding towards revolution. Lenin seems to be in a hurry in every statue – his coat billowing behind him, his hand pointing forward, a whirlwind captured for an instant in stone. Even when he's sitting down, he's in a hurry to think.

Busts of Marx and Engels adorn buildings close by. Russia vowed that Communism would bury the West. But today in this square the bust of Marx is dwarfed by a billboard of an androgynous boy wearing a Carmen Miranda hat with multi-coloured fruit and flowers. It's an ad for a Xerox colour copier, one of many Western products to have flooded into Russia since Communism collapsed. The funky Xerox boy looks out suggestively from under his hat, as if he knows it's Marx and Lenin who've been buried, now no more than relics of that other, incomprehensible time, when workers were going to rule the world.

Now this glamorous old Moscow street has reverted to the rich. I trudge through the snow past the Reserve Bank, a beautifully maintained building painted yellow and white, undergoing yet another expensive re-fit. A glittering sign on the roof proclaims 'Centralni Bank', in old Slavonic lettering, another nod to history. Armed guards stand outside, as with many other businesses here, but the snow makes everything magical, unifying the street and its past.

As new flakes flutter down, I almost believe that a horse-drawn carriage will turn the corner and a Russian count will step down. Maybe he will turn to his beautiful countess, swathed in furs, and help her down too, and together they will sweep past me and the armed guards into one of these grand buildings, to attend a party held by the Czar.

I smile at this image as I walk up a hill and left into a small side street, the snow squeaking underfoot like sand. 'Sandunovski Street'. The street is named after the bathhouse, I realise, when after only five minutes of careful reading I pronounce the word in Russian.

I feel as proud as the ancient explorer who first crossed Siberia. I've made it – on my own. Australian crosses Moscow in winter and Survives!!! Now I'd better just make sure the great explorer locates the women's section of the bath-house . . .

It turns out there are two women's sections, Upstairs and Downstairs, and just like in Olde England, Upstairs is more expensive. I decide Downstairs will do for this first venture and I enter a steamy female world with very strict rules.

'Dyevushki – spaarom!'

'Girls – steam!' bawls a huge, naked woman stomping out into a large elegant room decorated like a 19th-century railway carriage with long mirrors and leather booths lit by side lamps. The pictures are the only feature spoiling the elegant tone. They're photos of the film stars who frequent the men's Banya. Beefy men with paunches and gold chains, posed in groups, holding up vodka glasses and smiling at the camera, revealing mouthfuls of gold teeth. At first glance they look like mobsters. They certainly wouldn't get a go on 'Neighbours'.

I'm shepherded to a long leather seat by an attendant who speaks no English. We pass the photos and the shouting naked woman who looks par-boiled. Her face and many rolls of fat are red and her expression is stern, but her announcement galvanises all the women relaxing on their seats. As if someone had called 'Surf's up!' at Bondi, the women jump up, troop into a large tiled room with pools and showers, and queue outside a closed door. Old and young, fat and thin, they stand patiently. Naked women, all wearing woollen caps. Orderly but determined goblins.

You can see they used to queue for food in Soviet times, I find myself thinking, as I fall in behind them, until I realise with a start that one of the goblins is talking to me. It's odd how you don't expect anyone to be talking to you if you don't know their language. This woman has actually been addressing me for some time, and she seems very concerned about something. I explain that I don't understand Russian and the women hustle someone down from the front of the queue to translate. My interpreter turns out to be a beautiful supermodel type with a perfect body and dark hair tucked up under her goblin cap.

'This woman is asking, *Didn't you bring honey???*' The supermodel translates, adding all the emphasis in case I missed it in the Russian.

I confess that I didn't bring honey. When this is translated back into Russian, the first woman is shocked. They have another concerned exchange and the supermodel turns back to me.

'She says, What will you put on your face? You need to protect your skin.'

The concerned woman offers me some of her own honey. She has brought it from home in a small glass jar with a peeling pickle label. She unscrews it for me and sniffs, gesturing for me to do the same. I inhale appreciatively and so does Masha the supermodel.

'She says, It's good – it's from her own bees. It comes from her *dacha*, that is her country house.'

My benefactress, Lena, is in her fifties and is a contrast to the willowy Masha in every way. She is short and stocky and cheerful, a standard Russian grandmother except that she has had a breast removed. It is hard not to stare as a woman with only one breast offers you a pickle jar full of honey. But Lena possesses the two qualities that I will come to love about Russian women over the next three years of visiting this steam-bath: she is innately generous and utterly unself-conscious about her body.

Everyone wanders around naked at Sandunovski's Banya. There is no undressing under a towel, no folding your arms over your rolls of tummy fat or skulking around with a towel barely covering your ripply hips. These women drop their clothes as soon as they enter and prance about, eating, laughing and talking. They parade their flawed bodies: fat, thin, wrinkled, sagging, blemished or with a breast removed. It's a temple to imperfection and I am hooked from this first moment.

Lena extols the virtues of her honey, which smells like wild flowers overlaid with pickles, while Masha the supermodel continues to translate. For someone so gorgeous, Masha is very patient. Her hair may be covered with a woollen goblin cap, but her face gleams with something more Christian Dior than pickle jar. She is about to tell me what when the door opens and it's every woman for herself. The orderly queue disappears as the women rush in, armed only with loofahs in the Battle for the Best Spot.

The heat hits me like a brick. I follow the crowd up tiled stairs into a large open sauna area with wooden benches. It's so hot the air throbs, and the steam makes it painful to breathe: the reverse experience of inhaling outside in the cold. I am forced to put my (uncovered) head down and squint to cope with the wall of heat, while groping sideways for a seat.

An oven by the wall is the source of the heat, so I sit as far away from it as I can. Lena and Masha sit closer. They chat with each other from time to time, but it takes all of my energy to focus on not fainting.

The oven is stoked by the fleshy woman who called us in. 'Her bark is worse than her bite,' says Masha. The large woman works in tandem with a tiny, tautly-muscled woman with rippling abs and calves. They are the Laurel and Hardy of the Banya.

'Now this little one, she is VERY strict – she's from the Bolshoi Ballet,' Lena tells me proudly.

'Shhh,' someone else hisses, 'this is the First Steam. There is no talking.'

The rules are very intricate. There is no talking or pounding with birch leaves until we have gone out and returned for the Second Steam. It seems that during the Second Steam, like the Afterlife, anything is possible.

We stay in the wooden room until we are the colour of lobsters. Which for me takes about 30 seconds, though I try to tough it out as long as my newfound friends. When I feel I am about to pass out, they finally indicate they've had enough. I run out ahead of them. It's time to undergo the essence of the Banya experience – the make or break moment that lets you know whether or not this is for you.

Lena and Masha fill buckets with icy water. I watch with

interest until they throw them over me. One from each side. That's what new best friends are for. As the liquid snow hits my boiling skin I fear – no, I am certain – that my heart will stop. I feel like a cooked lobster who's been dropped into freezing water. Just to make sure there's no life left.

I gasp, a sound repeated all over the white-tiled room. Along with the *thwick thwack* of birch leaves, that yelping intake of breath is the second characteristic sound of the Banya. Minus 20 degrees outside, where this water comes from, plus 40 inside where we've just been – it's like being attached to a defibrillator. Only I haven't had a heart attack. Yet.

Maybe this will bring one on. I feel my heart contract, but once I realise that it won't actually stop beating, I become strangely energised. Like so much in Russia, it's the extremes and the contrasts between them that make you tingle. Lena tells me that this combination of hot and cold is good for you as well. 'Very good for your health, very good.' The men drink throughout their visits to the Banya, but the women warn that it's not ideal to mix this process with alcohol. Lena makes one concession. 'Well, a little vodka maybe . . . a little bit can never do you any harm. It's medicinal, you know.'

Lena and Masha look at me expectantly. 'Another bucket?'

Whatever it takes to become accepted in this strange, steamy, female world, I vow I will learn the rules.

I'm living in Moscow as a foreign correspondent, which means I'm part tourist, part resident – a permanent itinerant in search of an anchor. Russia is a different world – or so it felt from the moment the plane first touched down at Sheremetyevo Airport. It was minus 10 degrees Celsius the day I arrived, and the snow on the tarmac made it look as if the steppes reached all the way to Moscow. Gazing out of the aeroplane window, I felt desolate. *What have I done?*

I endured the bureaucratic ordeal of Sheremetyevo, where they treat you as a potential importer of nuclear weapons rather than a visitor, my passport finally being reluctantly stamped by an official wearing a flat, Russian military cap, medals shining on his chest. Welcome back to the Cold War. I was ferried to an expensive hotel in central Moscow owned by the Chechen mafia. The hotel gangsters didn't really help me to settle in.

It's a search for a sense of belonging that has sent me out on a cold evening, to find something essentially Russian that I can adopt – and maybe that will adopt me too.

Just to show they understand and want to help me fit in, Lena and Masha lift another wobbling bucket of freezing water and tip it over me. I give that involuntary gasp – *Christ that's cold* – though this time the feeling that I am certain to die passes more quickly. It's a medium-sized jolt instead of shock therapy. As I shake the water off, I suspect that this thrill of survival and revival could become addictive.

Suddenly Lena is concerned again. She says something in Russian which sounds harsh, but Masha translates as, 'Didn't you bring coffee?'

I am about to smile, but even Masha's beautiful face is troubled. I confess in a more sorrowful way, suitable to the gravity of the omission, that I haven't brought any coffee. They both sigh.

Lena scolds me – kindly – for my lack of preparation. She pulls out another pickle jar, this one filled with Nescafé. Obviously you couldn't bring coffee in its own jar. Maybe one day I'll learn why.

Lena rubs the Nescafé over her body in swirling black arcs. She explains with hand actions that coffee is an exfoliant. The idea is slightly perverse and the smell is great, somehow unexpected in this gleaming white environment. Soon the top half of Lena's body is brown, including her chest where her breast is missing, and she indicates that I should use her coffee too. I hesitate for a moment, because I have nothing to offer her in return, but Lena is so exuberantly generous and so insistent that I am soon rubbing her coffee granules all over myself.

I like the crunchy feeling but it melts easily, and I see that Masha is using a different concoction. Unlike her small pot of Christian Dior Something Expensive, this also comes in a glass jar from home.

'I have mixed coffee beans and kasha – it is grains, like wheat, very popular to eat for breakfast here. Then I grind them together. Please to use also.' She offers me her homemade exfoliant. It feels rougher and grittier than the Nescafé and I decide that I like it better.

When we are covered in coffee and grains, we move towards the showers. They are running full pelt and no one bothers to turn them off when they are finished. I ask why and the women appear baffled. 'Why you worry? Someone else will use.'

This is very different from Australia, I tell them, trying to explain about drought and the importance of not wasting water, as the coffee and kasha swirl down the drain. I turn off the shower, out of habit, and they indulge me as you would a batty old relative. Lena rubs her fingers over my shoulder to indicate that my skin is smoother. I try too. She's right. We both smile.

Lena is by now calling Masha 'Mashinka', a Russian endearment meaning 'little Masha'. As a sign of respect, Masha is more formally calling the older woman by her patronymic, 'Lena Andreyevna', meaning 'Lena, daughter of Andrey'.

They are from very different social strata. Masha is young, beautiful and wealthy. She works for a Western company and, more importantly, has a wealthy boyfriend, who, she proudly tells me, is a 'biznyessman'. In Moscow, that covers a multitude of sins. Lena is older, much poorer and recovering from a serious illness, and she mentions a standard-issue drunken-wastrel husband. But for a short time none of that seems to matter as they introduce a new person into the world of the Banya. They become Lena and Masha, Torchbearers of Female Knowledge.

I feel like a religious initiate, learning the first phase of the secrets, which the Raiders of the Lost Ark will one day come to seek. I smile involuntarily at the thought of Harrison Ford in the women's Banya, but I just know this is a joke that won't translate.

'Now, we go back inside for the Second Steam,' says Lena, opening the heavy wooden door.

I guess this means some beating should now be possible.

'I have left my birch leaves in water, to soften, so now they will be ready,' says Masha. 'You can use them too,' she smiles her Supermodel smile. 'We will hit you,' she promises.

It sounds more sincere with her Russian accent: 'Ve vill heet chou.'

This is turning out to be the most wonderful evening, I think, as she disappears before me into a cloud of steam.

The Banya is my induction into Moscow. It isn't simply that I feel cleansed and revived – which I do – or that the pedicures are unbeatable – which they are. Falling in love with this traditional pastime somehow eases me into Russian society, making me feel that on some level I fit into this perplexing 'other' place, maybe even that I belong.

I soon get to know Alla, the woman in charge. She always smiles, happy to see me, one of her regulars; concerned if I've been away for a while.

'Where have you been this time? Not Afghanistan again? Australia? Very good! And how is your lovely country? Your family must have been happy to see you.'

Our conversations become longer as my Russian slowly improves. I speak very haltingly and talking to me has all the pleasure of conversation with a six-year-old child, but Alla pretends not to notice. I chat to her before unpacking my things, now bringing my own honey and coffee in small glass jars. I mark my acceptance into Moscow by these small steps.

Russian women come to the Banya with their friends, and sometimes their daughters, laughing loudly as they order pickles and salami from the Banya restaurant. It's usually accompanied by the house specialty of refreshing herbal tea with lemon, and occasionally a little vodka, because a little can never hurt . . . They drop their clothes, put masks on their faces, conditioner – and often eggs – in their hair and sit back and enjoy themselves. Steam and laughter provide a respite from the harsh world outside.

On one visit, I plonk my things down onto an empty seat and return from the steam room, the regulation over-boiled crimson, to find myself encircled by five Georgian and Armenian women. I climb between them and sit surrounded by shrieking laughter, wobbling flesh and vast quantities of food. They don't need to order from the Banya restaurant as they've packed their own picnic, a feast of Georgian delicacies. They bring out platters of fruit and vegetables, plump grapes and apricots and figs, tomatoes with coriander and purple basil, followed by mounds of roast chicken, fresh bread and bowls of Georgia's most famous dish, slices of fried eggplant rolled up and stuffed with walnut and garlic paste.

'You must eat with us,' one of my neighbours offers. 'You can't come to the Banya and not eat!'

I accept the generous offer from this group of strangers. They work at Moscow's largest market, selling jewellery, and invite me to come and see their wares. 'Please promise you will come! Of course we will give you a discount.'

I tell them that my first and only visit to these markets involved buying a Red Army watch which started losing time within 12 hours and lost its minute hand, with a definitive clunk, by the next day. They shriek with laughter.

'Ah, that sounds like Slava – we won't let you buy from him again,' they promise comfortingly.

Then, as a sign of true Banya closeness, they offer to try to get my money back. Or maybe I would prefer a new watch?

I tell them it's fine, and that not everything I bought was bad. The Russian dolls were great. They were updated versions of the *matrioshka,* where a large painted wooden doll contains many smaller ones. I bought a set with President Putin on the outside enclosing five previous Communist leaders including Lenin and Stalin. There was a set with all the Simpsons inside a big Homer, and – possibly my favourite – the British Royal Family *matrioshka*, where the Queen contained Charles, Diana and Dodi, and the smallest doll was the burning car.

To enjoy the Banya properly, you have to go with a friend, because beating with birch twigs is something you can't really do to yourself – or not at a tempo to do you any good. Now I often go with my American friend Eve, who has been working as a journalist in Moscow for five years. She has a Russian grandmother and her family spoke some Russian at home, but Eve is a quintessential California girl. One generation in the west-coast sun seems to have bleached out all the *Russky* heritage.

Eve drew the map on the envelope for my first visit, and teaches me more Banya lore.

'Wet steam is better for you than dry, which is why people here prefer a steam bath to a Finnish sauna,' she says knowledgably, sitting inside the steam room, naked except for a cream goblin cap with 'Sandunovski's' stencilled on it in blue.

'And the proper way to use the birch twigs, the *veniki*, is to hit along the body, but AWAY from the heart.' She moves the dense steamy air as she demonstrates. 'You improve circulation by doing it, and you increase the heat at the same time.'

The feeling is pleasant and not remotely painful as the wet birch comes down on my arms and back, the leaves trailing their scent behind. Then Eve changes the rhythm, beating along my body at an increasing pace, from the soles of my feet to my neck. It is fragrant and invigorating and I want to sign up for flamenco afterwards.

We return home bubbling with enthusiasm and send along our male friends – various boyfriends, husbands and colleagues – but it's not as big a hit with them. Some like it, but most don't. I've noticed that men never seem to enjoy environments where they are naked together quite so much. 'I did feel great afterwards,' one Australian journalist explains, 'but being naked with all these thugs walloping each other, and then drinking more vodka and then walloping each other again – it wasn't really for me.'

But it remains popular with the gals. Another personal milestone is the first time I drive to the Banya – me, driving in Moscow! I don't have to consult a map anymore, and I park not far away, outside another grand building, the rococo blue and white architecture school. Unfortunately this turns out to be an illegal spot, and when I return to the car, a parking policeman is nearby. He sees his prey, and comes up rubbing his hands with glee.

Traffic infringements in Moscow tend to be settled by on-the-spot fines, enraging drivers and keeping the traffic police happy and well-fed, since the fines take the form of a cash bribe.

'Well, *dyevushka,* why have you broken the law in this terrible way?' the policeman begins his routine rouble-extraction speech.

Dyevushka means girl and is the standard form of address for any Russian woman you don't know – until she is venerable enough to merit the title *babushka*, grandmother. When I first arrived, this 'Hey, girl' used to drive me spare, but I've been here long enough that I don't waste time feeling insulted.

Instead, I launch into a convoluted explanation in bad Russian of how I didn't realise it was illegal and was only away for a short time. Things are looking grim until I hit on the magic words: 'I was just going to the Banya.'

The traffic cop surprises us both, himself as much as me, by forgoing his dosh and letting me off.

'Oh, to the Banya . . . well, off you go, but don't do it again.'

And it's a sign outside the Banya that makes me feel I've finally made it into Russian society. I'm driving there looking for a parking spot, when I notice that stencilled on the wall are the words 'Parking for Clients of the Banya only.'

That certainly applies to me, I think proudly, my jars of honey and coffee clanking in my bag. I'm no longer an Australian battling to master Russian and scrabbling to find a toe-hold on the edges of Moscow life. I am a Client of the Banya.

I am very pleased with myself as I gaze at the sign. The spot is right outside the Banya, and it's legal, making me even more smug, although parking here requires reversing uphill in a narrow lane. As I start this complicated manoeuvre, a huge black Landcruiser with black tinted windows bears down on me. In Hollywood these cars belong to the studio execs; in Moscow to the mafia. Turns out I'm not quite as savvy a Muscovite as I thought, since I decide I want to fight them for my spot. *I'm a Client of the Banya and I was here first*, I think, in my 'fair go, mate' kind of way.

Just before I start playing Russian roulette in earnest, I glance in the rear-view mirror and see two huge men jump out of the Landcruiser in giveaway gangsters' gear – closely shaven heads, black leather jackets, their guns plainly visible as they start running towards me. I look up to see three more identical black cars with black windscreens in the tiny street ahead of me – *where did they come from?* – and six more identically dressed and armed men standing on the pavement.

It seems I've arrived just as some mafia boss wants to come in for some off-duty whacking – hopefully, birch leaves only.

In the face of his overwhelming fire-power, I abandon my silly Australian ideas about who was here first and scurry down the hill as quickly as I can. I park and walk back up to the Banya. *That was a close shave!* I have to weave in and out among the 10 bodyguards now cluttering up the pavement, talking to each other through their earpieces and giving me dark looks. Two reach for their guns, but their boss calls them off.

'Naah, she's just going to the Banya.'

That's right, I'm just going to the Banya. I saunter by, bursting with pride. *It's obvious, even to gangsters.*

I never do learn which VIP was going into the men's section. Just another Client of the Banya . . . Why shouldn't the mafia stay clean too?

It takes all types, I think, saying hello to Alla. She smiles her lovely welcoming smile and comes over to see how I am.

SWEAT

When you live away from home, there is no bar where everyone knows you because you've been drinking there for 10 years; no café where you read the papers on Saturdays, and they bring your coffee the way you like it without you needing to order; there's no one who's been a friend since childhood. You're fresh minted with each exchange.

This has pluses, but the edges of your personality can get blurred when you're away for a long time. Doing familiar things in unfamiliar surroundings helps you to retain a sense of identity. Playing cricket or painting – in Vienna or Venezuela or Vladivostok – reminds you who you are.

I like exercising, so I look for a gym to join – and learn a lot about Russia in the process. The first one I try is a proper Communist outfit with threadbare carpet, peeling paint and antique Soviet dumbbells. There is a queue for two exercise bikes and a 1980s step machine. The gym's main selling point is that it's incredibly cheap.

The second is the in-house gym at the Chechen mafia hotel where I stay when I first arrive in Moscow. It has more equipment than the first gym, but there are no classes or instructors and everyone working there tends to grunt at you. But it's close to the office, so even though I don't much like it there, I stay on. Then the hotel closes the gym for six months for repairs, unfortunately the day after I've paid them to renew my subscription. Guess they just forgot to tell me. While I'm hunting around for where to exercise next, my friend Eve discovers *Planyeta Fitness*. 'It will change your life,' she promises, carting me along to inspect her lavish new find.

From the moment I see the purple 'Planet of Fitness' sign above a grand old Moscow house, painted pink on the outside, its inside gutted and fitted with mirrored studios in pale wood, I am overwhelmed. It has an utterly non-Russian feel. In fact it's so chi-chi and Western, it's like a mirage. Or maybe a visitation from another *planyeta*?

There are hundreds of running machines, bikes and weights, classes for boxing, Pump and yoga, a swimming pool, a crèche and two cafés. 'And it's open 24/7,' Eve sighs ecstatically, as if either of us has a burning need to exercise at 3 am. A woman passes us wearing a T-shirt that says 'Believe in miracles, but don't rely on them'. Back downstairs we find that there's the added Moscow touch of armed security guards and sky-high fees. A casual visit costs 80 dollars – more than a doctor or a soloist at the Bolshoi theatre earns in a week. Probably more than any of the women working front of house or stoking the oven at the Banya earns in three weeks.

Only a tiny sliver of the population can afford to exercise here. The *Novi Russki*, as Russia's new rich are known, are often old Communists who were in the right place at the right time to profit from the collapse of the Soviet Union. Plant managers who suddenly ended up owning the whole factory after the bodgy privatisations of the early 1990s – which most Russians still describe bitterly as outright theft. Or businessmen who bought monopoly industries for a fraction of their value from the Communist Party bosses who ran them. They both got rich – the Party hacks had mastered the rules of the free market sufficiently to make sure they received a slice of the action in return.

Oh, and mobsters too, of course. The first thing you need when the economy is in freefall and national assets are up for grabs is muscle – that's how gangster capitalism works. The shaven-headed thugs from Russia's *maffiya* are instantly recognisable in the Planyeta Fitness weights room.

I join immediately. It almost bankrupts me but I can't resist – and it turns out to be the best exercise I ever get, anywhere in the world.

On my first day, I luxuriate in being able to choose between more than 20 treadmills and climbing machines. A heavy-set, pock-marked man in his fifties is on the treadmill across from mine, sweating heavily. He has dark hair and pasty skin and is plainly suffering. One glance reveals he's a gangster. Can't get away from them. On the next treadmill along there's a gorgeous 20-year-old blonde. Her perfect body is encased in white lycra, and in case that isn't shiny enough, she gleams with stuck-on spangles: a heart on her shoulder, a dove on her ankle and a few non-defined shapes sprinkled across her collarbones. The transfixingly beautiful girl runs listening to a walkman, working hard without raising a sweat.

I don't realise they're together until the gangster almost falls off his machine. The lithe blonde instantly hops off hers and lovingly wipes his sweaty face, holding him up as he collapses against her. It's so nice to see a mafia boss spending time with his girl.

The manager comes by and asks me how I am enjoying myself. Alexandra Orgutsova is also tiny but perfect, with the muscle-to-fat ratio of a natural athlete. You can't exercise your way to looking like her: you're either born that way or you're not. She has a winning smile, and speaks English, so I tell her the truth – 'I like it very much' – but can't resist asking about the clientele at Planyeta Fitness. She looks across at the blonde nymph still holding up her gasping 50-year-old boyfriend, and says demurely, 'Our clients are mostly businessmen and housewives.'

I've never seen housewives like them. Head-turning gangsters' molls and models, who lope in on slinky stilettos, clad in Versace and loaded down with gold jewellery. The colours are gaudy and the patterns clash: checks, stripes, houndstooth, birds, horses, horseshoes, and logos, logos, logos, all swirling together. In summer there are acres of bare skin, and no one seems to wear any underwear – where were these babes hiding during Communist times?

Then women aspired to be engineers and road workers. Photographs from the Soviet Party congresses show pudgy ideologues with their hair in buns, wearing horn-rimmed glasses and elastic-sided sandals with socks. You still see them on the bus, including the one I caught to get here this morning. But inside Planyeta Fitness, it's perfect bodies with all-over tans, even in the middle of a Russian winter.

And, like at the Banya, the Planyeta Fitness change rooms are crammed with women who never seem to get dressed. They do their hair and make up naked, sitting at the mirrors for hours wearing only high-heeled sandals. And perhaps one gold anklet. I go out to exercise and when I come back 90 minutes later, the same girl is sitting in the same position, minutely examining her perfect face and languidly applying another coat of mascara. Being gorgeous is obviously a full-time job.

If those security guys downstairs were smart they'd figure out a way to get some closed circuit cameras in here. Hmm.

Since this is Russia, they probably already have. I wouldn't be surprised if we were being beamed out live on the Internet, and it serves you right, I think uncharitably as I watch a woman wrap her taut, brown, muscly legs in gladwrap. She wants to lose more weight while she exercises, and at the end of this amazingly complex operation, she looks like a frozen, fat-free chicken.

'Have I missed anywhere?' she asks, turning around to survey her perfect butt.

I'm one of the gym's few Western clients, usually professional women with flat shoes and cellulite. We instantly stand out amid the 'new Russia' glittering and prancing all around us. These rich, freakishly gorgeous women don't pay any attention to us – we aren't in their league – and they start giving me a complex. Who are they, so different from all the other women I know in Moscow? My Russian teacher and my producer and office manager have moderate figures and hard lives. Better-paid women in broadcasting or business jobs don't look like the gym girls either. No one does, except in pockets of Hollywood.

When I'm around the corner one night after midnight, I come in to see if anyone does actually exercise here during the wee small hours. The girl behind the desk looks up from her book and hands me a towel.

'No thanks – I just want to know if there is anyone here.'

She looks bemused and goes back to reading.

I go upstairs. Most of the gym is empty. There are three men and one woman – a reversal of the daytime ratio.

The woman is pumping iron as enthusiastically as if it weren't – I check my watch – 1.30 on a Saturday morning. Kristina is an ex-model who's joined Planyeta Fitness this week, and says she's thrilled to find a gym where she can exercise after midnight.

'I have no time during the day, you know, I have so many meetings,' says the red-headed 30-something. That's meetings with friends. Kristina – the girlfriend of a Moscow banker – doesn't have a job.

'No, but today I was busy windsurfing. I was out on the river all day, so I didn't have time earlier. I have to come here now.'

She adds, between squats, that another reason for the late visit is that she went out for dinner tonight – and ate dessert. 'I like sweets, you know, "no honey, no funny", but now I have to pay for it.'

She has a great body, but says her boyfriend told her she needed to lose a bit of weight. They were his last words tonight, before he went home – to his wife.

Kristina looks sad for a moment, then shakes her sleek head and goes back to working out.

So that's what's really going on. There's always a story behind squats at 2 am. At least she's spending her night alone in a stylish location.

I ask Kristina if it's important to be beautiful. She looks at me as if I'm mentally defective.

'Of course.'

She has the added pressure of being six years older than her banker boyfriend. She *has* to stay in shape.

'Maybe I'm falling in love with him. Maybe he will leave his wife. He wants children, but she doesn't. She's a career woman,' Kristina spits the description out disdainfully.

Kristina is divorced, with a four-year-old son, Mikhail. She doesn't have to go home to him because he is spending summer in the country with his grandmother – her ex-husband's mother. Kristina says that though she doesn't know her mother-in-law well at all, she has sent Mikhail away to her for three months. She stops to pull out a photo wallet and shows me a picture of a small blond boy with wide Russian cheekbones, squinting at his mother in the sun.

'He looks very sweet,' I say, though I can't help adding that in the West we wouldn't send a small child away for such a long time.

Kristina looks at the photo for a moment longer, then goes back to her squats, and I let her. While young stud bankers who pay your bills don't grow on trees, Kristina is starting to depress me. And I need some sleep. I'm coming back for a class in the morning and exercise at Planyeta Fitness is not for the faint-hearted.

The routines they teach may be Western, but the instructors here are Russian – and it quickly becomes apparent why this country produces so many Olympic gymnasts. The instructors are ferocious. They want that 100th repetition and they're going to get it. There's no interest in protecting your knees or your spine. There's none of the mantra of the Western gym: 'If you feel any pain in your back, just stop for a while.' Here, it's '*Now, do another 100.*' This is the take-no-prisoners, we-can't-be-sued method of staying in shape. '*Now another 100.*' Basically, it's the battle of Stalingrad.

'Is it good or bad? It's simply the Russian way,' says the manager, Alexandra, showing how she stays a slender size 6 herself.

And it seems to work. Even if you find yourself crippled, you'll be a cripple with firm thighs. My friend Eve says, 'I've gone to gyms for years, and nothing much has happened. But here – I'm actually losing my butt. You know, I'm going to miss my butt when it's gone.'

Gangster's moll or merchant banker, in Russia or in the West – who could resist that?

LOVE

Eve is on a mission for self-improvement – well, at least she intends to get thin. She's been infected by Planyeta Fitness. She's slimmer and stronger than when I first met her, and can lift staggeringly heavy weights in a gruelling floor class and then still have enough energy for a 45-minute bike ride. She tries to push me into becoming as fit as she is.

'Just come and do some spinning,' she wheedles, after we've completed a weights class and are standing, sweating, outside a dark room with blaring music and riders in lycra astride their stationary bikes. 'Even 20 minutes will be good for your legs.'

I deline but then Eve finds us another local treasure.

'You lose weight through massage – all the Russian girls do it.'

I've never heard of anything so unlikely – or so inviting. And since Russian deep tissue massage is the Eighth Wonder of the World, I'm happy to give it a try. In Moscow, the masseurs come to you. You provide the oil and they do you on your dining room table, which feels strangely illicit.

But Galina is so popular that you go to her. Her apartment is in an old Art Deco building in the centre of the city, midway between two Moscow landmarks, the Foreign Ministry and the Hotel Ukraina, Gothic piles built by Stalin in the 1950s. It's BYO oil with Galina too, but she provides her own instruments of torture to dissolve the fat.

At first meeting, Galina doesn't look like the type to achieve the ultimate magic and Make You Thin. A large-breasted, sturdy woman with strong hands, she laughs a lot but you can see in her face that she's had a tough life. I will soon learn about it as we exchange confidences in what turns out to be the best part of the deal.

Galina is a gifted masseur, with a healer's hands. She also works on your cellulite, enthusiastically poking and prodding you with a succession of plastic kitchen implements. One is a food processor attachment for kneading dough, about the size of a fist and with five rounded spokes; another is a small suction cup. I never learn what its original purpose was but Galina now pounds and scrapes both of them up and down women's thighs in her anti-cellulite assault course. It is incredibly painful at times, but at least you feel that it's worth it, for surely no fat could survive that.

'It has been shown to be effective,' Galina promises at the end of the first session. 'Try not to eat white bread and you should also exercise.'

Galina may talk the slimming talk, but it soon seems to me her heart isn't in it. Russian generosity and love of plumpness are in conflict with her war on lard. After the first session of pummelling she offers me tea and sweet biscuits, 'to revive you'. She frowns when I say I don't want sugar in my tea. This is my kind of diet massage.

I take the lazy approach. A massage every now and then to ease my conscience. Eve is more committed.

'If you don't do it four times a week, it's a waste of time. Tell Galina you want more appointments.'

Four times a week is yielding results for Eve – or something is. 'I'm using anti-cellulite creams as well – but I haven't told Galina, I don't think she believes in them.'

I don't believe in them either, but Eve is definitely losing weight. Over sweet tea with lemon, Galina confides that she's worried that Eve is melting away under her hands.

'It's not right. She is too thin. Her boyfriend will say "Where has my girl gone?"' Galina laughs, shaking her whole frame.

You have to love such an ambivalent slimming guru.

We send Eve's boyfriend along because he has back pain, and I suspect that Galina promises him she will go easy on Eve, so that he'll have *some* of his girlfriend left.

I keep going because Galina is a great masseur and I enjoy listening to her. And maybe I am getting just a little bit thinner.

There is something of the confessional about Galina's room, which is actually her living room with a massage bed stuck under the window. In summer the light is grey-green, filtered through the birch trees outside. In winter, when the trees are bare and the ground is covered in snow, the light is paler but still conducive to confessions. The room has an old upright sofa and a grandfather clock which chimes erratically. Plastic bags are lined up against the wall where Galina's regulars leave a change of clothes. There is also a tape recorder on which Galina plays Russian pop songs.

Sometimes she plays the radio. Once, I recognise a 1980s hit by Sting. I listen to his beautiful ballad about the Cold War, ending with him questioning whether Russians love their children too. Did we really think that, I wonder with Galina's hands on my neck. How had we reached the stage of believing that other human beings didn't love their children? It's wonderful to be here now that that time has passed and we can see each other just as people – happy, sad, successful, angry, talented, spiteful, small-minded, big-hearted *people* – once more.

Galina tells me about her husband. She divorced him many years ago, but has recently taken him back because he has been diagnosed with cancer.

'Someone has to look after him,' she says, 'and I think it is the right thing to do. Maybe God will reward me. Do you ever think like that?'

The Communists tried hard to eradicate God, but without much success. I tell Galina that I seem to have less faith in God than she does and ask her about her life as a young girl in Soviet times. Like many here, she found things easier then, though she has done relatively well out of the post-Soviet reforms. She's an independent businesswoman and her clients include foreigners and famous Russian actresses. I meet some of the most popular women from the Moscow stage on my way in and out.

Massage has also taken her places. She's travelled to Europe to give lectures and instruct in salons there. 'I went to Venice,' she tells me. 'Oh it was so beautiful, like a fairy tale. You can't believe that people live like that all the time.' Her eyes are shining.

Galina reached this point via an unorthodox route. She studied geography at university in Moscow in the seventies.

Many describe this as the best period during Soviet times, since the murderous convulsions of Stalin's era were over and there was a bit more money in the system. Life was grey but predictable. People owned apartments and televisions, and some even managed to buy cars, when their name came up on a list.

After graduating, Galina landed a job mapping the far reaches of the Soviet Union. She was away from home for months at a time, seeing Russia's vast empire and producing maps that remained classified for years. (The Soviets didn't even print maps of the Moscow city centre, in case they fell into enemy hands. This probably didn't make much difference to the CIA, but certainly made life more difficult for Russians who just wanted to get across town.)

But after Galina married and gave birth to a daughter, she realised that this lifestyle was no longer practical. With characteristic initiative, she retrained as a masseur. Retraining is a common feature of post-Soviet life – everywhere you meet engineers who drive cabs, scientists who work as bankers. One of my favourite Russian cameramen told me he was actually a neurologist. Since we were in a war zone at the time, this was comforting news. 'Oh good, you'll know what to do if one of us gets some shrapnel in the brain.'

Galina put her heart and soul into her new career, studying for six years.

'Six years!' I exclaim, 'You could have been a doctor!'

This is the wrong thing to say. Galina is hurt.

'This massage is medicinal you know. And,' Galina uses the word that Russian professionals most value, 'it is also *scientific!*'

She rubs my feet to show me how well-rounded this massage is. 'These pressure points come from Indian massage, and there are other components from all over the world.'

I try to mollify her. As we discuss life and especially love she relents. I can tell I am forgiven when she looks up from the pressure points on my feet and asks, 'Do you believe in Fate?'

Only a Russian could inject so much meaning into this question. Fate – *sudba* – was one of the first words I learnt in Russian. Hello. Goodbye. Fate. It's an important concept, explaining the inexplicable, reassuring everyone in this country with its cruel history that suffering is destined, written in the stars. So I know this is not a simple question and that an important confession is coming. You have to open up when discussing Fate. I tell Galina about my true love; she tells me about hers.

'He was also a geographer,' she says dreamily, pausing to look out the window, the grey-green light falling on her face. *He was also a geographer* – who would think that a love story could start like that? But I know better than to smile, and as her hands sweep up my back, the lovely Russian phrases about love pour out. She tells me about the trembling beginnings and the painful end.

'He was married, of course, so it had to end, but even now all these years later, I know I couldn't bear to see him. He rang on my birthday last year. I could hardly speak.'

This vulnerability is so out of keeping with Galina's tough exterior. Love softens us all . . .

The room is quiet, and her hands on my shoulders are sad.

So I measure out afternoons with Galina, her hands healing, her words soothing and fascinating in turn. She becomes a surrogate mother, a local who is on my side in this large, unfriendly metropolis, until the time comes for me to leave Russia.

I'm no longer a complete outsider, terrified that the steppes start at Moscow. Now I know my way around the Metro without a map, and recognise gangsters and politicians, and know that sometimes the two are the same. At the open air vegetable market, the Chechen woman who sells fresh herbs always saves me a bunch of basil. The Russian women have my jar of homemade yoghurt waiting when I walk up, and let me taste their fresh honey, on a twist of paper, straight out of the jar. I have favourite museums and concert halls and cafés. And friends.

Galina is one of the people I am saddest to leave behind. I go to see her after my final trips to the gym and to the Banya. When the time comes to say goodbye we are both in tears. I am flying away back to the ease and opportunities of the West. She is remaining to cope with the uncertainty and danger of life here, where people sigh and say they have been buffeted by 'too many revolutions'.

'*Nye pasledni ras.*' We exchange the lovely Russian farewell: 'It is not the last time we will meet.'

She looks at me thoughtfully and says, 'No, it won't be. I feel that too.'

We stand at the door of her apartment. Her last wish for me is '*Bolshoi lyubov*' – a great love. Even as she nurses a dying man she no longer cares for, trying to earn Brownie points in heaven, she romantically hopes for better for me.

I went to Galina looking to get thin. I found something better.

Galina is sending me away from Russia, with love.

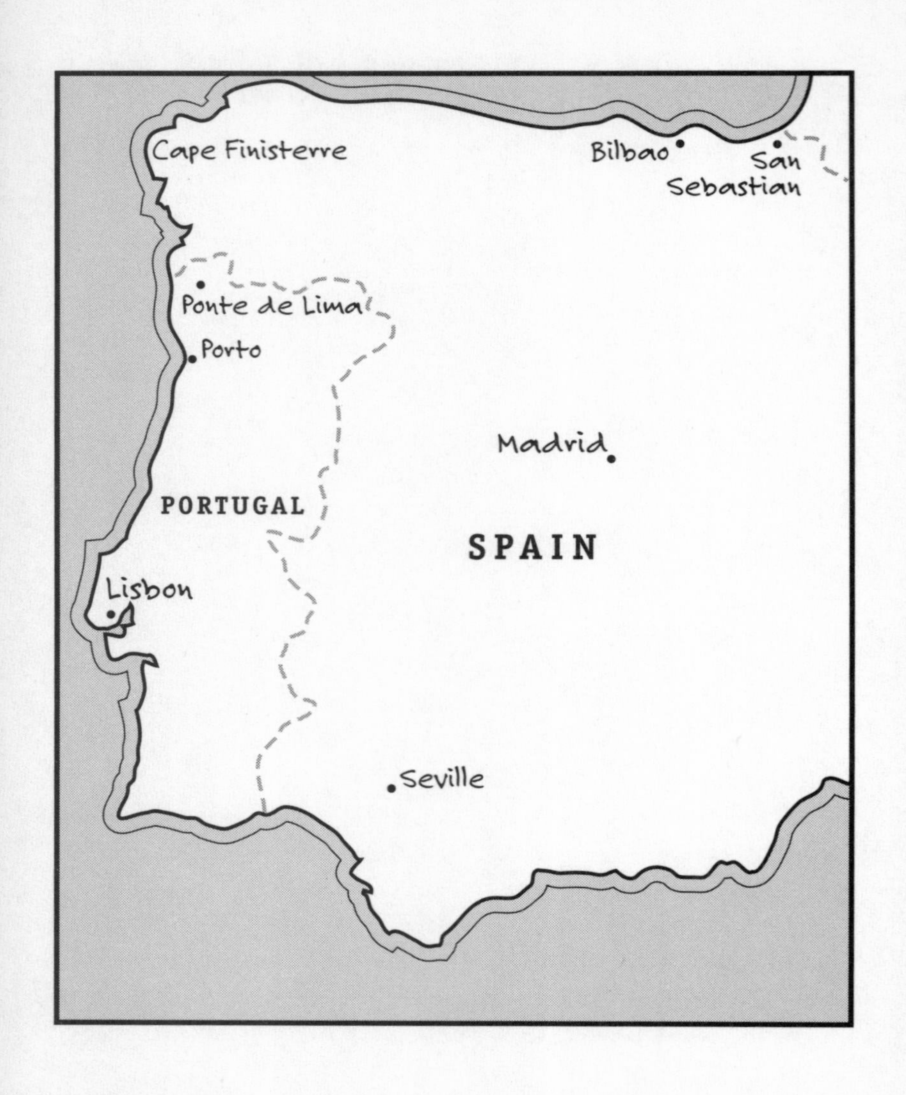
Cape Finisterre
Bilbao
San Sebastian
Ponte de Lima
Porto
Madrid
PORTUGAL
SPAIN
Lisbon
Seville

The Global Empire of the Heart

CHRISTOPHER KREMMER

IT RAINS almost every day for ten months of the year in north-western Spain. The Costa del Muerte (Coast of Death) is emerald green, but treacherous to shipping, and even at the height of summer the Atlantic waters are chilly. The people are deeply, some would say darkly, Catholic, and live in moss-covered stone houses. Millions of pilgrims flock there each July from all over Europe to visit the shrine of a saint beheaded in the third century.

We had driven from Paris on a whim, wrongly assuming that in July anywhere on the Iberian peninsula would be carefree and sunny. Just as my French fiancée and I were preparing to leave the capital for six weeks over summer, an old friend had accepted an open invitation to visit us. Mark, who had recently broken up with a girlfriend in Australia, had scraped together just enough money for a plane ticket to Europe. So, rather than leaving him alone in the apartment, we drafted him into our quest for a beach in Spain. We launched ourselves bellies-first, eating and drinking our way through the Loire Valley. Then, one very merry night in Bordeaux, Danielle decided to change her hair colour to claret in honour of the local reds. Accepting her dare to join in the makeover, we departed for Spain the following morning, Mark as darkly continental Marco, and me, Roberto with Alsatian blond flecks.

We were crossing borders, swapping identities, escaping the everyday. There were surfers in the bay in sunny San Sebastian, raising hopes that soon we would be lazing somewhere quiet, further west along the coast. Somehow the surfers' wetsuits managed to escape our attention. An hour beyond the seaside resort, the geographic and historical realities began to sink in. Driven from one benighted village to another by incessant rain and swarms of overwrought pilgrims, we realised that there would be no beach in Spain, at least not the kind we were looking for. Our holiday mood was quickly evaporating, replaced by a growing friction between Mark and Danielle. In Bilbao, when she had tried to help navigate through the wet and gloomy industrial city, Mark took issue with her choice of route, stabbing his finger impatiently at the map and countermanding her instructions. Then, her habit of reading aloud from guidebooks began to irritate him, and he became a cruel mimic. Finally, in the pilgrimage town of Santiago de Compostela – after an argument about the plight of the Palestinians – Danielle had a teary fit, accusing Mark of anti-Semitism. Caught in the crossfire, I hunched over the steering wheel and drove in a panic towards Portugal.

Phantom holiday brochures haunted my imagination: 'See Europe, and destroy your relationships,' they read. The constant need to smooth things over and avoid fresh hostilities was exhausting enough, but the prospect of having to choose between my two closest friends mortified me.

'That boy needs a woman . . .' Danielle fumed in our hotel room in the Spanish border town of Túy on the night of Mark's *intifada,* '. . . and if things continue like this, so will I!'

Descended from a long line of advocates, Danielle was the first daughter in her family to be admitted to the French equivalent of the bar. Her zest for wine, food and adventure concealed a calculating mind and a fiery temper. She had built a career by using the former, and controlling the latter, but she hadn't met many of my old Australian friends. Since school, Mark and I had been more than just friends. Ours was a club to which no one else was admitted. We spoke a cryptic language that only we understood, only we found amusing. In our twenties we had assumed that we'd become famous writers or actors, famous somethings. But the years passed and it didn't happen. Mark settled into a hand-to-mouth existence as a casual teacher of English to migrants and refugees while I learnt French and joined an international firm of accountants. Mark trudged through a thicket of disastrous affairs: I met Danielle. While previous partners had puzzled over my loyalty to Mark, she knew him only as my most reliable and entertaining correspondent, a status he maintained as other friends disappeared off the radar.

Over breakfast on the terrace of our hotel, high above the Rio Minho, I launched a peace initiative. The Mediterranean beaches of the Algarve were too crowded and too far away, I told my troubled travelling companions, yet to turn back was an even less appealing prospect. We were in too deep, with no option but to unite and press on into northern Portugal. Across the river, the cannon and battlements of the Portuguese town of Valença sneered at us. For centuries its stubborn inhabitants had been punishing invaders from France and Spain. In the 1880s, Gustave Eiffel forged a truce of sorts, building a bridge over the river at Túy. But his Puente Internaçional, a grimly angular structure of grey steel lattice, lacked the grace of his famous tower. Rather, it resembled one of those Bailey bridges used by armies during invasions – not the best look, given the history of the area. Yet the bridge marked a turning point in our struggle, and as the car rattled across it, the clouds quite literally parted, and a blaze of sunshine poured through Eiffel's iron armature. Finding nobody on the Portuguese side to whom we could surrender our passports, we misread the map and turned left into the mountains, rather than right down the coast.

Big adventures often turn on small mistakes, and by the time we realised ours we were deep in a landscape of plunging valleys and terraced hills. The small farm plots were tightly cultivated with oranges and figs, olives and maize, and cabbage patches sprouted under grapevine trellises. Long-horned cattle grazed at the verges, and octogenarian women rode in ox carts. On a sunny Sunday morning, the villages we passed could be distinguished by the tone of their church bells, the size of their haystacks and the number of dogs slumbering outside their cafés. It was as if summer had a border, and the season only existed across the Minho. After a week of futile trawling along a dismal coast, we had stumbled into the heart of a gentle country. It was Spain with a machismo bypass. For 500 years, the Portuguese had turned their backs on Europe, preferring Asia, Africa and the Americas, and their explorers, traders, missionaries and colonists fanned out across the oceans, winning plunder and glory. But the thrusting ambition that won Portugal an empire was long gone, and the empire itself had shrunken back to the core, and would soon be a mere province of the European Union.

According to Danielle's guidebook – and for once, Mark didn't snipe at her reading – we were heading towards the valley of the River Lima, reputedly the most beautiful in all Portugal and marked by an 'air of sleepy indifference to the wider world'. Celtic fortresses still crowned many hills, and Roman milestones marked the roads. In 135 BC, a legion commanded by Decius Junius Brutus had mutinied on the southern bank of the Lima, refusing orders to cross over. So beautiful was the shallow stream that the soldiers believed they had reached the Lethe, the river that in Roman mythology marks the boundary between this world and the next. Heaven and Hell awaited them on the other side, and anyone who drank from the river would forget his earthly life. Terrified, the troops hesitated. With his career on the line, Decius seized the standard and plunged in alone. When he called to his men by name from the other side, they realised that this was only an earthly paradise and marched on. A bridge across the river in the town of Ponte de Lima marked the spot where the spell had been cast and broken.

Danielle spotted it first, a series of arches in stone, toiling in gently magnifying repetitions across glassy, slow-moving waters. Five of the original Roman arches had survived, the rest having been added later to replace fallen ones. It was an understated structure, no great leap of faith being required to span this broad, shallow stream, just a steady incline to the middle, collapsing in unhurried steps to an equally unhurried town on the other side. Beneath the bridge, women carrying head-loads of laundry trailed across the sandbanks, dumping and scrubbing at the water's edge. An open *praça*, or square, linked the town to the river, the square surrounded on three sides by restaurants and cafés. Along an avenue of sycamores that followed the riverbank, we found our way to the covered terrace of the Restaurant Encanada, where we ordered lunch and watched the laundry drying in the warm mountain air.

I can't remember which came first – the soup or the women. The *caldo verde* – a cabbage and potato broth – came with a slice of sausage and nutty maize bread; the women came in a gust of perfume and chatter. They smiled at us politely and seated themselves a couple of tables away. Asking Mark to pass the bread – and not getting a response – I saw him staring at one of them, a tall, pretty brunette in jeans, sunglasses and a bright red top. She was regaling her companions in Portuguese with some anecdote that they all found highly amusing. Now and then, she would glance across to our table, where Mark sat transfixed, apparently unable to take his eyes off her and oblivious to my repeated demands for bread.

'Danielle,' he said in a distant voice, still looking at the Portuguese women. 'What do they drink here?'

Consulting her Michelin Guide, Danielle quickly found the answer.

'*Vinho verde*,' she said, archly raising an eyebrow in vindication at finally being consulted. 'Green wine. They drink it young; slightly acidic and effervescent.'

'Order two bottles of it, will you.'

'No worries, *mate*,' she said in a fake Australian accent that – combined with her haughty summons to the waiter – was as implausible as it was humorous.

When the wine came, Mark asked the waiter to deliver one of the bottles to the women's table, a grand gesture that elicited thanks in three languages. Only the woman in red – the one with the wedding band, the one he was interested in – said nothing, nodding and smiling graciously at us instead. But Mark wasn't finished yet.

'To your beauty,' he said, raising his glass to her only.

They hadn't heard that line in Ponte de Lima since the Romans, judging by the chorus of playful 'oohs' and 'ahhs' that rose from the girls' table. Remarkably – at least, I found it remarkable – it worked. Soon, the woman who had inspired it was standing beside our table.

'May I?' she asked in English, taking a chair, and a discernible radiance took its place at the table. 'Welcome to Ponte de Lima,' she said, and on *her* lips, it became a single word: *PON-tuh-day-LEE-muh*.

Sophia Rodriguez was a fair-skinned descendant of the Celtic tribes who had dominated the Iberian peninsula before the arrival of the Romans. She was intelligent and vivacious, but not onerously so, wearing her qualities with a casual, earthy elegance and possessing a throaty laugh that was almost bawdy. When she apologised for her English, Mark took his cue, offering his expertise to make her more fluent. She was dropping her aitches, he told her, a problem he could fix easily.

'So you are an English teacher? 'Ow wonderful,' she said, stealing glances at his dyed black hair.

Sophia, it transpired, ran the Biblioteca Publica Municipal, the town's archive and library. It was housed in a watchtower, a remnant of the old Roman walls, she told us. Their festive lunch was to farewell two staff members who were taking leave over summer. Among the archives' holdings, she mentioned casually, was the original royal charter granted to Ponte de Lima by Queen Dona Teresa in 1125.

'We 'ave so many scrolls and parchments written in Latin, and only a few of us to take care of them,' she said, playfully seeking sympathy.

Again, Mark volunteered his services.

It was impossible to tell whether the warmth of Sophia's welcome was just part of the local culture or something more specific, but Mark's reaction to her was unmistakable. He was lonely and, I suspected, rapidly getting bored in the company of a middle-class Parisian couple. Still, I was shocked by the sudden reminder of how quickly he could monopolise a woman's attention. The intensity and directness appealed to their vanity, or so I told myself. Having been sidelined on countless occasions, I knew better than to try competing with him, and instead occupied myself by squeezing olive pips off the balcony. Soothed by this inane pursuit, I had forgotten all about them until one of the pips landed in the ear of an elderly gentleman strolling along the Alameda, and I had to pretend to be listening again.

'Do you like to swim?' I heard Mark say. 'We're looking for a nice beach, not too crowded. Can you recommend anything?'

'Of course,' Sophia said. 'You should try the Costa Verde. It's not far from here.'

Had she suggested surfing on the River Lima he would have nodded no less eagerly. They took a decade to say *adeus*.

When Sophia returned to her colleagues, Mark called for the

bill – that was a first – and he lagged in the cobbled streets on the way back to the car, looking somewhat dazed by it all. It *was* another world, seductive enough to halt a Roman legion. Danielle, too, was unusually quiet, but I had learned not to underestimate that silence. She was hatching something. Sure enough, as the Renault clambered over the bridge towards the onion-domed church of San Antonio de Torre Velha, she swivelled in her seat, feigned a coquettish smile, and said to Mark:

'She liked you, lover boy.'

He so wanted to believe it.

'I suppose I have you to thank for that,' he said, tousling his hair and laughing for the first time since Bordeaux.

'No, honestly,' Danielle persisted. 'She *really* liked you.'

Where the River Lima meets the Atlantic in a tangle of docks at Viana do Castelo, we turned right and headed north along the Costa Verde. The afternoon had turned muggy so, rather than waste it, we'd decided on a swim. The coast between the Minho and Lima rivers forms a chain of dunes and beaches, some despoiled by railway lines, casinos and slapdash housing, others pristine and surrounded by farmland. Choosing a turn-off at random, we followed a crippled lane that squeezed between dry-stone walls delineating a swathe of small agricultural plots, then rose into a pine forest and came to a dead end at a lighthouse. The view stretched down across cornfields to where a crumbling fortress defended a crescent of sand and ocean. To our north, Cape Finisterre, the western extremity of continental Europe, recalled our troubles in Spain. But we had triumphed over geography and affirmed the essential truth of travel: you *can* leave your troubles behind – at least some of them. The simple act of grabbing our towels and running down the rocky track to the beach felt like victory.

I'd been meaning to have a word with Danielle about something, and the water seemed a good place to do it. It was cold in, and Mark fled within minutes, wandering off alone up the beach and disappearing around the point. Danielle, who was a strong swimmer, stroked evenly through the surf, daring me to follow her. We'd been missing our privacy, and when I caught up with her, the warmth of her kiss made my teeth stop chattering.

'That was cruel,' I said.

'Really?' she replied.

'Not the kiss.'

'Then, what?'

'Why did you tell him she liked him?'

'It was obvious. She was smitten.'

'Obvious?'

'Yes. It was the black 'air. Irresistible,' she said, backstroking away from me with mischief on her lips. 'You boys need *much* more romance in your lives.'

Provoked, I chased her back to the beach.

We had been lazing amorously for a couple of hours and were beginning to wonder what had happened to Mark when, from the forest skirting the lighthouse, there came a buzzing sound like a chainsaw. Looking up, we saw him at the top of the trail, perched regally on the pillion seat of a small motorcycle. The bike was piloted by a man half his size and twice his age, wearing a helmet like the ones they give cannonball daredevils. They were bucking and lurching down the track, then got stuck behind a peasant's ox-drawn cart. After much probing and tooting, the harassed farmer pulled over, allowing the bike to squeeze past with a spurt of acceleration and a few fishtails, delivering Mark to the beach.

'Allow me to introduce you to a local identity,' he said, getting off the bike with conscious fanfare. 'Danielle and Robert – meet Senhor Grillo!' Sheepishly, the tiny man with stubble-clad cheeks removed a black cloth cap and bowed his head with a muffled '*Bom dia*'.

'Senhor Grillo is the keeper of the lighthouse that you see on the point above us,' Mark said.

Then, as if by prior arrangement, he smiled at his new

friend. 'In English, his name *Grillo* translates as . . .' and they both raised limp hands in front of their chests and cried, 'Grass 'opper!' in unison, before collapsing in laughter.

As Grillo fell against me, wiping away tears of hilarity, my nostrils were filled with a pungent odour. He reeked of alcohol.

'We've just had a few *vinho verdes* at the local *cervejaria*,' Mark said. 'Grillo's found us a house.'

Mark's offhand way of announcing it didn't fool me. He was obviously feeling very full of himself.

We had passed the house on our way to the beach. It resembled a stone and glass bunker dug into the hillside on the forest fringe, probably quite contemporary when it was built, by my guesstimate, in the sixties. Fallen pine needles matted the rocky terrace and there were no outdoor tables or chairs to suggest recent habitation.

'*Alugar-se* (for rent),' said Grillo, smiling as he fumbled with a hefty key set while we peeked though the windows.

The door gave an arthritic crack and he beckoned us to follow him inside. In a spacious living room, a stone fireplace commanded the attention of some distressed leather sofas, and wicker baskets overflowed with old copies of *National Geographic* and *The New Yorker*. An expanse of checkerboard floor tiles led to a well-worn dining table for 12, and a gangway like the ones used to board ferries rose steeply to an enclosed mezzanine above the living room. A half-flight of stairs led from the dining room to a country kitchen, bathroom and several bedrooms crammed with bunks out back. Climbing the gangway, past framed posters of retrospective exhibitions at the Tate and other London galleries, I entered the master bedroom. It was a quiet space of meditative stillness, furnished austerely under an exposed timber beam roof. A small writing desk looked out across the pine tops, and a locked wooden sea chest branded with the initials 'R.A.L.' stood at the foot of the bed.

When I went downstairs, Mark and Grillo were waiting in the living room. The fortified Portuguese was teetering in his cups, counting his keys as if he'd lost one.

'Well, what do you think?' asked Mark.

'It's comfortable enough,' I said, determinedly non-committal in the face of his enthusiasm.

'They want ten thousand *escudos* a week.'

'That's reasonable . . . Does he own it?'

'No, he's just the caretaker. It belongs to the family of some dead Portuguese writer. They're in Lisbon. Should we take it?'

The easy flow of blessings ever since we'd entered northern Portugal was creating the illusion of speed. Only that morning, we had actually discussed abandoning the trip and returning to Paris. Now, the bad weather and bad blood of Spain had evaporated, replaced by good fortune. Only Mark's careless comment – that we had found paradise without a guidebook – recalled the tensions of the road journey. When Danielle emerged from the back of the house she was beaming.

'This place is *fantastic*,' she said, wide-eyed with wonder. 'When do we move in?'

Then the fog horn sounded its warning.

Lighthouses are lovely, sirens less so. While the *farol* at Sargaço crowned the point with its noble white pillar, its grumpy horn lurked in an ugly concrete block on the edge of a nearby cliff. The siren would be our constant companion during the coming weeks. An alarm would trip if Grillo was away for more than four hours and, given the lighthouse keeper's gregarious personality, this happened quite often. Frequently, the siren would wail on a perfectly clear day. However, the shipping authorities and people of the nearby village seemed unperturbed by this eccentricity. From that afternoon onwards, Grillo moonlighted as our providore, showing up at the house unannounced with cans of olive oil, armfuls of dried cod, loaves of flour-dusted maize bread, bags of vegetables and fruit and, later, mail. Contrary to regulations, he smuggled us into the *farol* for night-time viewings, and in his spare time showed me how to catch bass off the beach. He was, at all times of the day and night, happily drunk or drunkenly happy. It was difficult to tell which.

Although the gold, spices and slaves of a far-flung empire had at one time made the Portuguese monarchy the richest in Europe, the people of the north – the *Minhotos* – still eked out a living from tiny landholdings, pooling their oxcarts and labour during the planting and harvesting seasons. Conservative, devout and deeply superstitious, they celebrated feast days in honour of rodents, so that the mice might spare their granaries, and left certain sacred hills untilled in the hope that others would remain fertile. The local church, where navigators had once been blessed before setting off in their *caravels*, now dispensed the same blessings to fishermen, and the cemetery was fragrant with the scent of candle wax and freshly cut flowers. The local grocer was a corpulent man with a green-and-white-checked dishcloth fixed permanently over his shoulder, who offered every customer a glass of *vinho verde* poured from a blue and white ceramic jug. Not surprisingly, customers lingered, watched intently by the shopkeeper's one-eyed mother.

We had found our beach, chilly but sun-drenched, and thought we might spend the entire month there in the curious, slightly insecure space inhabited by people whose dreams come true. Apart from Grillo's buzzing motorcycle, the only traffic sound was the creaking of oxcarts' wheels as they lumbered down to the fields in the mornings, and back again each afternoon. Danielle and I came and went from the beach, reporting our sightings of tankers, our adventures inside the fort's ramparts, or just the way the sun fell into the ocean. With a fully-stocked kitchen at our disposal, Danielle was soon indulging her passion for cooking – and our passion for eating – as we celebrated long dinners at the long table, awash with cheap wine under the flickering, Gothic light of a cast iron candelabra. Mark had won the toss for the upstairs bedroom, and at the end of each night would take a bottle of port and climb the gangway to his room, spending hours at the writing desk penning letters and diaries. All night the lighthouse beacon rhythmically swept a dark horizon, and the scent of pine and murmur of ocean crept in through the open windows as we slept.

A fortnight after arriving, on a night cold enough for Grillo to come armed with firewood, Mark was perusing the bookshelves when he found a dusty 19th-century travel book by an Englishman who had toured the region, including Ponte de Lima. It was, wrote the traveller, 'a very rich and picturesque country' inhabited by 'black-haired peasant women of the Minho Province, with their rich olive complexions and fine eyes'.

Next morning, Mark took the train to Viana, and there boarded a bus to Ponte de Lima. When we met later that afternoon on the beach, he told me what had happened.

The road from Viana was narrow, barely wide enough for the state-owned bus company hulk that listed on its axles as the driver swerved outrageously, skuttling dogs and farmers' milk cans left out for collection on the verges. As a bright sun burnt off the morning mist, the bus arrived at Ponte de Lima. The river still flowed gently but the sandbank now bustled with vendors who'd flocked there from all over northern Portugal for the town's famous Monday market, a local institution for 800 years. Struggling to find a path along the crowded Alameda, asking directions as he went, Mark eventually found his way to the tower that had functioned as a prison until the 1960s, and which now housed the town's archives. Entering the keep, he saw Sophia, standing alone in an adjoining room, talking on the telephone. She was having trouble being heard, so was speaking quite loudly, holding the handset at an odd angle to better insert the words. Caught in this comical posture, she blushed violently, covered her face and crossed her legs in joyous embarrassment, wagging a finger at him and promising to be only one minute. She looked sporty in a light woollen red-and-white-striped top and white skirt, and tossed him a flashing smile. As he waited, he watched her fingers toying with a crucifix suspended on a thin gold chain around her neck.

That morning Sophia guided Mark around her beloved home town. Her work seemed entirely optional, and in the anonymity of the market crowds she was totally uninhibited, walking arm in arm with him along the river. At Café Gaio, they practised her English and his Portuguese, and avoided difficult subjects like her marriage and his break-up. He was content to appreciate the music of her voice, with that little croak in the larynx that broke the back of every sentence, opening them to playful subversion. Her colleagues and friends came and went from the restaurant, the women unable to hide their girlish glee at the presence of Sophia's admirer. The rest of the patrons, old men mainly, were content with their newspapers or poker games. Long after Sophia left, Mark lingered there, joining in the drinking and card games. By the time he wandered back to the bus station, the traders and craftsmen had packed up their wares and departed, leaving the deserted sandbank strewn with garbage.

At Sargaço, I had spent the afternoon with Grillo, who, on closer acquaintance, turned out to be a bit of a fascist. He had supported the late Portuguese dictator, Dr Salazar – still did – and had a fetish for security. His home was barricaded with iron bars and grilles welded with a dubious oxy-acetylene outfit of his own manufacture. As he escorted me around the village, he would point out proudly all the mesh and steel shutters he'd installed on various homes and buildings.

'They don't call you "Grillo" for nothing, do they?' I said, condescending in English. But to my surprise, while not getting the slur, he enthusiastically embraced the word play.

'Dr Salazar *grille* man. *Strong* man,' he said, showing me a fist, and I realised the purpose of dictators: they give solace to once-great nations and hope to wannabes.

Grillo didn't just hold strong opinions about the need for law and order. He also kept a shotgun in a long box at the lighthouse.

'*Pour la securite*,' he told me, patting the weapon like a baby, an authoritarian in several languages.

Heading off alone to the beach near sunset, I felt enormously relieved to have escaped him. I was drying off after my swim when a voice called my name and Mark's black hair bobbed above the sand dunes. He'd been running.

'How was your day?' he asked, breathless with the rush to tell me about his.

'Fine,' I said, then added, 'To tell you the truth, it was a little weird. Grillo and I conquered the world.'

'Oh, Dr Salazar.'

'The Man of Iron.'

'Pity he couldn't make the trains more efficient. I swear that *regionais* service from Viana stops at every house. It took hours to get here.'

'Nice day with Sophia?' I ventured.

'Glorious.'

'How old is she?'

'Don't know. Mid-thirties maybe.'

Danielle and I had been thinking of driving down to Porto and spending a few days there, before returning via Aveiro, where a *corrida* was scheduled for the following Sunday. Earlier in the trip, the idea that we might do anything without him would have plunged Mark into a funk of conspiracy theories and self-pity. Now, he barely noticed.

'Actually,' he said, 'I hear these bullfights are not like the ones in Spain. The bull's horns are padded and they just torment it publicly and then take it out the back to be killed. It's a sanitised version. Good for the tourists I suppose. Anyway, I'll be here.'

'Or in Ponte de Lima, maybe?'

'Well, now that you mention it . . . I might need a favour.'

Frankly, I was surprised it had taken him so long to ask. The favour concerned Sophia. Part of her job required visiting the smaller libraries in the hill country, delivering books and documents on loan from the central service in Ponte de Lima. In her old Ford Anglia, and driving herself, the trip took a full day. So Mark had offered to drive her on the following Monday, in my car. With the time saved, she could show him a bit more of the countryside and they could have a picnic in the hills. He'd been bargaining for the use of my various cars ever since high school. In return for this latest loan, I got a week in the master bedroom at Sargaço for Danielle and me.

Our holiday wasn't turning out exactly as I had expected. Instead of a carefree month together with two of the most important people in my life, the trip had become segmented, almost partitioned. With Mark I played cricket on the beach and visited the *Concho Cervejaria*, a bar in Viana where they served scallops in the shell and little fish pies that nicely complemented the draught beer. We'd stay late, watching live broadcasts of *corridas* under floodlights from Lisbon, complete with action replays. After the bullfights, we'd repair to a pool hall called *Tac Tac Tac,* taking on all comers until the local toughs got sore at losing and provoked a brawl. Old enough to know better, we nevertheless carried our cuts and bruises back to Sargaço like trophies.

Travels with Danielle were more cerebral. Every few days there would be a *festa* in one town or another, summer celebrations as old as antiquity. We became adept at identifying local handicrafts by region, and the house began to fill with artworks and furniture destined for our apartment in Paris. Danielle's knowledge of design and history spurred our quest for examples of Manueline Gothic architecture and we photographed dozens of these bizarre buildings festooned with sculpted anchors, rope and other nautical follies. In Porto we found another Eiffel, the strangely beautiful Bridge of Dona Maria Pia that spans the Rio Douro and connects the city to the port-wine lodges that have traded Portugal's most famous export for 500 years. In the quayside restaurants we dined on freshly caught seafood and light wines, strolling back to our hotel in the evenings along cobbled lanes hung with the flapping laundry of entire neighbourhoods.

Still, I couldn't shake the nagging feeling that there was something rather pedestrian about the way Danielle and I were travelling. Were we, as Mark had implied, just tourists, sunning ourselves on the beach and buying our trinkets, but never really knowing Portuguese people? There was much to share, travelling with a partner, but it did tend to insulate you from all the adventures you could have alone. Like a splinter, Mark's offhand remark about the *corrida* had gotten under my skin. In fact, his critique was deeper and more longstanding. The way he had chosen to live his life – 'no safety net' – had always gently mocked the way I'd lived mine. Somehow, secure in a loving relationship about to be sealed in marriage, I had managed to become jealous of a loner's freedom. Danielle and I could own all the apartments in Paris, could travel the world 10 times over, but the global empire of the heart belonged to the reckless navigator.

The *corrida* was a disaster. Aveiro was a polluted and malodorous fishing port in the grip of a hepatitis epidemic. You could almost feel the virus hatching in the seething lagoon. The arena was a shambles and the bulls were so lethargic that not even the feckless *forcados* could stir them. As they led one wounded animal from the ring, I turned on Danielle, holding her responsible for our presence at this malignant entertainment, and stormed out with a splitting headache. We argued vehemently on the drive home, narrowly avoiding several oncoming cars whose drivers had clearly observed the Sabbath in the tavern instead of the church.

It was a relief to return to our sanctuary at Sargaço. The house looked unusually neat and tidy, cleared of all the sandy towels and empty wine bottles, and I wondered if Mark had been entertaining in our absence, but he denied it.

'I've been living like a monk,' he said. 'Just me and my pal Grillo.'

He'd cooked dinner, a soothing Sunday roast, and had splurged some of his own meagre funds on a bottle of La Grima, a spirited aperitif with a label featuring the Sacred Heart of Jesus. Candlelight wavered on the walls, playing on the faces of painted wooden cherubs suspended in the higher reaches, and the haunting melodies of Portuguese *fado* filled the room. It was Amalia Rodrigues, the tragic queen of the genre, revered as a saint from the Mediterranean to the Minho. It is said that the music's bottomless melancholy recalls the separation of lovers across a once-vast empire and the many deaths that were required to maintain it. We were all getting suitably sloshed when a knock at the door interrupted our maudlin reverie. It was Grillo, out of hours and holding a lantern that cast a haunting light on his face. There had been a telephone call for Mark on the lighthouse extension, he said, his tone onimous, as if announcing an assassination or coup. Most shocking to him, it seemed, was that the caller was a Portuguese woman, Senhora Rodriguez from Ponte de Lima. She had asked that Mark call her at home. Looking quite out of sorts, the lighthouse keeper handed over a scrap on paper on which he'd scrawled her number.

'I 'ope nothing is wrong,' said Danielle, but when Mark returned from the lighthouse the mystery of Grillo's dark night of the soul was resolved. The call had simply confirmed Monday's hills tour with Sophia.

A swallow tapping at the window woke us the following morning. The sun had been filtering through the pines for several hours, and when I stumbled down the gangway to the kitchen for coffee, I found a note from Mark on the counter.

'Hope the car didn't wake you,' it said. 'Will tell all when I see you this evening.'

But it would be years before I heard the story.

When Mark arrived at Ponte de Lima that morning, Sophia had not yet come to the office, and an earnest younger colleague ordered him to take a seat and wait. Arriving late, breathless with haste and apologies, Sophia immediately set to work shuffling books and harassing her subordinates in an imperious tone, giving the game away with occasional devilish glances at Mark.

'Would you work for this *terrible* boss?' she asked him, giggling and dumping a boxful of books on the counter. 'Please, be a good worker and take these to the car.'

He was waiting outside, trying to interpret the shape formed by a patch of missing cobbles in the road, when Sophia emerged, juggling more books, a pile of paperwork and a handbag. She was taller than most Portuguese women – taller than most Portuguese men, for that matter – summer incarnate in a sleeveless flowing white crepe dress, her ease the most beguiling mystery, a secret that might free him. As she neared the car, she stepped awkwardly on the uneven cobbles and he caught her before she fell, noticing a slight dampness in her hair.

They were out of town within minutes, driving into the hills towards a quiet country of maize fields and vineyards, the road a necklace strung with quaint villages. Hoping to impress, Mark inserted his *fado* cassette into the tape player, but at the first chords Sophia recoiled, begging for the music to stop. *Fado* was miserable, fatalistic, she said, the source of all Portugal's woes, and she couldn't bear to listen to it. Hastily switching it off, Mark was momentarily at a loss, staring at the road ahead, wondering how to recover from this embarrassment. Then, against his shoulder, he felt the gentle fall of her hand. She had relaxed, surrendering a bare arm to the slipstream of air rushing past the car, as a delicious smile spread across her mouth.

As the road followed the contours of the hills, the Lima would appear in glimpses, twisting hypnotically backwards to its source in the wild country beyond the mountains. In Ponte de Barca, they stopped to drop off some books before turning north towards Monção, pausing on the lonely heights of Extremo Castaneiro to admire the view. Here and there, Sophia would lead him off the road to inspect an unlocked church or a house decorated with the blue and white tiles that date back to the time of the Moors. In the car, her English lessons continued. When she asked about the word 'love', he spelt it out on the dashboard.

'You are a good teacher,' she said, teasing.

'Good teacher, bad pupil,' he countered. 'What else can I teach you?'

'Are you scandalising me?' she said, theatrically huffy. 'You should know that in Portuguese, we have three words for 'saint' – *Sao*, *Santo* and *Santa*. We are the most saintly people!'

He asked how to apologise in Portuguese.

'*Perdoe-me*,' she said.

He could ask her anything now, even her age, and was shocked when she owned up to 25, not the older woman he'd imagined. Having breached the battlements of her private life, he demanded more information as tribute. Her husband was 20 years her senior, she revealed, a professor at Coimbra University who spent only the odd weekend in Ponte de Lima, leaving her to rear their four-year-old daughter alone.

'Big job,' said Mark.

'But as you see, my work is not so hard,' she said. 'It takes my mind off the problems of my life.'

In Monção there was another library to visit, and a teenaged librarian girl who was a niece of Sophia's.

'Pretty, no?' Sophia said, nudging Mark with a wolfish leer. 'Single, too.'

Before leaving the town, they stopped at the 14th-century shrine of a local heroine who had foiled invaders by hurling loaves of bread at them. Convinced by her profligacy that the town could withstand a long siege, the invaders retreated.

'That lady pretended that the people were 'appy and well fed. Since that time, the women of Portugal keep pretending,' Sophia said. 'Once we ruled 'arf the world. Now, not even our-selves.'

'You see that over there,' she continued, pointing to a *pelourinho*, one of the stone pillories that in every Portuguese town recalls the public thrashings once meted out to those who flouted the laws of convention.

'Be good,' Sophia warned him. 'Be *very* good.'

By late morning they had reached Lindoso, the furthest town on their itinerary, where a 13th-century castle commanded fine views across a Rio Lima swollen by a dam close to the Spanish border. Excited by the slow pace of life there, Sophia dragged Mark around a market where cowbells and clogs were big sellers, and after that found a secluded spot overlooking the river, where they spread a rug and unpacked their picnic lunch. Sophia could not wait to spread herself on the blanket, kicking off her shoes and laying on her back to survey the powdery blue sky. As he prepared a plate of olives, cheese and maize bread for her, Mark noticed for the first time that she had great legs. Lots of women had great legs, but Sophia was ageless, moved by an immaculate spirit without which all physical beauty fades like an unwatered garden. They were entirely alone, surrounded by beauty, and he wanted to tell her of his feelings. But in the end, her childish joy in the moment seemed sacrosanct.

After lunch, they went back into Lindoso to call her office and get some coffee before returning. In the café, a group of diners at one table were in high spirits, enjoying some kind of reunion or celebration, when one voice rose above the others.

'*Descuple-me Senhora. Incomodá-la?* (Excuse me, madam. Am I disturbing you?)'

It was a handsome, prosperously-dressed young man seated at the head of the table, calling out to Sophia. When she saw him, she smiled and winced like the victim of a practical joke.

'*Não, não incomoda nada.* (No, not at all),' she responded, and as the young man rose from his seat, she crossed the floor to embrace him.

Standing at the counter waiting for the coffee, Mark watched them launch into an animated conversation. Sophia was obviously familiar with the man, and with most of the other people at the table, raising her eyebrows and smiling warmly as she recognised each one of them in turn. Several times she pointed to Mark, waving her hands flamboyantly in some kind of explanation, but made no move to bring him across, leaving him to nod and smile in mute confirmation of whatever she was saying. Then, pointedly looking at her watch, she made to leave, exchanging kisses with the young man, who made a waggish little salute in Mark's direction. When Sophia returned and saw the barista pouring their short blacks into small cups, she told him she had ordered take-away, and they left after the 'mistake' had been corrected.

'That is my husband's younger brother and his family,' she told Mark as they walked to the car.

The relatives were in Lindoso for the festival of Santa Maria Madalena, when an effigy of Mary Magdalene, the prostitute who washed Jesus' feet and dried them with her hair, is hoisted on a palanquin and paraded through the streets by devotees. Mark had already wondered how his relationship with Sophia might be viewed by the conservative, Catholic people of the north. In Ponte de Lima, he'd noticed the odd, elderly head turning as they passed arm-in-arm, but Sophia had remained unfailingly casual throughout. Now she seemed distracted and subdued, and for the rest of the drive home his morbid imagination became fixated on the image of the stone pillory she had shown him in Monção. The intensively cropped, stone-enclosed farm plots that they passed now seemed claustrophobic to him. Even the vegetables had no privacy in this country, and the houses clinging to the hillsides appeared precariously balanced.

When they reached Ponte de Lima, he drove down the cobbled laneways to her office and brought the car to a halt. She learned across, touching his shoulder, and kissed him once on the cheek.

'Today was very beautiful,' she said. 'When will I see you again?'

'When are you free?' he asked.

'For my English teacher? Anytime.'

At Sargaço, I had been lazing around the house all morning, confined by a fog that had rolled in off the Atlantic. The siren was wailing – for once, with reason – but we were so used to it that Danielle was managing to sleep in. Leaving her, I'd had breakfast alone with my short-wave radio for company, then spent a few hours playing with an antique stereoscope and box of 19th-century view cards that I'd bought in Porto. I had toured the Grand Canyon in sepia, and was heading for the Pyramids, when the radio announced that Portugal's railway workers had begun an indefinite strike over wages and conditions. Then, I heard Danielle cursing in the upstairs bedroom. At first I thought she was abusing the rail workers.

'Fucking bullshit . . . Fucking asshole,' she was shouting in English, as if French was too good for the gutter.

When the stream of invective continued, and she had ignored several requests to explain, I climbed the gangway to the bedroom. She was sitting up in bed, peering at the handwritten pages of a spiral-bound notebook that Mark had apparently left in the bedside table drawer when he'd vacated the room for us the previous day.

'Look at what this bullshit friend of yours writes,' she was fuming. 'Fucking asshole. Bastard. Smug wank-*er*.'

'What do you think you're doing?' I asked, trying to snap her out of it. 'You have no right to read Mark's notebooks.'

'*Pourquoi pas? Il parle de moi!* (Why not? He speaks of me!)' she cried in a wounded scream of outrage.

Whoever he'd been writing about, and whatever he'd written about them, I had no intention of reading it. So Danielle read it for me.

'"Danielle is tediously insecure,"' she began. '"Whenever Robert and I are enjoying ourselves, she interferes, as if she and I are competing for 'is attention. All goes well, except for the presence of that STUPID COW."'

When I left the bedroom, she followed me down the gangway into the lounge.

'Wait! There's more: "I would not advise any-body to travel with a couple, at least not with Robert and Danielle. Everything is decided between them, and I am always on the out-er."'

When I left the living room, she followed me into the kitchen.

'Would you like to know what your good friend thinks about you?' she asked.

'You're going to tell me anyway,' I said, almost in tears.

'You bet I am: "Robert is acting like a com-plete worm. 'Ee's been totally domesticated by that FRENCH LAWYER BITCH. It's repulsive. They deserve each other."'

'Are you finished?'

'Do I need to go on?'

'No.'

'Then?'

'We'll leave.'

Five kilometres from Sargaço, on his way home from Ponte de Lima, Mark had driven into the fogbank, a rising blizzard of droplets defying gravity and the efforts of a pallid yellow sun to break through. He had stopped in the village to buy wine as a gift for the loan of the car, when a passing wedding party in honour of the shopkeeper's daughter abducted him, the celebrants forcing him to drink a jug of green wine. Released only after undertaking to return with the rest of us, he entered the house in high spirits, but soon realised that something was wrong. Danielle was hunched up in a ball on the sofa, flipping way too fast through a copy of *Vogue*. I was halfway through laying the table for dinner, so Mark followed me into the kitchen.

'Problems between you two?' he asked.

'No, not really,' I said. 'But we have to cut short the holiday. A client in Paris is insisting I finish his tax return. All the data's on my hard drive.'

He knew it was bullshit, but played along.

'Oh. I see. So . . . when are you leaving?'

'Tomorrow. I'll go down to Viana in the morning and organise a freight company to get the furniture we bought in Porto back to Paris. Once that's done we should be on the road by the afternoon. Anyway, the rent's paid up until then. What will you do?'

'God, I don't know. I'd like to stay here, but I can't really afford the rent alone. And without a car . . .'

'You know about the train strike that's just started?'

'No, I didn't know that. Without the car, or the train . . . I could get around on buses, I suppose.'

'Do me a favour?'

'Sure. Anything.'

'Danielle's a little sore about the whole thing. Best steer clear of her for the next day or so.'

'All right, I will.'

Dinner was funereal. Danielle and I hardly spoke a word, leaving Mark to fill in the gaps with descriptions of the castles and bridges he'd seen that day. After dinner, he took a torch and walked up to the lighthouse to call Ponte de Lima. Sophia answered. He told her he needed to see her urgently, and asked if she could make lunch in Viana the next day. She said she would try. He could hear in the background the plaintive voice of a little girl. By the time he returned, Danielle had retreated to the upstairs bedroom and I was tidying up. We both needed a drink, and there being nothing else, broke open the wine he'd bought, a slightly fuller red called *Dao*.

'To the taxpayer,' I said, raising my glass in a derisory toast.

But Mark had something more serious to get off his chest.

'Robert . . .' he began somewhat uncertainly. 'I wanted to thank you for inviting me to come with you guys. It's been a fantastic experience.'

I tried to brush it off, but he persisted.

'Really, I mean it. It's been a rough patch since the break-up. I guess Danielle bore the brunt of that. I must have been down on women, or Spain, or something, especially during that first week.'

In my determination not to violate his diary, I'd neglected to check the dates of the entries Danielle had read. Not that it would make any difference now.

'Anyway, she's been great, and you're a great couple. I'm . . .' his voice teetered and thickened. 'I'm sorry,' he said. 'I didn't mean to be such an arsehole. I've been wanting to make up for it in some small way.'

Reaching into his pocket, he produced a small piece of filigree silverwork in the shape of a heart. I knew he couldn't afford such things.

'It's supposed to hang on a silver neck chain. But I couldn't find a decent one today. Tell her this is just the first instalment. Once I get myself sorted, I'd love to come back here with the two of you. We've still got to play our final test match on the beach at Sargaço. We've got to walk that rocky path down to the ocean through the pine forest and the cornfields once more before we die.'

'And Sophia?' I asked him. 'Will she be there?'

His head rolled back on the sofa and he exhaled deeply.

'Good question,' he sighed. 'You know how easily I get carried away. I mean, I know I'm on the rebound, but why did it have to be with a married, Roman Catholic, Portuguese woman? Those are small towns up there.'

Before turning in, we agreed that I would drop him next morning at the Jardim Marginal in Viana, where he hoped to meet Sophia. We were sharing the bathroom – me in the shower, Mark brushing his teeth at the basin – when I heard him curse. Pulling back the shower curtain, I saw him frowning at himself in the mirror.

The hair dye was growing out.

Next morning, Mark had shaved, polished his shoes, borrowed a tie and, for the first time during the entire trip, donned a jacket. He looked like he was heading for a job interview. At their last meeting, Sophia had asked whether he had ever taken the funicular to the top of Monte de Santa Luzia, overlooking Viana do Castelo.

'It's where lovers go,' she had said.

So that's where he was taking her.

The fog had cleared overnight, and a stiff breeze was bending the trees along the road as we drove into the largest town of Alto Minho province. Viana was a fishing village that had struck it rich, and lacked the history of the smaller towns of the region. With the discovery of the New World, its estuary had grown into a busy port, only to decline again when Portugal lost most of its overseas colonies. Its buildings were overly ornate, typifying a gauche, temporary prosperity. The gleaming white, faux Byzantine church crowning Santa Luzia's hill, in particular, gave me the willies. I dropped Mark at the entrance to the municipal gardens and went off to find a freight agent.

The rail workers' strike was a bonanza for the truckers. It took me two hours at the crowded freight company office to organise the uplift of our furniture, pottery and miscellaneous knick-knacks to Paris. In about the same amount of time, Mark and Sophia decided their destiny.

They met, as agreed, under the statue of Viana, a place

immortalised in thousands of photos because, from there, the statue, the city hall and hilltop basilica can all be captured in a single frame. Despite the buffeting breeze, Sophia looked glamorous in sunglasses and a shortish skirt with a crocheted woollen top, but she deflected all compliments, declaring Mark to be the smartest man in Portugal.

'I feel undressed beside you,' she said.

'Under-dressed,' Mark corrected, but she insisted that her English was better than his.

'Undressed will do fine,' she said, turning every word to her advantage.

Sophia's laughter turned to fear, however, when they reached the funicular. Swinging on its cables in the high wind, their decrepit, empty carriage shuddered over its stanchions. Whispering Hail Marys, Sophia clung to his arm. Then, when they reached the top, they found the café inexplicably closed.

'No matter,' said Sophia, quickly regaining her composure. 'Come, I will show you the *castro*, the stronghold of my Celtic ancestors.'

She led the way through a wood, emerging in an area of bleached stone ruins, remnants of the double-walled Celtic roundhouses built all over the Iberian peninsula in the two thousand years before Christ. An enemy who successfully penetrated the *castro*'s outer perimeter found themselves trapped in a killing field between the two walls. The Celts lived securely in these lofty fortresses until the Roman conquest, when they were forced into the valleys to grow food for the Roman legions. Mark and Sophia nosed around in what remained of the ancients' living rooms until the arrival of a tour group of Brazilians and Chinese forced them to move on.

They came to a secluded corner of the hilltop and found a bench seat with a magnificent view over the port and estuary where the Rio Lima pours into the Atlantic. In the distance, sandy beaches hugged the coast and the horizon bent under an unblemished sky. Feeling the heat of her exections, Sophia stripped off her crocheted top and fanned herself with her hands. Now she really was undressed beside him, except for a skimpy singlet, smiling dreamily at the view.

'You mentioned problems yesterday,' Mark reminded her, his breath slightly irregular from the walk. 'What problems are those?'

Immediately he regretted the impost for what it did to her smile.

'I love my daughter,' she said, 'and my husband is a good friend. He used to be a good lover, but now he is a good friend.'

Although he cared for her happiness – perhaps because he cared for her happiness – it was exactly what he wanted to hear. With the mouth of the Lima at his feet, he could see only the mouth that had spoken those words, only the face that illuminated his world. Drawn by her breath, he was on the brink of a kiss, when she raised a hand, not in surrender.

'Mark,' she said. He could see that her fingers were trembling.

'Nothing is better than love. To love and be loved by somebody who needs you. Yes, it is difficult sometimes. But when you are given this gift, you shouldn't throw it away, not even for the most beautiful moment. Look . . .'

She pointed at Portugal – the nation that had it all, then lost it – laid out below them.

'We are the owners of this world. It sits in the palm of our hand.'

One hand held his, the other caressed his face.

'Sophia . . . I . . .'

But before he could say it, her fingers stopped his lips.

'And I also,' she said. 'But I have a daughter.'

Driving back to Sargaço, I was thinking about Mark and his many disappointments; the lacklustre career and dead-end romances that we would always joke about, before the years became judgmental. Yet he had never abandoned hope that life would one day reward the poet in him. Inviting him to Europe, I had wanted him to see how well I'd done – the business, the apartment and the wife-to-be – never for a moment believing it would impress him, and yet somehow needing his approval, or at least his understanding, as he needed mine. Noticing a cassette cradled in the stereo, I pushed it into the deck. It was Mark's *fado*, and all at once the car became a vehicle for the Portuguese song of longing and surrender, of hope regimented by fate, and the fragile heart's separation across far-flung dominions. Pulling off the road, I stopped the car and sat there listening for quite some time. If you believe that life is a struggle between dreams and reality, then *fado* is your song. It had always been ours. Instinctively, I turned the wheel, and headed back into Viana. It was going to be difficult reconciling past and future, but I knew I couldn't leave Mark behind.

As I waited at the entrance to the funicular railway, I could see a carriage dropping into the base station. If Mark was on it, I would offer him a lift back to Paris, but when the first carriage disgorged a mixed group of foreign tourists, I decided to wait for the next one. It hung suspended, rocking in mid-air before descending.

Sophia emerged first, striding briskly away from the funicular, at one point almost stumbling and dropping what looked like a pullover. Gone was the self-possessed elegance I had seen in Ponte de Lima. Clearly distressed, she ran right past me to her little car and drove off erratically into the traffic. Mark followed her, walking, his head and shoulders sagging as if his jacket and tie weighed a tonne. Had I not been there, I think he might have found his way to the ocean and waded in, never to return. Instead, I led him to my car, in which he deposited his crumpled body. We drove back to Sargaço in silence, with no more need of *fado*.

Still smouldering with hurt, Danielle did not look pleased

to see us. She had packed my things and was ready to go. She couldn't believe it when I told her Mark had suffered a blow and would be coming with us. The task of saying *adeus* to Grillo fell to me. He was grief-stricken over our sudden departure, refusing the generous tip I offered him, and was only placated when I promised we would return one day to Sargaço. When I got back to the house, Mark had packed his few possessions into his backpack and was sitting quietly on the end of his bed.

'Danielle read parts of your diary,' I told him. 'Just the bits about her.'

Exasperated, he looked to the heavens, but saw only the ceiling, his face contracting in a painful grimace.

'Just in case you were wondering,' I said.

The Renault bucked and groaned as it climbed the rocky path back to the main road for the last time. At the lighthouse gate Grillo stood to attention, saluted, then raised his shotgun and fired a volley of buckshot into the air to mark the solemn occasion. All three of us smiled and waved like happy campers, in our happy car, heading home from our happy holiday. At the highway, we turned north and set off on the long drive back to France.

Only then did the volcano of Danielle's pent-up rage and frustration erupt. Swivelling in her seat, she fixed Mark with her wildest glare, and in a voice that burnt like molten lava said to him:

'Okay, Mr Bull-*shit*. But I swear, if you say one more *fucking* word before we reach Paris, you're OUT OF THE CAR.'

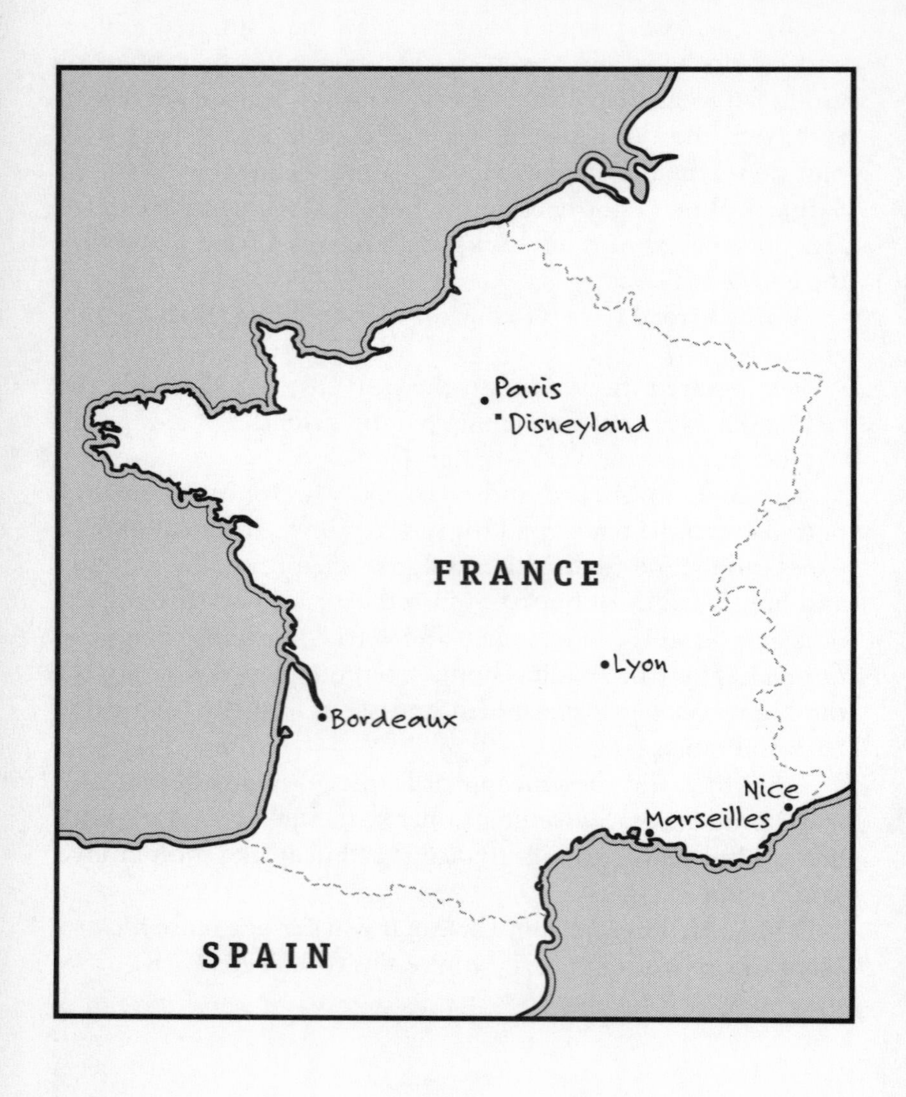
Paris
Disneyland
FRANCE
Lyon
Bordeaux
Nice
Marseilles
SPAIN

Disneyland Paris: A Notebook

NIKKI GEMMELL

> 'I had ceased to ask that terrible question – what is the good of it all? Now it seemed quite plain and simple: the proper object of life was happiness, and I promised myself much happiness ahead.'
>
> — Leo Tolstoy

And so to Disneyland Paris – that bracing handshake of a theme park, that bright and brash foreigner who looks Europe straight in the eye and bellows a cheery hello. The quintessential stranger in a strange land. And this makes me curiously open to it. For I, too, am a stranger in a strange land, and I know the glittering loneliness of that existence. I'm also moved by this intruder's eagerness, and ignorance, in thinking it can so boldly do things its way, as opposed to theirs. The innocence of that! Excuse me, Disneyland, but this is Europe.

Well, bring on the new world, I smile. Just as bring on the New World, I've lamented more than once, as an Australian living in this creaky, burdened continent. Bring on people who smile when they talk, showers that work, cleanliness, optimism, enthusiasm.

It wasn't always like this. Once, smug and knowing in my homeland on the other side of the world, I'd dismissed the idea of a Disneyland in France as an abomination never to be consumed; like put-put golf or World Series Cricket or K-tel records. Fifteen years ago I'd sympathised with an appalled French intelligentsia who'd shouted 'cultural Chernobyl' when the Disney company first announced its intentions for some muddy farmland south-east of Paris. Ah yes, I nodded, a travesty indeed (and I do believe I was wearing a black turtleneck). That most exquisite of nations – reduced to this. *Quelle horreur*! It was as unthinkable as Jacqueline Kennedy Onassis being snapped at a supermarket in a velour tracksuit with her hair in rollers.

Well, that was then. And this is now.

Being driven to London's Waterloo Station from our home in the city's west. In the back seat of a minicab with my three-year-old, Lachie, exuberantly pressing a button that makes his window go up and down while my 18-month-old, Ollie, tries to climb on my shoulders and lick his window, having wrestled himself free of the seatbelt containing us both. I do not discipline either boy for a rude, slippery exhilaration slips from all three of us: We're all going on a winter holiday. And there's not a tantrum or tear in sight.

Andy, husband, is blissfully alone and relaxed in the seat next to the driver. Now and then he stretches, luxuriously, and turns, luxuriously, and bestows a serene smile upon the chaos in the back. I tell him to enjoy his moment while he can. A tongue lands in my ear. The baby giggles. We all giggle.

Blowsy flakes of snow billow around the car, colluding with the euphoric atmosphere. It's the London of my imagination and I so rarely see it: unfurl the snow rug, carpet the earth!

I could love London if it was like this more often. We're having too much fun, already, we're playing.

Oh dear, again. You see, we've been playing rather a lot lately.

As an expatriate family in Europe our lives have never been quite 'proper'. There's no weekend that's taken up with a cousin's birthday or a visit to grandma and we never go to christenings – ours or anyone else's. For all those rituals belong to a grown-up world of responsibility and obligation and friendship mulled over decades, to a family life that's settled, stable, certain. Ours is not. We move in an anchorless expat's world and know all too well the suspicions of school admissions secretaries who never quite trust we'll hang around, and Easters with just, well, us; in a hotel. We're a tight little pack of four, bound by blood and love and exile. It's lovely and lonely and one day it will have to stop. When the parents grow up.

Uncertainty has leaked into my life over the past couple of years and is in danger now of ruling it. Uncertainty about what accent our children will grow up with. The choices I'm making. The tension between the two professions in my life: motherhood and writing. For you see, I can only write when I'm alone.

'The centre of our story is the tension between the yearning to create a home and the urge to get out of it,' wrote the American writer Gail Collins recently. Ah yes – her story, my story, the female story.

Once upon a time in Australia, Andy and I ran away from where our lives were leading us, at an age when we shouldn't have been contemplating such things. I was thirty, and could see just over the horizon the frantic waving of a very sensible existence involving long service leave, contents insurance and a proper fridge. We set up shop in a tiny room on London's Fleet Street. When Andy's mother saw our reduced living circumstances she cried. It was all in her face: 'Two Australian professionals in their thirties – in this?'

We'd reverted to laundromats and backpacks and bar fridges but were having an enormous amount of fun staving off adulthood. One day we'll go home, we said, and start cooking, and decide what we want to do with our lives.

In Europe, Andy and I reinvented ourselves. We were bolder and braver than we'd ever been back home. We brought to our new country a cheeky, reckless energy, a feeling we could do anything here, by ourselves: we could do what we really wanted to. And if we failed, well, no one had to know.

The Brits bought it. We've had the best careers of our lives in England – perhaps because we didn't care as much. If something didn't work out, well, we'd just reinvent ourselves again.

What could possibly lure us back?

Vaulting skies. Light that bashes me, hurts me (in Britain it licks me). The smell of Alice Springs (how can I cup it in my hands? How can I bottle it?). Sleeping in a swag under the stars, being caressed by the air rather than huddling against it (the cold in England curls up in my bones like mould). Flinging sun into my lungs. Driving somewhere I've never been, with just the sky and a map and a shoebox of cassettes. Dust that's red and as soft as flour claiming my boots. The shrill of cicadas. Bush taut with sound. Nicknames. My grandmother telling me she can make a salad sing; my grandmother calling a scourer a 'scratcher' and home videotapes 'walkie-talkie photos'. A Bondi supper with Mum. Brothers. Dad. Mates.

As we speed through our Dickensian London of dancing snow this trip to Disneyland feels like a last hurrah; a last play. And I'm giddy with the prospect of that.

Salman Rushdie described exile as 'a dream of glorious return'. But that return is so very complicated if it's to Australia (as

I'm sure it is, in its own peculiar way, with every country). But what of my beloved homeland that loves nothing more than cutting down to size its bolshie expats, grubbied by the disloyalty of assuming that life could be better somewhere else? Does one slink back too soon, tail between one's legs, to face the cynical smirk: couldn't cut it, eh, in the Big Smoke? What if the answer is as simple as: I'm done. I know I should stay longer but actually, I just want to come home.

Children have changed me. My three-year-old has an English accent and yet Andy and I want our boys to grow up as Australian men. To have a childhood like we did – where a backyard's a given and not a luxury. Where playing barefoot is a signifier of freedom, not impoverishment. Where sunshine and fresh food grow children tall. Where the kids know what a rash shirt is, and a boogie board. Where they can swim that beautiful Australian Crawl. Where they learn confidence, curiosity, reach.

Andy is not ready to return. I'm not sure he ever will be. And this has become a question mark between us.

We have first-class seats on the Eurostar train from London to Paris – a ridiculous luxury, but this is typical of our life of European play. We know we should be paying off mortgages and investing in shares and saving for pension funds, but any surplus money we make seems to be spent on making the most of Europe while we can.

Craving a dazzling, cramming in the loveliness.

'Life is only given us once, and one wants to live it boldly, with full consciousness and beauty,' wrote Anton Chekhov in *An Anonymous Story*, and I'd jotted it in my journal the night before leaving for London.

What better place than Europe to live with full consciousness and beauty? And what better city than Paris? It assaults you with its beauty. I go there just to . . . look. To bask. It's not a smiley city, it's never been that; but like a sullen lover it only makes me crave it more. (I have a more sober, fractious relationship with London, perhaps because I know it better.) Henry James declared Americans 'too apt to think that Paris is the celestial city'. Well, yes, Mr James, but it is. Still. It embodies a common human hope that the world is more beautiful and romantic than it can ever be – aren't we all aspirational when we go to Paris? Andy and I visited often before the children arrived. Like an Indian summer we grabbed at its glare, swallowed it complete before the settling closed over us.

It's Jean Seberg in a little white T, Simone de Beauvoir in a smoky café, Mona Lisa's sexy inscrutability, Coco's pearls, *The Story of O*, Hemingway at the Flore, Diana at the Ritz. It's not, God help me, a hot dog with yellow mustard.

'Have a great trip,' says our gentle minicab driver in his Afghani headscarf as he lets us off at Waterloo Station, not a hint of irony in his voice.

Ah, that familiar scratch of travel anxiety, post 9/11, as we pass through security at the train station: in a corner is an Arabic-looking man with NYC on his jacket and four bulging gym bags, being questioned intently by three policemen. My belly does the little twist of alarm it always does now when international travel is endured. 'Please let this suspicious-looking man not be on our train,' is my selfish, silent prayer. I'm not proud of this wish, which is also, by extension, 'Please let him blow up someone else's train, if that is what he is going to do.' But ours is a train of children, the only one of the day that goes directly from London to the gates of Disneyland. There will not be an adult travelling alone upon it. Would al Qaeda really focus on such an innocent target? I cannot answer that. The ferociously angry radical Islamists take issue with the very idea of Western modernity – its shameless pursuit of pleasure, its audacity, its optimism. And here we have a trainload of mainly affluent Brits travelling to a symbol of American cultural imperialism in a country that's just banned the wearing of Muslim headscarves in schools. A train with the most emotive cargo imaginable: a Western nation's young. Hmm. And we all know al Qaeda's got a great eye for a story.

A bomb in the train tunnel under the English Channel – immolation and drowning – what could be worse? Andy is second-guessing my thoughts and waves Lachie's passport photo under my nose. It never fails to make me laugh: our five week-old son looks like a younger version of Tony Soprano and bears no resemblance whatsoever to the boy before us now. My husband, God love him, is always trying to jolt me from my fears; he's always implying that I'm imagining too vividly and worrying too easily, that I just need to relax.

'Women who write feel too much,' the poet Anne Carson said, and I've wanted to tell Andy this more than once in my defence – see, this is why I feel fluttery and fragile at the direction in which the world is heading; it's darkening around us. Can't he feel that? Wouldn't it be safer in Australia?

'God no,' he's said more than once. 'Look at Bali.'

(Actually, I did tell him once about that Carson quote. 'Yes Sylvia,' he replied; adding, 'that's for the gas,' with his wonderfully dry Australian smile as he threw a box of matches at me.)

Are the choices in my life suddenly being dictated by fear? I never used to live like this. Motherhood has changed me; a cautiousness is closing over me.

Why do we seek cages in which to imprison ourselves, why do we seek the comfort of the known?

The euphoria scuttles back once we're settled into our sleek Eurostar carriage with its complimentary newspapers and French *Vogues* – the man in the NYC jacket couldn't possibly be among all these chattery, cluttery, bouncy families; he'd stand out like a sore thumb, he wouldn't dare. I feel so close to these travellers, all bound by a common, humble hope: to live, and to experience pleasure. Such a simple, innocent, raging want.

As the train glides away from the platform Andy and I smile conspiratorially, wishing each other luck: we never know how these trips with the children will unfold. All four of us could emerge at the gates of Disneyland distraught, hungry, hysterical and bursting to go the loo – or for the kids, worse: with soaked pants. But Disney has ways of making the three-hour journey as easy as possible, and a man swiftly appears with colouring-in packs, snack boxes and some extraordinarily vivid, American-style enthusiasm. It works – the children are instantly absorbed with crayons and croissants. Andy and I share smiles once again: God knows how long this miraculous peace will last. Or who will get the first nappy change.

Ah, thanks mate. And this is where Eurostar and Disney fall down. I can't locate any child-changing facilities so end up removing an extremely pungent nappy while Ollie stands in the swaying train, gripping for dear life a none-too-clean toilet rim with his deliciously plump hands that I always – except for now – want to kiss. There's no other way to do this.

He doesn't utter a sound, God love him.

I do actually kiss his hands. I can't resist, I'm so proud of him. He looks at me as if I'm disgusting.

Outside the window the joyous snow flurry has turned into the England of snivelly, drippy, relentless greyness, the England I know so well. There goes the country of my imagination. My heart soars to be leaving the rain-soaked, suburb-walled city, the row upon row of pebbledash houses with their satellite dishes, the cowed and tamed land. My heart soars to be going to muscular Paris; such a heart-lifter of a city. It does not feel like it's bowed down by the cram of its people and the weight of its history; it does not feel irreversibly grubby; it does not feel like it's cracking apart.

We barely notice the Channel tunnel – the boys are so absorbed. They have a surprising appetite for contentment on this trip. They eat and draw and befriend other children in the carriage. Andy dares to pick up a newspaper. He never gets to finish a newspaper anymore.

In France the snow is thick; it blankets the fields and pitched roofs of the villages. They look empty. There's little traffic.

I've always loved the peculiar silence of the French countryside. We stayed in a village in Provence last summer and it felt as if all its middle-aged and young people had left, for good. The shop hours were languid and luxurious, as was the sole waiter in the town's only restaurant. Even the church bells, tolling every morning for the daily service, were languid and luxurious.

It reminded me of nothing so much as Venice; another European place strangely emptied of proper, messy, bustling life; half-abandoned, not quite real. Given over to people like us: the curious.

Ollie falls asleep, jammed hard against me, limpet-stuck. As if this is the only way he can sleep, as if he will never let me go. I dare not move him for fear of waking him. I gaze into his face and hover a kiss on his forehead and gaze into his face again and a great calm washes over me.

At home, at night, I often go into the boys' bedroom and just stand there and listen to them and breathe in their sleeping. The happiness burns through me.

Lachie falls asleep too, on the seat beside Andy. We look at each other, breaths held: we have our lives to ourselves, for goodness knows how long. We seize the calm while we can.

This is how I work now: in stolen moments, while the children are asleep. I've annexed a new writing life of short chapters and snatched thoughts, of three-line paragraphs and fragments on shopping dockets, for I never get a long stretch of time to myself. Gone are the 14-hour writing sessions fuelled by champagne and chocolate; the luxury of sixty drafts; the week-long sojourns in distant cottages with Andy protesting, 'You're leaving me for a book.' Now I leave him for his children, too many moments of too many days. And I know I am remiss.

I'm always trying to find wily ways to separate, from all of them, to find some restorative pocket of me-time. It's difficult, and it carries a burden of guilt: these precious moments I've snatched for myself are moments when I should be with someone else. Yet I have to write. I feel like I'm living spiritually when I'm working; absorbed, focused, lit. When I can't glean the space to sit at my laptop I feel fretful, lost.

The theme park opened in 1992. The Disney Company originally planned to set up its European showcase in warmer Spain, but the French government stepped in with a lucrative deal on some farmland near Paris. It offered an area one-fifth the size of the city, keen for the tourist revenue and the 14,000 jobs the venture would create. But the French populace was not so keen – Parisian communists threw eggs at Disney chairman, Michael Eisner, several years before his grand European baby opened.

When the gates first swung wide you couldn't get a glass of wine in the park or smoke in the restaurants. That has changed. This, after all, is Europe, and there are some things you cannot budge. But the park's heavily in debt and at the moment it's threatened with closure. A European recession is blamed – and French snobbery.

The French intelligentsia still feels threatened by this interloper in its midst (and it's human nature, of course, to belittle what threatens you). But the park's been caught up in a much larger battle – the fight by the French chattering classes to keep their country unique. The American domination of world culture is seen as an appalling error, a virus run rampant. Not long ago it was French, not English, that the elite of so many cultures deemed the requisite language. Just recently the highly influential *Le Monde* newspaper lamented the decline of the French language. The government's taken strong measures: it's introduced laws making it an offence to use Anglicisms such as '*le weekend*'.

Mr Eisner was hoping to emulate the wild success of Tokyo Disneyland with his shining new park. But an advisor to the Parisian mayor in the early nineties cautioned against foreign arrogance: 'The Japanese are sponges of foreign culture,' Pierre Lellouche warned. 'It will be harder here.' Indeed.

After touring America for several months, the writer Jean Baudrillard declared 'the U.S. is utopia achieved'. And to the French, well, that's not such a good thing.

It's only as we glide into Disneyland's soaring, extremely smart glass and steel terminal that I realise the train journey's revealed absolutely nothing of Paris – we've merely stopped at its edge. All we've seen are the fields and freeways of northern France. Not a glimpse, as anticipated, of a honey-coloured building, the spires of Sacre Coeur, a blue and white street sign, a Mercedes cab (in fact, where are the cars? Ingeniously hidden, of course, in this über-world. Such dirty, noisy things that they are).

Disney music greets us as we step onto the platform, followed by Elton John's 'Your Song'. Welcome to France.

Le Monde would be appalled.

Outside the station the light streams through the clouds like tent ropes from heaven. As we step into the fresh air the sun slips from behind a cloud, beautifully on cue, and the world brightens and we straighten our backs and feel taller and fresher; responding as obediently as seedlings to the jolt of ultraviolet. People are wearing sunglasses even though the temperature's hovering around zero. Exuberant sunshine like this never seems to occur, mid-winter, in England – the land of soft weather and no shadows. Disneyland would never work in a place where the sky is so low it almost brushes the rooftops. This hard, bright light of France complements Disneyland's hard, bright colours. England's light is too milky, diffuse. It's not optimistic.

I feel like I haven't worn sunglasses for years. Or squinted.

'My days burn with the sun', wrote Judith Wright, and how I dream of that. Of breathing in the sunshine like the desert with rain. A friend once wrote, 'Where is your home, Nik? I guess it's where your bed and your laptop are.' And where the light is, but Andy doesn't understand that. He flinches from light; he tells me it's because he's from Melbourne.

I can't write about Sydney, just as I find it difficult to write about Paris. Both cities are too dazzling for me; it's hard to find the grit within them to make the pearl. Unlike London, or Alice Springs, or Antarctica – places that have had to work hard to seduce me.

The boys dart and dance in delirious circles on the vast concourse surrounding the station. They can run, they have space, and they're instinctively seizing the possibility within it. Their London lives are hemmed in, contained by the cram all around them. Our house is a tiny, two-bedroom mews cottage that once stored vegetable carts for the Portobello market. There's no garden. Lachie's kindergarten has a strip of paved pathway at its entrance as its outside space and this is not unusual for a London school. Here in France it seems the boys are suddenly using muscles I've never seen in action; they've become bolder, brighter, incandescent with delight. My heart cracks as I watch the children they might be, if they were raised in another place.

> 'To the English . . . Americans are a sort of mutant breed, whose optimism is a sure sign of emotional aberration. The English are constitutionally unable to fathom it, and for good reason. American optimism has its root in abundance and in the vastness of the land . . . Britain, on the other hand, is an island the size of Utah. Its culture is one of scarcity; its preferred idiom is irony – a language of limits.'
>
> — John Lahr

I'm ready for the muscularity of another way of life.

Disneyland is smiley. It lowers itself, tries too hard, gives you the gift of enthusiasm. Everything Paris, and Europe, does not; and that irritates me about this continent of patronage and privilege. The Italian designer Emilio Pucci was the first person in his family to work for a thousand years – such a European story. Walt Disney was the son of an abusive farmer, newspaper deliverer and jelly factory worker – such an American one.

Disneyland is anti-Europe, anti-history, anti-literary. How on earth can I write about this, I wonder, as I enter the park. It just . . . exists. How can I find inspiration, in all honesty, in a swirling teacup ride?

I'm a stranger in a strange land here but my boys are instantly at home. Andy too – as he chases after his sons and scoops one then the other into his arms; holds their little bodies flat as ironing boards in front of him and sings, 'We can fly, we can fly!' while whooshing them around in the bright air. My three Peter Pans.

'Come on Mummy!' Lachie sings and runs up to me and holds his palm quietly to my cheek, so tender and grave and curious. 'Come *on*, Mummy,' he says, softer.

My love for them is weighty, voluptuous.

How could I rupture this little unit? Even though at times I'm screaming inside to break out. To live life my way, as opposed to someone else's.

There's no black in Disneyland; no darkness, no poetry. And Europe is all about darkness and poetry. So much blood seeped into its soil: Flanders' fields so close, Normandy, Auschwitz. Kosovo, Dresden, St Petersburg. The burdened continent.

Yet in this gleaming park Europe is scrubbed. So many of Disneyland's stories are based on European ones – Pinocchio, Sleeping Beauty, Snow White, Beauty and the Beast – but they, too, are scrubbed. Everything in Disneyland is bright, ordered, unthreatening; the America of the imagination, the image America wants to present to the world. Look at Main Street, USA – how lovely and pure and innocent it is!

The park is optimistic. Nothing looks worn or cracked or grubbied, like so much else in Europe, especially its tourist attractions. It is scarily clean.

Disneyland erases reality and that's strangely comforting if you surrender to it; for humans instinctively shrink from too much reality. There's no point in Disneyland where you can glimpse the outside world. The park's ringed by an artificial rise upon which grow trees that obscure what's beyond them. It's a shock to hear a small plane overhead, to raise your head to the intrusive jolt from the real world. In our little island we bask in the solace of fantasy. It's an island of reassurance, of cleanliness and efficiency and politeness. That's the lie America takes to the world.

We do not know what is beyond this place. What future awaits our family; what land, schools, friends. What peace, what security we can lay claim to.

Where is France in all of this? Disney has modified Sleeping Beauty's castle at the park's centre to look more like a French chateau, in deference to the host country (every other Disneyland has a Bavarian-looking one.) But I can't tell the difference; it just looks like a fairy-tale Disney castle to me for that is what I expect castles to look like, ignorant child of the New World that I am. (And I had the audacity to be disappointed, several years ago, by my first glimpse of a real French chateau – because it didn't look just like a Disney one.)

The company's not interested in reality, but a prettified version of it. 'Things as we think they ought to be rather than what they actually are,' explained one of the park's designers, helpfully, in the early nineties.

It's a shock to catch sight of a pair of red Doc Martens under a ticket collector's replica-Victorian coat, a walkman's earplugs under a train driver's puffing-billy hat. Aha, reality intrudes! These slippages would definitely not have been included in the designer's vision. But I love them for the subversive thrill of them – they're signs of messy, leaky, complicated real life.

It's an architecture of candy-pink pretence – Walt Disney's idealised re-creation of where he grew up (the American Midwest of the late 19th century). Our hotel's built directly onto the park entrance. It's a vast edifice of fake Victoriana, painted a gooey pink and cream and topped with gold-tipped turrets. It's so ugly, fake, bizarre it's compelling. As buildings go, it's the antithesis of the black turtleneck.

I head straight for the known: the shops. They all have the same merchandise (Minnie Mouse dolls, Mickey backpacks,

Buzz Lightyear costumes, Nemo pencils). The windows do not tell you this, for each one has a sparkling display of something else, enticing you inside with the promise of the new. But once you're through the doors, nothing is different. By the time you realise you've been fooled your children are running off to various displays and grabbing at yet another toy to buy.

Embrace the mystery as a parent, throw away the map, relinquish control – I'm still struggling.

Once I was a neophiliac, moving restlessly from landscape to landscape every couple of years, succumbing to the relentless gypsy within me, searching for fresh fuel for my fiction.

And I have the chafing again.

But I'm a mother now. And perhaps I just have to embrace the mystery of being settled; find the courage to surrender to a new way of life.

Ollie runs off, ignoring my cry; dropping his mother without a backward glance now that he's found something bigger and brighter. I feel unburdened yet melancholy that a phase of motherhood – utter dependence – has come to an end. A strange exhilaration and devastation shoots through me as I just stand for a moment and let my youngest child run. Lachie, in horror, rushes to Ollie and takes his hand and leads him back, admonishing him as he thinks his mummy would.

In Disneyland I'm not an Australian or a Londoner, I'm that most universal of species: parent. There's a commonality of experience all around me – European, Arabic and Asian mothers and fathers rush children off to toilets, pull them from shops, hold weary bodies in queues, wipe noses, adjust hats.

There's no woman here whose beauty I want to gulp, as I so often do in Paris. Here we're all just . . . mums. Worn out, harassed, faded (I recognise the set of that face). Once upon a time, perhaps, these women would have made more of an effort with how they looked, just like me. Have they been pushed to the side of their own lives? Do they feel that all the vividness and promise of their youth, all its loudness, has been rubbed out?

You're invisible in Disneyland. You never feel invisible in Paris; as a woman you're always being appraised – and that makes me feel feminine. But here among nothing but mothers I relax into being unnoticed. I don't feel feminine in Disneyland, don't care what I wear, don't reapply my lipstick. I give myself over to the kids.

'There was nothing but land: not a country at all . . .' wrote Willa Cather in *My Antonia*. 'I had the feeling that the world was left behind, that we had got over the edge of it.'

Mathilde checks us in to our hotel. She is one of those beautifully fragile French girls with sad, speaking eyes. She's dressed in an ill-fitting Gibson-Girl outfit that's utterly wrong for her figure; she's much too slender for it. What is the peculiar sadness in so many French women? It's as if they've endured, stoically, a lifetime of being let down. There's so much history – emotional history, sexual history – in her face. It's too complicated for this place.

Mathilde leads us to our room. Our bags have already been checked in from the train station. Lachie and Andy go back to the park, determined to squeeze every minute out of it that they can.

Peter Pan on the door handle, Tinkerbell on the bedhead, hippos in tutus on the bathroom tiles, Mickey on the shampoo bottle and engraved in the soap. It's all fascinating and vile.

Ollie points and goos at everything he recognises. He seems to recognise a lot. I'm not proud of that: too many videos, too many days.

Oh tender eve! While my wee general plays with his colouring book I lie on the rug beside him and fall asleep. Suddenly, an empty baby cup is put in my mouth. I open my eyes, smile, close them again. A minute later an unpeeled banana is pushed between my lips. Dear, kind boy, flood my heart! I'm overwhelmed by the realisation that comes to every parent, at some moment, that these little creatures will one day give something back. The realisation that all the giving, giving, giving – the relinquishing of all your own selfishness from the day they were born – is suddenly, beautifully returned. It's the simplest of kindnesses, the simplest of lessons.

Andy and Lachie return to the room brimming with stories of rented strollers and Smarties ice-creams and half-hour queues for the rides. We have a room service dinner of rubbery pasta and semi-cold chicken nuggets which the kids love and the adults do not. But I eat because the meal's much more substantial than what I often have now – a slug of milk, if it's a night when Andy's late from work. Too tired to cook just for myself, too tired to eat.

In the grown-up section of the park there are cinemas and restaurants and discos in a steel and plastic complex designed by Frank Gehry. I know I should visit it for the architecture alone. Are you kidding? I'm a mother. The prospect of bed by nine, in Egyptian cotton sheets on a king-sized mattress, is a luxury that can't be relinquished. Our big night at Disneyland involves *My Favourite Martian* on the Disney channel, all four of us jumbled on the bed.

Lachie refuses to accept the movie's called anything but *My Favourite Russian*. Andy and I are too exhausted to explain.

The tiredness is deep, dragging through me. It's the tiredness of always going to bed too late for there's so much to do and the day's never long enough; the tiredness of never getting a sleep-in beyond seven. Because you have no family around you to give you a break, ever; no relief.

I need to find some way to be enchanted again in my life. It used to be with walking into the unknown and poetry and the smell of Alice Springs and my husband's hips and his laugh and Europe, the dream of it; and right now, I'm too tired. For any of it.

We wake to a white blanket outside; the park's been softened by a heavy fall of snow. 'Is it real?' asks Andy, the cynic, painting a picture of Hollywood snow machines working tirelessly overnight. 'They've had a huge problem attracting visitors in winter. Maybe this is their solution.' The pillow's aimed at his head.

I'm defending Disneyland. The worm has turned. Andy is incredulous.

We're greeted at breakfast by a phalanx of strangely-sized adults in costume: Minnie Mouse, Mickey, Pinocchio, Tweedledum and Tweedledee. They're all petite women – picked for their size, which is non-threatening to small children. But Ollie takes one look at their plastic heads, foam shoes and cartoon clothes and runs, appalled, in the opposite direction. (He won't go near his brother's garish Wiggles pyjamas either. The European sensibility is deep within him.)

He's the only child among a throng of children who's reacted in this way; the only child who refuses to believe. Our three-year-old, on the other hand, hugs every character like a long-lost friend and imagines conversations with them, even though not a single Disney character utters a sound. He turns to us, face beaming, then turns back to his friends. Lachie's an appreciator. He has a New-World enthusiasm and openness, a naïve friendliness, he's always had it in him. God help anyone who tries to break his spirit.

Mickey Mouse tries again with Ollie, who's ventured closer while clutching my hand. But a metre away my son's having none of it; he buries his face in my skirt and keeps it there, as if the sight of this cultural abomination, so close, is too much to bear. Mickey knows instantly to melt away – it's official Disney training. Never linger with a traumatised child: not a good company look.

I want to be cynical, I really do – there's so much to be cynical about. But as I watch Lachie cuddle Minnie and kiss her nose and chatter about his toy rabbit I have tears in my eyes. He believes; this creature kneeling before him is utterly genuine. For Lachie, and all the children around him – except the cynic – it's totally real. They'll talk about their trip to Disneyland for days and weeks and years afterward. These cartoon characters bowing their heads and listening so attentively to the children are their first pop stars, their first gods; and the gods love them. I'm surrounded by pure, uncomplicated happiness. And you can only smile at it; you have to surrender the cynicism. I envy the children's capacity for enchantment, the certainty they have in life. It's so fresh.

'The need to go astray, to be destroyed, is an extremely private, distant, passionate, turbulent truth,' George Bataille wrote. What is marriage doing to me? Losing me? And here I am in Disneyland, a mother, just that, with a dangerous feeling that I have to crash catastrophe into my world. Open the floodgates to rupture.

'I feel that a kind of retreating has dictated all my choices in life,' a friend said recently and I felt a chill at her words, for it had begun to dictate my choices, too. Once, not too long ago, it had never been like this.

Yet here I am. 'Exuberance is beauty,' said Blake, and all around me is exuberance. And I realise that at some point you just have to embrace it all. The park works; it's the joy on the kids' faces. Whatever gets you through, is my grandmother's catch-cry. This does.

So, again, to the rides. I'd hoped that because the sky was heavy with another payload of snow I could be like a Michael Jackson in Harrods – have the place to myself. I'm dreading the legendary queues, in the bitter cold, with two little boys who barely understand the concept of patience.

The park's busy. Of course. I always underestimate the sheer density of Europe. And it looks like the company has had no trouble attracting visitors in winter. Worse luck.

Our first queue is for the steam train that encircles the park. We board after a 20-minute wait (not bad going, I'm told). We're greeted by a loudspeaker: 'McDonald's welcomes you.' How strange – there's no outside branding anywhere else (how much did they pay for that?). The rattly, open carriages shunt forward in a puff of smoke that shrouds the platform. I close my eyes and for a ridiculous moment the clank and squeal and protest of the open carriages lurching into motion, the biting cold, the hard wooden benches and smell of burning coal evoke nothing so much as the cattle trains of the Holocaust. Europe, soaked in blood; and Jews were deported to death camps, perhaps, not too far from here.

But the train is painted a cheery green, McDonald's is welcoming us, and everything will be all right. We always seek certainty; we want to so easily forget; we are so very good at erasing.

Reality, a writer's reality, intrudes: I take out my notebook, I'm here to work. When I write a change comes over me, a retreating, a disconnection from the world that's almost violent. Yet in Disneyland I can't hear myself write and the notebook is barely touched.

A painter friend in Alice Springs told me recently of her new studio that was like living in a white balloon. I dream of that. I can write in Alice, in the hum of its silence. I found it also, a long time ago, in Antarctica.

What has become of my life?

And yet as a mother I'm at the coalface of living, and for a writer that's a good place to be. Motherhood didn't turn out to be the professional impediment I expected, for the children have hauled me into life. I'm no longer in control – I've had to let go, had to relinquish my own raging, wilful identity as a single woman. But perhaps I'm a better person for it.

'I don't want to underlive,' I'd written in a journal as I left Australia. And here I am now, six and a half years later, living to bursting with the kids. In a different life. I have to participate as a parent. A writer stands back, and motherhood doesn't often allow you the necessary distance to do that.

The food! We succumb because we have to – we're all starving. There's no alternative to an unremitting offering of hot dogs, hamburgers, nuggets and chips, at every café and kiosk. We're in France, God help us, and there's not a pain-au-chocolat in sight. The only European aspect I can find of the park's food industry is the way people are contentedly eating on café chairs outside, on ground that's frozen to a frosty paleness. We can't. I'll never get used to this mongrel cold, rattling and growling around us. I've never learnt how to dress properly for a European winter, never learnt the secret of layers.

We eat in a cavernous hall called the Videopolis for no other reason than it's warm. Correction, not quite warm, but warmer than outside. It's a barn-like place with tiered seating and giant screens running classic *Looney Tunes* cartoons. People buy their fast food and take it to a table and watch the screens, almost in silence. Would this scene be the same if Disneyland had been built in Spain, or Italy? I fear so, for I suspect this is a universal pose of the 21st century: eating, in silence, by the telly.

Everything here is almost – almost a burger, almost a hot dog. We eat an approximation of American fast food and because of that nothing is completely satisfying (except for the French fries, the only item cooked to perfection. Of course.)

Almost a burger, almost a Disneyland. The park is like French rock and roll – a fair approximation that doesn't quite possess the heart and soul of the original, doesn't quite do it right.

No matter, because the kids couldn't care less.

Everything is simplified, reduced. I'm anticipating the Australia display in the 'It's a Small World' section with a keenness undignified for a woman my age. What signifiers has my country been distilled to?

Of course: kangaroo, koala, cork hat. Same old story.

I don't even notice England's display, my home for the past seven years. Andy does. He insists that England is home. That it will be for many years to come.

The only area of the sparkling park that looks tired and dated is Discoveryland. It's a Jetsons vision of what the future's meant to be, and nothing is outdated as fast as an imagining of what is ahead.

But there's a wonderfully inventive movie celebrating technological achievements of the past 150 years, and as I watch the glories of the Concorde and the Eiffel Tower I realise that the best in the world is often the result of a collaboration. Disneyland Paris is itself a collaboration. I look around at all the faces staring up at the screens encircling the room – the European ones next to me, Arabic in front of me, Japanese behind me – and I realise that this is Disney's beauty; the collaborative aspect of it, the universal embracing of simplicity, story, reassurance, pleasure. And it's the kids who get that. Yet the adults here among them are collaborators too, for we are accepting it.

'I opened my eyes and here was the world. Here was this

great human and divine enterprise,' wrote Vasily Rozanov. And that is why this whole experience has been so unexpectedly moving. Disneyland is so complete, so sure; in a fragile world where I'm striving to make my children's future anchored and secure. They recognise and respond to the certainty of Disneyland, just as I do now. It's the certainty of childhood, a state of grace before cynicism, fear, doubt.

Late afternoon, tantrums imminent. The Pinocchio, Dumbo and Peter Pan rides have all been ticked off, as has the Swiss Family Robinson tree house that looks alarmingly real yet is made entirely of steel and plastic. It's time to go home.

'*Parlez-vous Anglais?*' I ask the waiter in the hotel bar, an hour before boarding the train. It's my one, clumsily spoken French phrase. He looks exasperated, as if no one's ever bothered before with this courtesy of enquiring whether he speaks English. 'Of course,' he replies curtly, implying I'm wasting his time attempting French in this place. Ah yes, they're used to dealing with doltish foreigners here, whereas in France, proper France, this simple query is always appreciated.

I've not found France on this trip. And curiously, my heart no longer aches for it. For I have learnt that this journey was not about France. It was about my children's happiness.

'Let's move to Paris,' I smile to Andy as we walk to the station. He grunts, and in that grunt I know it'll never be – at least as a couple. Paris to him is a bureaucratic nightmare and a decrepit political system. Perhaps he has a much clearer vision of the place than I do.

Graham Greene described childhood as 'a writer's bank balance', and I wonder sometimes about the relentless way Andy and I try to cram our children's lives with continual, seamless happiness. What defences will they develop for the bleakness of the world? How do I teach the boys bravery amid all this play; how do I spine their lives?

With good, kind, big hearts, I hope. Security will give them compassion, I hope, will give them a strength to cope.

As we wait for our train we huddle around an elegant cylindrical heater at the station – ah, France intrudes, finally, in the beautifully sleek, Phillipe Starke-like design. But I don't need my shot of Gallic beauty anymore because this Disney cynic from way back has actually been enchanted by the rude American interloper. For beyond mortgages and tax bills and school waiting lists, beyond the heartbreak of writing, beyond all the uncertainty about where we will live and what is ahead, there is this certainty: the joy in our children's faces.

As the little boys do silly faces at each other and giggle insanely about God knows what Andy and I look at each other and smile secrets. We live so much of our lives by reflected happiness now; but in doing so, we have found our own.

My abiding memory: the three boys chasing each other in ecstatic circles at the Disneyland entrance, and my heart cracking with love as I watch them. 'Come on,' Andy shouts, but I shake my head. It's my right as a writer to do this, to stand back. I take out my notebook and jot down what I so often forget, that the most intense happiness is to be found in the simplest of moments: the sight of your father laughing uncontrollably during a film, a bedroom filled with the sleep of your children, requited love. And this circle before me of delirious happiness. I pocket my notebook, and join in.

A gratitude
had begun
to sing in me.

— Denise Levertov

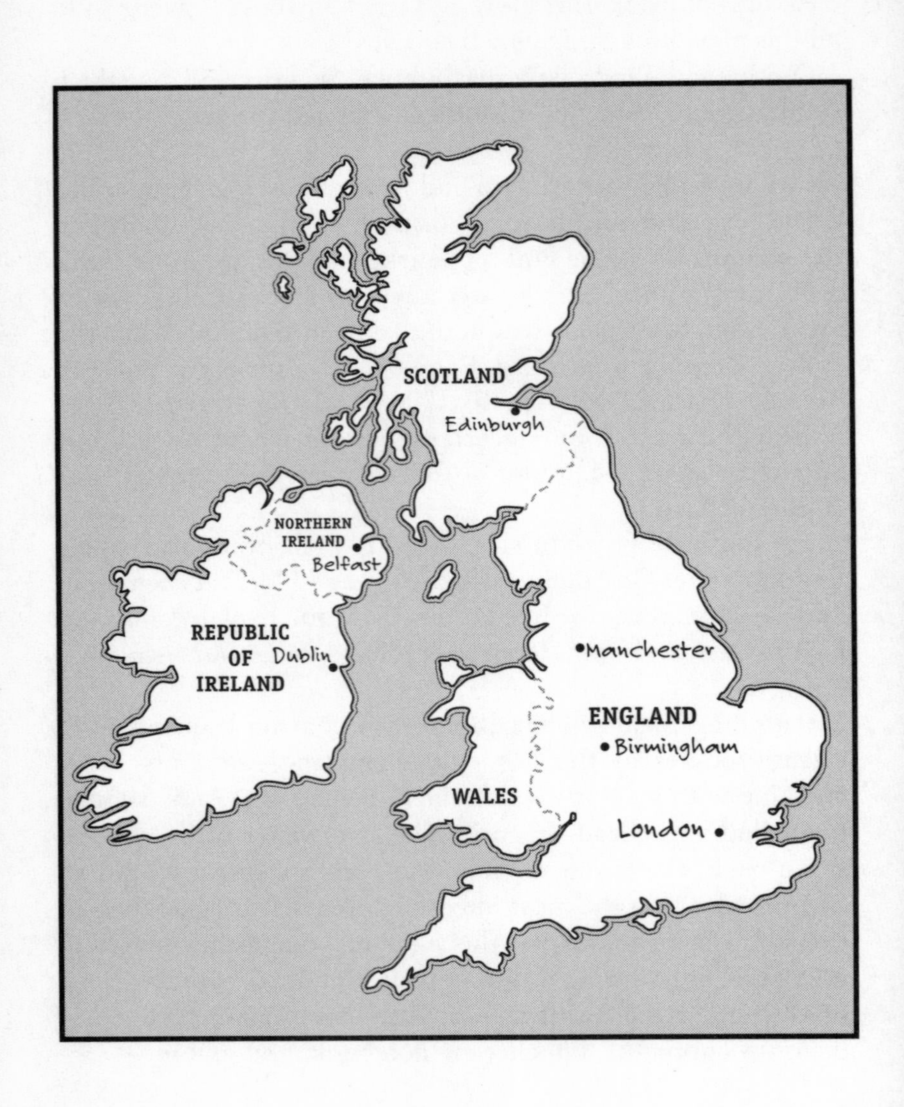
SCOTLAND
Edinburgh
NORTHERN
IRELAND
Belfast
REPUBLIC
OF
IRELAND
Dublin
Manchester
ENGLAND
Birmingham
WALES
London

A Battle with the English Equipment

NICK EARLS

IT'S NOT always easy to tell where you lost an evening once it's gone.

Things would probably have been fine if I'd been prepared to eat more chips. My body hadn't quite adjusted to London, and I ran into a bit of a food and beverage disparity. And the couple of glasses of wine, and the no food, and the last peculiar effects of time-zone slippage and the hectic interview schedule started to take their toll. I relaxed, in a biological kind of way – one that required close monitoring, or a good set of cue cards or a long lie-down – and, left momentarily unattended near the chips, the night came unstuck.

Weeks before, the invitation had told me that the launch would be at L'Equipe Anglaise, which my excellent French had promptly translated into 'The English Equipment'. I wasn't entirely sure what the English equipment was, and how or why it might differ in shape, form or function from anyone else's equipment – the French's most obviously – and

I fought to put the idea out of my head, but not with much success.

'Ah, yes, the English equipment,' I'd say knowingly to the plain walls of my magnolia-painted shed in Brisbane, but there was nothing knowing about it. And I'd turn the invitation over in my hand to read both sides of it, but nothing became clearer. The steam engine and the spinning jenny, the pin-stripe suit and the Gladstone bag . . . all these came to mind as famous pieces of English equipment, but they couldn't be L'Equipe Anglaise. Not if we were launching books there.

I started the month with interviews at home for *Bachelor Kisses*, then flew to the UK to promote *Zigzag Street*. On the plane, when I should have been reacquainting myself with the novel, I met Claudia, a BBC journalist on her way home. We talked all the way to Singapore, about the suitcases and wooden giraffes and exuberant pieces of crystal people bring on as cabin baggage, about the really unappealing Bette Midler movie screening, which we decided would work far better if we took the headphones off and made up our own dialogue. 'I never talk to people on planes,' she said, and I said I didn't either.

Claudia stayed in Singapore. I travelled on, my designated Singapore-to-London sleep sector now given over to re-reading *Zigzag Street*, the London dawn hitting hard when I got there. So that was partly to blame for the haziness that dogged my next few days, in and out of interviews, in and out of big black cabs, four new novelists and their four publicists touring around in search of attention.

But, general haziness aside, the problems really begin when I'm next to the chips. Next to the chips in L'Equipe Anglaise, its name still a mystery, our books freshly launched, the wine not so much kicking in as ambling across and befriending me. I'm holding my framed Fab-Four-Abbey-Road-zebra-crossing shot of we four authors. I'm watching the event go on around me; I'm feeling quietly good about myself, but mainly quiet.

I'm here. My book's being launched in London – right now, present tense. I'm the only Australian and the only male in a Fab Four that's as manufactured as the Spice Girls, but I'm here – and it feels like an achievement, though I'd quite like to lie down and read about it later.

And that, of course, is when people decide they want to talk to me, and Gina, my publicist, sights me and steers them my way – social columnists from newspapers and a fiercely attractive blonde woman who might be called Amanda and is something to do with TV and has lips so precise I think they must be stencilled. A woman who says she's from *The Times*, presumably as a joke, and then hitches up her skirt to show me the motif at the top of her stockings. This, it turns out, is quite an ice-breaker. I relax more. We chat.

And I'm thinking, surely you didn't say *The Times*? I recall that my underpants have a rather fetching logo at the front, but I'm not *that* relaxed. It strikes me that introducing things like that to the conversation could easily lead to misunderstandings, even though she's already done the skirt hitching thing. Plus, I'd only be copying. I don't think there are any prizes for being the second person in a crowded room to show your underwear, particularly when the first has flashed a label so upmarket you didn't even recognise it. I still, I reassure myself, have some judgment left. The music gets louder.

We talk about how the tour's been going. She asks me how Manchester was yesterday. She asks me something else, something I can't quite hear. It's about Australians and, I think, about stereotypes. I've been waiting for days for questions about Australians and the closest I've got so far is a couple of passing references to 'Neighbours'. So, Australians and stereotypes. My chance to do my bit for my country overseas, to dispel some myths. Make us look considered and reasonable, versatile even. I tell her Australians are a lot more versatile than people give them credit for. And, bland though this is, she seems to find it much more interesting than my views on the Manchester leg of the tour.

She says she thinks versatile is good. She says a lot of people look for versatile. She asks me if I'm versatile, in a way that makes it seem like a joke, so I tell her, 'They don't come much more versatile than me.' Which, of course, is untrue – I'm a control freak in a shed, most of the time, but she doesn't need to know that. Versatile? I only ever wear one brand of underpants. Rather fetching logo though, it occurs to me again. But again, I say nothing, stay discreet.

And it's just as I'm saying 'They don't come much more versatile than me' that enough of the parts of her previous question about Australians and stereotypes fall out of the noise and into place for me to work out that it was actually a question about Australians and sexual practices. I've just told her 'They don't come much more versatile than me.'

Of course, that's when I see the notebook. And this could be *The Times*. And she's writing it all down.

'So, Mr Versatile,' she's saying, 'What would you be best at, do you think?'

Not a good question. I try to stall her by asking if she means personally or as a nation. She says that she understands that, as a nation, the Australian male considers speed a virtue, but she's sure that with my versatility I must have more to offer. I know I have to answer, I know I have to say something. Versatile? Surely I'm not versatile. I can't even really imagine what versatile people do. The idea of a nipple clamp, for example, makes me wince. Is that versatile? And as if I could ever say 'nipple clamp' convincingly, even if I wanted to. Which I don't. She's got me with this. I simply should not be having this conversation. Conversation.

'Conversation,' I tell her. That's the part I'm best at.

And she says 'Excellent', writes it down in capital letters

and tells me that about wraps it up, though what it's wrapping up I'm not quite sure.

When she's gone I wonder what I am best at. I've never thought of it that way before. To hope you're some kind of gifted all-rounder probably suggests only a lack of insight, and that you aren't actually up to much. And I keep hoping, surely she didn't say *The Times*? Best at . . . I've never thought of 'best at' before. And maybe it actually is conversation. Would that be a good thing or a bad thing? Some hopeless slack cop-out, or something people might actually quite like. Or could great conversation turn the ensuing straight-down-the-line, medium-quality sex into a disappointment? How did I get to be 34 and married for years before I've had to address this? How did I get the idea that I have a gift for conversation, when I know that this desperate scrambling debate is one of a great many conversations that will never leave my head?

Anyone with a clue about conversation would have sorted this all out long ago and moved on. Anyone with a clue about anything would at least step away from the chips, cut their losses when it comes to *The Times* and make a fresh and unambitious start with another group of guests somewhere across the room.

I don't do that. Most of the next half-hour, I imagine myself having sex. And it's not a great thing to be doing. I should be working the crowd. I should have eaten more food before drinking the wine. I should have come to this country a few days earlier so this strangeness would have passed by now. I should get out more at home, rather than spending my work days living by email.

I begin to realise I might be pretty dull. I begin to think that the best thing about me might be my underpants logo and, sure, it's not a bad underpants logo – slightly scratchy but not bad – but I never wanted it to be better than the rest of me. You should always buy pants that make you feel good, I realise, now too late, of course. Pants that make you feel good about yourself, not about the pants. The moment you think you can't live up to your underpants, you're out of the game. That's one thing I'm certain of.

And that woman from *The Times* – she had those stockings, she had that brazen motif upper-thigh-high. Great underwear, heaps of confidence. And I get all mine at Kmart. Till now, I'd always thought it was because of the shareholder discount, but I'm beginning to think I might just be a Kmart guy. Bad vision: Kmart underpants, Kmart sex. With 7½ per cent off because of shareholder discount. In the shed, when applied to a range of products – paperclips, stapler, glue stick – this looks good. Out in the world, maybe not so good. And what is 92.5 per cent of Kmart-standard sex anyway? I'm just guessing, but I don't think the word would be versatile. I think I could be letting my country down.

It might be kind of reliable, but there probably wouldn't be much flare. But you wouldn't be expecting to be particularly impressed, would you? You're expecting Kmart. You're expecting value, something functional, nothing fancy. And maybe that's not such a bad thing to offer. You're expecting the elastic to survive a couple of years, and if it did any better you'd be thinking 'Hey, these are good underpants', and you'd appreciate them. It's probably largely about expectations.

Gina finds me and takes me to the nearest group of people. It includes Amanda, the high-octane, blonde TV woman, and I just know she has totally confident underwear. I do my best not to imagine her underwear. I do my best to say sensible things. I do my best to resume control and I completely lose the capacity for conversation. Various other TV people gather around us. I can't imagine any of them values a shareholder discount half as much as I do, and I'm sure they all outrank me seriously when it comes to garments, inner and outer.

Gina senses that I'm flagging, and suggests a meal.

We head for the Groucho Club, because she says she owes me after last night. Though she bought me dinner last night too. But dinner last night was a bowl of cereal with M1 motorway vistas at 10.30 pm on the way back from Manchester, followed by a bit of a nap with my head tapping away against the minibus window on the way home. We – the Fab Four authors – had done our 'show' earlier that evening in a Waterstone's bookshop that was proudly the second-biggest anywhere. We'd started with a press conference, a term which also in this instance could justify inverted commas. So, 'press conference': the Fab Four of us sitting in old olive-coloured vinyl arm chairs in different parts of the tea room, speed-dating five Mancunian journos with dictaphones.

'So, how do you like Manchester?' three of them asked me, and I told them it seemed like a great place, though in fact I'd arrived there, in the dark, for the first time in my life only 20 minutes before being led to the tea room. 'I'm looking forward to seeing more of it,' I said, having seen Australian airport press conferences – the real thing, no inverted commas – go right or badly wrong depending on how some American star has handled the equivalent question minutes after passing through Immigration.

Gina and I go to the Groucho Club and meet Charles, an artist and cartoonist, and she says to me, 'This is the friend I mentioned earlier, you know, steaming mug of tea,' and Charles says, 'Yes, that was someone I knew.' Which is what you would say, since the story Gina's alluding to was about a 15-year-old who arrives home from school, greets his mother in the kitchen, goes upstairs to his bedroom, shuts the door, puts on his headphones and plays The Stranglers good and loud, drifts away into the fantasy, tosses himself off thoroughly and opens his eyes to find, on his bedside table, a steaming mug of tea.

In this man's company, then, I feel less awkward. He seems used to being introduced with the aid of references to a story about masturbation. I suspect his underpants could be pretty bad, or at least unlikely to have a flash logo.

I'm able to persuade myself that I'm not doing so badly. My mother might have once said to me, after going to an adolescent medicine seminar, that she'd been told that day if your teenage child is alone in their room with the door shut they're almost certainly masturbating, but I never copped the steaming mug of tea. I did eventually get used to doing all my study with the door open. I still have no idea if telling me the door thing was her way of giving me the all-clear, or if she was being strangely hip just by bringing the subject up, or if she was actually trying to freak me out, but I have to admit my marks did improve.

At the Groucho Club the evening gets more surreal. I seem to recognise most of the people here. I've seen many of them regularly for years, on TV and in magazines. I know none of them, but it takes some effort to believe that, some effort to convince myself that I haven't left a roomful of strangers at L'Equipe and turned up to a roomful of friends, where conversations could begin in the middle, picking up from where we left off last time.

I'm a long way from my regular life – my three-person, one-cat household, my magnolia walls, my inflexible brand-name specificity when it comes to groceries and garments, my deep attachment to Coles Myer and to 7½ per cent off. It's as though I've now stepped into a TV, and I'm looking out at everything else, at my actual life.

We sit a table next to the cast of 'The Bill', who seem to dress better than they do in real life, except this is real life, the place where all the stars are. And Sun Hill Police Station, which always struck me as very real, is, of course, the made-up part. But at least in this unreal real world they seem to have none of those difficult interpersonal conflicts that trouble them at work, so that's not a bad thing. As the evening goes on, though, one of them does approach a diner at another table, take him in a playful headlock and shout, ‘You’re nicked. You’re nicked.’ He’s messing with my sense of boundaries, and I don’t even know any more whether he means to or not.

We finish our meals and take the rest of our bottle of wine to a small table near the bar. Gina begins a debate with a film producer about the ethics of making a movie about the sinking of the Titanic, then admits that for years she’s had an idea for a knitwear label called Madame Defarge, but she thinks that’s completely different, and in much better taste. She can’t say why. She says a Titanic movie’s just wrong, even if they built a great boat, and it’s worse because they made it a love story.

‘What next?’ she says. ‘The moors murders?’ And she promptly outlines a plot, works on character profiles and drafts a shot list. We all agree, of course. We’re all appalled. No-one would dare make a movie about the moors murders.

A couple of minutes later I notice the film producer making a few furtive notes on a serviette and stashing it in her bag. She shrugs and says, ‘Well, Gina’s not going to make it, is she?’

A friend of Charles’s comes up. She’s married to a famous artist. Not that anyone should be defined by who they’re married to, but I’m not told much else. She has well-worked-out arm muscles and an accent that seems to swivel and point in different directions. And the only problem with that is I seem to have some compulsion to keep up with her, as though we can’t converse unless we shift accents at the same time. She’s probably well-travelled; I’m three days away from home and making it up as I go along. She’s cosmopolitan; I’m adrift. It’s a noisy room, and maybe the only accent-switcher in it is me.

Is this some fitting-in problem that I’m having? Have I so little control now that I’ve lost my own accent? Have I spent too much time in my shed in relative silence, despite being led to believe that that was the kind of thing a writer would do? I really haven’t been the same since the encounter with that woman from *The Times*. I find a public show of underwear disconcerting and things haven’t felt normal since.

'So, what have you been doing lately?' I ask the partner of the famous artist, as though I've just edited a line out of a conversation with someone I actually know, and put it to her instead. As though I've any idea what she's done *other* than lately. As though, since we both seem to be from the Upper East Side at the moment, it's okay to seem a little familiar so far from home.

London has destabilised my accent. The partner of the famous artist, who can use three different accents over the course of a medium-sized word, gives me almost no chance of getting it back. I listen less and do my utmost to talk in my normal voice. I find my way back there and I force it, and I can't believe how nasal it sounds. How unsophisticated. Surely the sound coming out of me now is not my normal voice? Not anywhere in the world could it be a normal voice. I can't believe I've done so much radio in the past couple of days with this shamefully crappy voice. I'll probably never sing again, not even along to things, not even in the shower. If there's one thing I take away from this night, that should be it.

And what has the partner of the famous artist been doing lately? Well, surfing, actually. However unlikely that might seem to me. Surfing off the Devon coast this morning. And, sure, I can see her on a board pretty easily, but this is England, this is winter. I ask if it was cold and she says Barbados a month ago was better. And they'd had a weekend in Maui, but the weather was bad the whole time.

And I'm beginning to think that this *is* what she's been doing lately. Surfing. Surfing recreationally. Pretty much everywhere, pretty much all the time. Perhaps that's what she does, that's why she's got the well-worked-out arm muscles. And, I have to admit, while I thought the artist was doing well, I didn't realise his success could support a global surfing habit (assuming that's where the support for the habit comes from).

Your partner, I want to say to her, he puts sheep in tanks. Have you ever thought about that? People pay him heaps for, like, large dead animals that he hasn't done a whole lot with. You surf all over the world because a guy put a big dead animal in a tank, and put it in a place that houses art. And since he was the only person putting big dead animals in tanks that day at the art place, the man's a genius and his work is highly prized.

He designed a restaurant with a 10-foot tube of Canesten to decorate the women's toilet. What about that then? What about that as an observation about the late 20th century? Is it one? Isn't it?

But this line of enquiry comes with a querulous tone, even when it's still in my head, and I don't like to think how it would end up sounding if I actually tried it aloud. Which I don't since the tone is wrong and it's entirely possible I'm wrong about the artist's name as well. She might be married to someone altogether different – an animal-loving vegan, famous for his arty black-and-white photos of breaking waves, for instance. I keep finding myself in loud places tonight, and I should stop making assumptions about things I haven't quite heard and offering my best tentative observation in reply.

But all's well this time. She's still talking about surfing and, since it's a surf conversation, I hardly have to pay any attention at all to be participating as fully as is expected. I'm slightly worried, though, that the only thing that makes sense to me at the moment is what she's saying about waves. She's telling me more of what she means about Barbados, Barbados and Devon, how there's more to surfing than just the waves. Barbados had better surf, *and* she'd surfed better. And I know what she means. The others don't. It's a difference they don't appreciate. They think it's automatic. Better waves, you have a better day. 'It's timing, isn't it?' I say to her and she agrees. 'It's you and the wave.' And she says, 'Exactly, you and the wave.'

So, we're getting on well now. And the others can't go with this. They couldn't have said 'you and the wave'. At least not in my accent, which was clearly coastal, though possibly from both sides of the Pacific. And I'm calling her by name now, in a way that you don't have to in a two-person conversation. A way that perhaps suggests I'm pretending to be formal and intimate at the same time, when I'm probably entitled to be neither. I call her by name three times, I think, two of them while imitating a spaced-out west-coast surfer giving bad advice, in case that might be funny. I wish I wasn't doing this. And I'm calling her Myra. And I realise we may not have been introduced by name, and I'm wondering where I've got Myra from.

Then I remember the topic of conversation when she came to the table, and I'm probably naming her Myra after the moors murderer of the same name. She doesn't seem to mind, but I wish brains didn't work that way. And it's not as though I can call her anything else now. I make such an effort not to call her Myra that I shut up completely, for the second time tonight.

Ten minutes of well-managed silence from me – 10 minutes of concentrating really hard on not apologising, and on not telling her I'd temporarily confused her with a moors murderer – and Gina calls a cab.

Back in my room, my compact magnolia-walled hotel room, I talk to myself – not loudly, but just to get some idea of where I'm from. And the answer, all too obviously, is that I am still from someone's blocked nasal passages, but whose, I have no idea. I make notes about Charles and the steaming mug of tea. It's a story that might one day fit in somewhere. The rest of the evening makes insufficient sense to write down yet.

I flick the TV on and give myself my nightly half-hour of Winter-Olympic curling. It's strange that this is what's becoming familiar to me now. Half a world away from my regular life – a life given over to more routines than those of an elderly housepet – this is the only thing I've managed to do three days in a row in exactly the same way. This, and the bowl of middling-quality muesli I start the mornings with in the hotel breakfast room downstairs.

I rearrange the pillows and get comfortable in front of the contest playing itself out on the ice. I think about how many stones Sweden has in the house. I think about it in a Scottish accent. Curling. I can't accept that my days begin with muesli and end with Winter-Olympic curling, and nothing predictable happens in between. As if the curling itself isn't weird enough. It could only be an ancient game. It could never be invented now. How could you invent it? How could you go, 'I think I'll invent a Winter-Olympic sport using only granite and housework'?

I sleep. I wake up. I take in the magnolia colour and for a second or two get things wrong. This is not the shed. This is Belgrave Road in London, a hotel. This is not where I'd expected to be. Not that I'm complaining, but I didn't think I'd get to places like this.

Years ago, I had a concept of the author as someone who would spend a lot of time in a shed. Roald Dahl did, writing in pencil on pages on a tray in his lap while semi-reclined in an old armchair. And Dylan Thomas wrote in a shed, some time, somewhere – I've seen a photo. And Thomas Mann, by the shores of the Baltic. The list goes on and on of authors alone with their thoughts in little rooms away from the action, their pages on some rough-hewn board as they connect once again with their genius and make copious notes in spidery longhand, crab-handed marginal notes about the world and its shortcomings, all without leaving home.

But it was never like that, I now realise. The Dickens *A Tale of Two Cities* tour rolled on through the American west by train day after day, and night after night he'd get up and read to packed houses. And the journalists would be there at the station when his train arrived and they'd ask him, the moment he disembarked and before his eyes had even sorted out the light, what he thought of Kansas City or Tulsa or Phoenix.

Despite that, I'd had an idea of the author as someone who worked away in an isolation that was, if not splendid, at least suburban. Someone whose phone would only ring when the time was right, who could play tennis several times a week during business hours, who could have big ideas in very small places. I *had* big ideas then. Big, complicated ideas. Grand and clever plans.

Now, in a way, my ideas have become completely, even determinedly, ordinary and it's some of my days that are peculiar. My nine-minute reading about a none-too-special Brisbane coffee shop conversation sustains me night after night on this tour. It's a five-page, anywhere-in-the-world, boy-meets-girl-and-nothing-happens story. Night after night, it begins like this:

> 'I go to a coffee shop. I eat a bagel and read. I always wanted to be cool enough to be one of those people who was comfortable sitting alone in a coffee shop and reading. I always thought they had a special allure.
>
> 'Just as I'm in the process of dismissing allure and deciding "loser with a book for company" is a better fit, a girl says *Mind if I sit here,* and indicates the other side of the booth. I tell her, Go ahead.
>
> 'She is twentyish. She is a babe. I glance around. There are plenty of free seats. She chose to sit here. And I tell myself this could be the knock of opportunity, and that I should put a lid on my very disabling ambivalence for once. I should say nothing more, go back to the book, pump up the allure.'

And so it goes. But somewhere – somewhere in going from an idea to a novel, in being transported around to other places and put in front of audiences – it's become a different kind of ordinary, a kind of celebration of ordinary.

And sheep are ordinary, and tanks are ordinary, and sheep's insides are very ordinary and are spilled on properties around the world on a daily basis without any idea of the missed potential for art. But in the place where vision beyond the everyday is expected, the place where people come for the vision that is art, the gutted sheep is the artist 'affirming life with deadly subjects'. The cow and calf bisected longitudinally and presented in two parts continues the artist's 'exploration of themes of mortality and isolation'. I know this because, the next morning I read it on the Internet. I know it's not just a man becoming famous on account of a big dead animal or two.

Because it's not as though that would make sense. It's not as though big dead animals are particularly rare. It's not as though he was the first to notice them. Give them a couple of days in the sun and everyone in the vicinity notices them. But he's put them in a place where people look for meaning, and there's something in the inevitable uncomplicated ordinariness of the displayed parts of the big dead animals that seems to allow them to mean something. Something about issues as major as life and death.

And I get the impression from the number of countries involved in the surfing of the last month that the artist's life, reliant at least partly on the ordinariness of animal viscera, is now far from ordinary. And my life's not like his, but I'd had ordinary notions of what a writer's life would be like, and sometimes it's less ordinary than I'd imagined. I thought I'd watch more daytime TV. I never thought I'd tour England and fall asleep watching Winter-Olympic curling night after night.

I did not envisage an evening involving the Groucho Club, the cast of 'The Bill', the wave-hungry partner of the famous artist, the forwardness of *The Times*, the stylishness of a journalist's underwear when all I've got to show is Kmart, and even then Kmart bought at a 7½ per cent shareholder discount. I did not envisage the minibus on the way back from Manchester the night before, eating cereal for dinner late, maximally tired and looking like crap, dozing mouth-open with my head clunking occasionally against the window. Or waking to the sound of laughter and seeing the word 'allure' written in the condensation on the glass and an arrow pointing to my head. All this was glimpsed in passing, and never made certain. I still don't know – I'll never know – if I heard the famous artist's name correctly. There are no pictures on any websites of a partner, whether named Myra or otherwise. I disconnect my laptop and go down to breakfast.

Today, even my breakfast routine is stolen from me. There's a newspaper editor to meet, no slow, quiet muesli to be had this morning. He orders sausages and beans, and he tells me his paper doesn't do author stories but he likes my work and has a proposition to put to me.

'You're funny, yeah?' he says. 'Bloody funny. I've read the book, well, some of it. And you were a doctor once, Gina said. Right? So, I'm looking for something on sperm. A feature. Funny. A bit informative as well, but it's got to be funny. You know, good sperm and how to get 'em. That sort of thing. How sperm counts are declining, and tight underpants and all that. Funny.'

He shovels in more sausage and more beans. I think he winks, but it might just be a facial tic. I tell him it sounds great, and that I'll have a think about it. There's lots of scope for funny when it comes to sperm. He tells me he'd like it in two weeks. I don't tell him I'll be touring for another six and it won't be happening.

Gina meets me in a cab for another morning of interviews at Broadcasting House. We sit in a small cubicle switching from one BBC region to another, sometimes every quarter of an hour. Accents come at me from all parts of the country. The same questions come through again and again. Where did you get the idea from? Is this what the Aussie male is really like? Do you ever dance nude in the office?

Gina says, 'Let's keep it interesting.' She writes a random

selection of words on a piece of paper and, while each question is being asked, she points to the one I have to include in my answer. Every time her finger hovers near 'hyacinth', I start to get tense.

In a break I have coffee with Claudia, who's on her first day back at work at the BBC. It turns out that after our Brisbane to Singapore flight each of us tried to strike up a conversation with the person next to us on the Singapore to Heathrow leg. My neighbour was a neo-Nazi and hers wanted to have sex with her under a blanket.

On Saturday, the *Zigzag Street* part of the tour is done and I'm back at the airport. I buy a cheap curry and a copy of *The Times*. In the Metro section, there's a column headed 'Arty Animal' and, next to it, a columnist head shot that looks entirely familiar.

But it's okay. The only writer mentioned is Louis de Bernières, in a context involving red wine and in which he seems to have been caught a bit off guard. There's a photo, and that's how he looks. Were stockings involved, I wonder? And a little notebook whipped out, just as he realised he couldn't hear her properly over the music? I'm grateful for the huge success of *Captain Corelli's Mandolin*, happy to let him be the more inviting target. It looks like I'm in the clear.

I'm not. A week later I'm in Adelaide for their writers' festival, and I'm in an Internet café checking my email. There's one from Gina about a *Times* review that slams all Fab Four novels, three of them comprehensively. 'And I wouldn't be too concerned about the Arty Animal piece,' she says at the end. 'I'm sure people will find it amusing.'

So I go to *The Times* site and find the article, in which the Arty Animal's stockings, proud though she was of them on the night, fail to rate a mention. The article in which I smile rakishly and the Arty Animal blotches fetchingly. The article in which I begin by keeping a low profile over by the crisps, but soon enough, certain bold claims concerning sexual versatility and conversation come to the fore.

And the reviewer does indeed slam the books, but comes unstuck by mentioning that the central character of one of them takes up worshipping Satan. Satan is, in fact, the name of her dog. A rather cursory reading of the books has revealed itself and, back in London, Gina goes into action. The Arty Animal, though, is on solid ground since she seems to have quoted me verbatim and it's hard to make a fuss about that.

That night I visit the Squeezebox, the Adelaide Festival party venue. It's a temporary roofless faux church, featuring a battery of accordion players down near the altar. Standing in the Squeezebox is like finding yourself in the middle of a mixed metaphor.

Someone waves at me from the dance floor – a Random House publicist I met earlier in the day. She's dancing with another publicist, and a man who looks familiar. I've seen his photo, his photo with wine. 'This is Louis,' one of them says, and it's Louis de Bernières. Louis de Bernières, far, far away from the nearest copy of today's edition of *The Times*, is dancing in the Squeezebox in Adelaide with two Random House publicists.

Will I ever be so important that I have a contract that gives me *two* publicists? As my surreal life becomes more surreal, there's some comfort in resorting to the petty.

So, we dance, but my first real conversation with Louis de Bernières takes another year to happen, and it happens in Perth.

The steaming mug of tea anecdote makes its way into *Perfect Skin*, where there's really no need for it but no one ever makes me take it out.

Claudia gets married in France, writes a book and produces a five-part BBC radio series about the digits of the hand, with one episode devoted to each.

I become involved in fundraising anthologies for the international aid agency War Child and, for the second anthology in Australia, I write a story about a guy from Brisbane who meets someone called Claudia on a flight to London. They talk about the wooden giraffes people drag on board as though they're slivers of balsa wood and they revoice the really unappealing Bette Midler in-flight movie from beginning to end. The story's called 'Cabin Baggage', and everything that happens west of Singapore is fiction. Claudia reads it and okays it, but says her workmates were hoping for porn.

Coles Myer announces the phasing out of its shareholder discount card, and says that it will be gone completely by 31 July 2004. Hundreds of thousands of people are mildly pissed off, but one, of course, is gutted. I suppose I will still buy my underwear at Kmart, but I will wait for those sporadic 15-per-cent-off, Monday-only doorbuster sales. That'll show them.

I become a co-editor on the third War Child anthology. An email arrives from England telling me a perfect fourth member of the editorial team has been found, and who should it be but the Arty Animal? We all meet for a drink in London. This time I remember to eat. No underwear is exposed. The Arty Animal remembers nothing of our earlier meeting but says, 'Oh, yes, that sounds like me.'

Two of the other Fab Four authors end up writing stories for the book, and my Claudia story ends up there, too, in the UK edition.

For the Australian edition I write a story about a person whose life involves travel and becomes confusing. No one knows it at the time, but it's a trial run for a novel.

At the start of the novel the character flies across time zones and finds herself alone in her hotel room late at night, watching TV. I find myself writing half a page on Winter-Olympic curling, at first with no recollection of where my expertise has come from. The half page amuses me greatly, but there's no place for it in the novel so it has to be cut. One day I'll use at least that 'granite and housework' line, I decide. One day someone will ask me to write something, and in it'll go.

And so it continues, I suppose, this ordinary and extraordinary clutter that comes along when we clear enough space in our minds to make room for it. It rambles along in a loosely connected or frankly disconnected way, and it breaks the control we like to think we maintain when we're home in the world we know best. Home among entrenched habits. Home assuming the best stories come from elsewhere, as perhaps I once did. Home writing with our trays on our knees, assuming at the start that it's all about big ideas and taking years to learn otherwise. Years to learn that some of our best ideas aren't big and might not be distant, and that they travel better than we do, better than we expect they will.

But that knowledge comes to us once we've gone away with them, and it comes home and irresistibly takes charge and we turn out animals in tanks, bisected, or stories about people, even if we started out thinking this should all be about something grander than us.

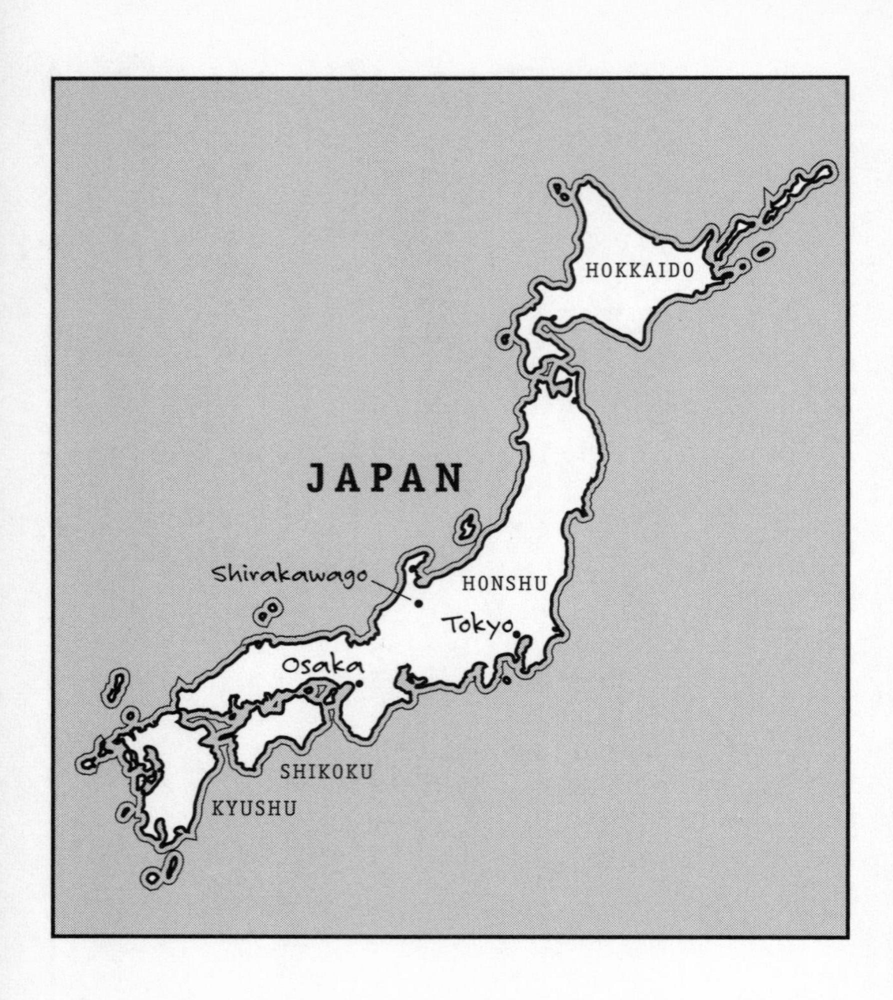
JAPAN
HOKKAIDO
HONSHU
Shirakawago
Tokyo
Osaka
SHIKOKU
KYUSHU

Exactly as I Remember

TONY DAVIS

THE COUPE was slipping backwards down the steep, icy hill. Nothing I did with the accelerator or brake pedal seemed to be making any difference.

We were about to smoothly, silently slide to the bottom, tail-first, then thud through the flimsy fence and glide over the edge of the mountain into the darkness. We would be quietly, fatally lost among the snow-covered fir trees somewhere down below. Or perhaps we'd explode in a million shades of red, yellow and purple like the baddies in a James Bond film.

It was so unjust. I was in one of the most crowded places in the world and there was simply nobody about. It was the richest nation in history, and I had rarely driven on such appalling roads. And I was right in the heart of a country I was deeply in love with, yet the very same country was doing its best to kill me.

Not only me, but Carolyn, who didn't even want to be here.

The whole thing was a stupid idea – and was becoming

more stupid by the hour. A few weeks earlier I had arrived at the notion of flying to Tokyo and driving through the mountains to a tiny rural village said to have scarcely changed in 400 years. I was in the middle of a personal obsession with Japan. Or, if the car slid back any further, the final moments of a personal obsession with Japan.

It was the mid-1990s and the country was in its maddest, most frenetic and most fascinating stage. It was so fat with funds that property experts calculated the walled plot of land surrounding the Imperial Palace in the centre of Tokyo was worth as much as every square centimetre of California. Residents complained that perfectly good roads were being pulled up and remade so local authorities could get rid of budget surpluses. The rest of the world was trying to change the way it did things to somehow tap into the industrial alchemy of the Japanese Miracle.

What few guessed was that the wagon was already out of control. The greatest economic success story of the modern world was about to spectacularly crash and burn. And on this sharp, snow-covered rise, 30 kilometres past Kisofukushima, we were on schedule to beat it by a full six months.

I had thought navigation would be the hard bit of driving in Japan. I hadn't even considered bravery and endurance. Yet we had been travelling through an apparently endless succession of narrow, poorly lit tunnels, around blind hairpin corners, over sections of dirt and single-lane bitumen and across flimsy-looking bridges spanning icy rivers somewhere down in the dark. There had been landslides too, which usually involved driving right up against the lip of a cliff to circumnavigate. At times the icy conditions reduced us to walking pace and I was struggling to keep our lumbering luxo-barge between the marker posts. The tail would swing out wildly, or the nose refuse to go where it was pointed, leaving us skating towards a sheer drop and causing my chest to thump, the back of my hands to prickle.

There was by now a knitting needle piercing through each of my temples, it was growing darker with every hour, the snow was becoming heavier and our destination still didn't seem any closer. I was openly speculating that the village of Shirakawago didn't really exist, that Old Japan was a myth. That the glitz and insane rush of Tokyo was the real Japan, the only Japan. And then, instead of its usual attempts to swap ends or jump face-first off a ledge, our car decided to simply spin its rear wheels and refuse to go forward. And then to start sliding backwards. Backwards towards a hairpin bend on the brink of a mountain . . .

In the modern world we can pick up countries and drop them like favourite albums. They fill a need in our lives or capture the mood of a particular time. Sometimes they even shape the mood. We can have them on constant rotation until we are sick to the teeth, then let them slowly drift to the edge of the rack. We can return years later and be instantly recaptured by their thrall. Or we can say, 'How did anyone ever think that was interesting, let alone me?'

Through the years I've picked up and dropped many favourite countries, cities and regions. Each provided an ideal in excitement, or relaxation, or exotic temptation to measure against the mundanity of another hot summer in the office or an early morning commute on a rainy, cold and windy Sydney August day. Or the rank stupidity of another rankly stupid decision by a government I helped vote in, or tried to vote out. At one time I considered Hong Kong the most vibrant, exotically exciting place on earth. At another it was New York. It has been France and northern Italy. On many other occasions I've wondered why you would want to go anywhere else in the world when you can sit for free at the very edge of Sydney Harbour in the autumn sun, reading a book and occasionally tilting your head up to gaze at the yachts.

But for five or six years, it was Japan. I read all that I could, and talked about *my* tiny, crowded, long-isolated country to anyone who would listen. Every aspect of Japan was different, exciting, shocking and perplexing. And the more I dug beneath its thin Western coating on a series of short working visits, the more different, exciting, shocking and perplexing it was.

The origins of my fascination came back recently while watching the film *Lost in Translation*. Not the implied affair, or near-affair, but the soulless hotels, the *Blade Runner* views out every window, the sense of time collapsing into a haze of hotel corridors and unreasonable work schedules and surreal encounters. The endless babbling around me in a language I was sure I could never possibly understand. The idea that when I met a Westerner off the beaten track there was instantly the sort of bond you might share with a fellow earthling encountered on another planet.

Lost in Translation was criticised because the Western characters didn't engage with the Japanese; the locals merely provided a show – Intriguing Asia, in Wide-Vision Surround Sound – for the amusement, bemusement and cemusement of foreigners. Yet that was exactly how it all was for me the first few times. They were rushed trips in the line of journalistic duty, usually to write about a motor show or new product, once to interview a test pilot who had flown Japan's experimental fighter planes in the final days of the Second World War. The pace was ludicrous, the prices outrageous. The artificial lighting ensured none of the surfaces looked quite real and none of the colours were anything close to true. Even outside, the sun never seemed to really make its way though the Tokyo smog to lift the country completely out of twilight. It was a parallel world to the one I lived in and, for its mysteries alone, far more compelling.

As with New York, my heart rate picked up a few beats per minute the moment I arrived in Tokyo. But unlike New York, the

Gotham City of the East was almost unnervingly safe and law abiding. People parked cars and left their wallets on the dashboard. There was no graffiti, no litter, no vandalism to be seen.

Memories of those trips are characterised by several things: following women with little flags to meeting points; long interviews through interpreters in which questions were never really answered; a permanent haze of cigarette smoke; the constant use of the word '*hai*' (or yes), even when the answer was obviously no; the mortuary-drawer-style businessmen's hotels near railway stations; huge dinner trays covered with tiny black bowls of mysterious substances; and vast quantities of Asahi and Kirin beer, handed out to Westerners at every occasion. There was always a bustle around me that didn't quite involve me. I could be within it, but never part of it. There were people I met everyday but came not one millimetre closer to knowing. And that just made it far more intriguing and captivating. So I hatched a plan to make scrutable the inscrutable. To find the real Japan. And to show it to Carolyn, my wife.

The idea was relatively simple. About 350 kilometres to the north-west of Tokyo is a small village called Shirakawago, considered one of the last relatively untouched parts of rural Japan. The houses are traditional *gassho-zukuri* designs with steeply pitched straw roofs. Even on a clear day you can't see a car plant. But for the odd satellite dish, little has changed in centuries.

I managed to book into a 400-year-old thatched-roof *ryokan*, or hostel, where the regional food was so authentic, it was said, Japanese visitors photographed it. And because there was no train over those mountains, getting there would involve driving, something very few Westerners do in Japan. It wasn't hard to see why – the difficulties were legion. The nation's population of cars, parked end to end, exceeded the total length of roads. Added to this were tens of millions of bicycles, mopeds and motorcycles, an absence of footpaths on most streets and a street naming (or non-naming) system so complex even the Japanese struggled with it.

Crawling through Tokyo's unsignposted and unbelievably crowded streets, we had managed to miss the turn-off to Expressway Number 4, a result of the peculiar local habit of putting the sign after the turn-off. A few (possibly illegal) turns later and we were back on the ramp, which quickly descended into a string of vast multi-laned tunnels, lit with a strange yellow light and filled with thick smog. Each tunnel cost about the price of a decent Australian lunch to enter. Between them were stretches of raised expressway lined with high concrete walls. The posted limit was 40 kilometres per hour but in practice there were only two speeds: stationary and flat biscuit.

Even in the 1990s, the sight of a Westerner behind the wheel was rare enough to inspire second takes among pedestrians and terrify other road users. They seemed to slow down, speed up or simply take the closest exit once they looked inside our cockpit. To add extra spice, we were – for no reason that made sense – in a battleship of a Japanese luxury coupe known as a Eunos Cosmo RE. It felt only 10 per cent narrower than many of its home country's roads.

Our challenge was to complete the 700-kilometre round trip without getting lost, hitting anything, tipping off the edge of a mountain pass or letting the Land of the $10 Orange Juice swallow all our resources. My personal challenge was to convert Carolyn, who had never been to Japan, and had never considered going. She couldn't quite understand the appeal of a country that had as its semi-official slogan 'the nail that stands out must be hammered down'. Or one where a couple of years earlier I had been expected to eat the flesh from the back of a lobster which was still alive and which – if chef hadn't thoughtfully de-socketed its legs – would have scrambled off the table.

My wife was humouring me. Even the travel agent had humoured me. 'We don't normally send people to Japan – it's too dear,' she'd said, reaching for a stack of brochures. 'Have you considered Bali?'

There is a peculiar joy, nonetheless, in sharing something big. Especially your city. My claim on Tokyo was slight, but I was going to cling to it. Things hadn't started well. On the first night, a very fresh prawn chose to leap out of the noodle hotpot it had been invited to participate in. It landed next to Carolyn's seat. She ran out of the restaurant and into the street, somewhere. By the time I found her she was in an alley, throwing up against a fence. And, simultaneously, being propositioned by a local.

Carolyn insisted it wasn't the live prawn. She was still queasy from the flight. As for the local? Well, a man with halting English asking an obviously ill *gaijin* if she wanted to go out with him was so ridiculous we should just ignore it. 'Let's pretend day two is our first day,' she generously offered.

I was relieved. I needed Carolyn to like Japan. Fortunately she was quickly absorbed in Tokyo's architecture with its singular mix of steel, glass, concrete, tiles, wood and paper, and what look like entire precincts made solely of neon. She marvelled at the Shinto shrines, the asymmetrical office blocks, the small shops with their ski-jump roofs and Tudor-like panelling, the avant-garde buildings in crazy colours with mock crumbling Roman façades or, in one case, with what looked like a massive golden turnip on top.

Carolyn had never seen so many people in one place. In every place. Schoolboys in uniforms modelled after those of Prussian military officers, city workers in haute couture, dark-suited *salarymen* with dark hair and identical dark cases packing literally by the million into train stations now decorated with billboards saying in English (and only in English) 'Import Now'.

Retailers had discovered a new fad called *kurisumasu* (Christmas) and were doing an even better job than any nominally Christian country of turning it into a commercial bonanza. On December 25 you were expected to exchange gifts, spend lavishly at an expensive restaurant *and* complete a normal day in the office or factory. 'Merry Xmas' was the message on every second banner in the retail districts. A particularly spherical Santa Claus, perhaps presumed to be a Western deity, was the pin-up boy of the moment.

Even on Expressway Number 4 some of the trucks had Santa Claus dolls tied to their roofs. The posted speed limit was now 80 kilometres per hour, but at 100 we didn't overtake anything except a police car. Later the police car overtook us at 110 kilometres per hour with lights flashing and two very serious-looking officers wearing pudding bowl crash helmets. They were unlikely to catch even the slowest semi-trailer out that day. Perhaps the reason I was coming closer than almost anyone else to obeying the speed limit was because I'd read that Japan had a purpose-built jail for driving offenders. More than that, the stratospheric price of fuel and the rapacious thirst of our twin-turbo, three-rotor Cosmo meant decisions about overtaking were ruled not by 'Am I able to?', but 'Can I afford to?'.

The scenery around towns was dotted with Pachinko Parlours and Love Hotels. The former are gaudy, neon-lit halls where chain-smoking Japanese gamble on a derivative of the poker machine filled with ball-bearings. The latter, characterised by Camelot-style turrets and drawbridges, are designed for amorous couples who can't get privacy in overcrowded Japan. Rooms are rented in two-hour brackets called 'rest periods'.

By the time we left the expressway for a secondary road, about two weeks' worth of said Australian lunches had passed through the right-hand side window into the hands or baskets of toll-collectors. But I was king of my domain. I had come, I had seen and, except for a missed turn-off or two (for which I could have easily blamed my navigator) and the occasional clutch of schoolgirls laughing at me behind the wheel, I had thus far conquered.

What *Lost in Translation* didn't show was that the people of Japan have a time-honoured approach to each challenge, an almost sacred dedication to every task, no matter how minor. It's all in the history (of which I had now read so much). Japan kept to itself through the centuries, perhaps more than any other country. It opened its doors (or had them opened) only in the 1850s when Commodore Matthew Perry and his legendary black ships turned up in Edo Bay with the demand that Japan sign a trade treaty with the United States.

The Japanese had never seen steam-powered ships before, nor such impressive armaments. They quickly adapted foreign technology to their own uses, creating a curious hybrid culture, onto which they overlaid their own tradition of miniaturisation and a complex series of harsh and unyielding rules. If so many people were to live in such a small place with so few resources, it had always been said, there had to be these rules. The people had to work as one; the nail that stood out needed to be hammered down.

And then, after centuries of austerity, they decided to build the Cosmo. Perhaps we should have guessed something was wrong.

At a fuel station – the Cosmo loved them – the attendant was so surprised to see foreigners that he walked an entire lap of the car, then looked us up and down as he dragged on his cigarette. Some may have thought the unusual thing in this scene was not two foreigners in rural Japan, but a man calmly smoking a cigarette while standing on top of several thousand litres of super. Not here.

The man may, of course, have walked around the car simply to check the tyres. If we had spoken Japanese, or he English, he might have pointed out what we were about to discover: that our tyres weren't up to the task ahead. We had one more surprise for him, a credit card. Although many places had a Visa or American Express sticker in the window, Japan was (and still is) largely a cash economy. The man hunted around for a dusty machine, tried to remember what he was taught when it had been delivered and, when he failed to get it to make the right impression, lit another cigarette, took a soapy cloth and thoroughly washed my card.

There was hardly a patch of the surrounding countryside not frantically producing income. If it wasn't a road, house, factory, farm, Love Hotel or Pachinko Parlour, it was a shrine . . . and even Zen monks would whack out a few lines of calligraphy for a fee. I bored Carolyn with every fact and anecdote I could muster about Japan, including the story I'd read about the Tokyo Love Hotel with a 'Space Shuttle Room'. The bed was edged with fins like a 1950s Cadillac, mounted on rails and fitted with a sound and motion detector. When this sensed a certain level of excitement, it sent the bed blasting across the room. And I regularly pointed out retrocars – a twist of history which saw Japanese manufacturers building copies of 1950s and '60s foreign vehicles not as they once were, but as modern buyers wished they had once been. The fact Nissan didn't build Noddy's original car had apparently become a source of national regret.

Carolyn had already collected stories of her own. She had discovered that the first people to arrive in a department store each morning were greeted by rows of bowing, white-gloved staff prepared to wrap and box even the smallest purchase to within an inch of its life. 'I'd come back again just for that,' she'd said with a grin. It wasn't just *kurisumasu* that had the retail world in a frenzy: the department stores were at the forefront of the national craze for the environment. This meant each layer of progressively more unnecessary wrapping had a little illustration of a seal or polar bear printed on it.

As we couldn't read any of Japan's three alphabets, our main guides were the little numbered posts beside the road every few kilometres. While driving along secondary roads to Shiojiri, then Kisofukushima, a rural town near the foot of Japan's central mountain range, Route 361 suddenly became

Route 461 without explanation. Forty minutes later we were still trying alternative sidestreets. In desperation we pulled into a service station and showed our map to staff. They smiled in a non-English-speaking sort of way and handed over a hand-drawn map that bore no resemblance to our published version.

Even with the new map we were soon lost again. It was 4 pm, the mid-winter night was already taking hold and we were a long way from our destination. This wasn't how it was meant to be. We should have been sitting around an open fire by now, drinking sake and discussing the amazing mountains we had passed through. Down an unlabelled road I could see the outlines of a few houses, but there were no obvious lights. I knocked on a door anyway. A woman opened it. The rest of her family, in view behind her, stared up in mild shock. They were sitting in a dim room around a *kotatsu*, a low table with a light bulb underneath and a heavy curtain around its perimeter to hold the bulb's heat in. These universal gadgets enable people to keep their hands and legs warm in the coldest months without wasting electricity that Sony could be using to turn out Trinitron screens.

The woman called up her ten-year-old son, who spoke a little English. He was able to point us back on track, yet twice more before the next big town roads were blocked and inexplicable deviations set up. At 5 pm it was dark, moonless and snowing lightly along Route 19 towards Takayama. At 6 pm it was snowing heavily. No one had told us to expect snow. Then again, no one had mentioned the narrow tunnels, unsealed roads, potholes or poorly fenced hairpin bends either. These hairpins were marked with convex mirrors, but such mirrors weren't necessary because there weren't any other cars or people. All of Japan's 120 million people, we could only assume, were sitting around their *kotatsus*, having quite rightly decided it was a silly time to go outdoors.

In daylight this road would have been a great deal more spectacular and a great deal less treacherous. The plan had been to see it then; the only view now was the constant, dark outline of one sheer cliff rising to the left and another falling to the right. It was below freezing. We knew because that fact set off a flashing light and a buzzer in the Cosmo. The gloomy and damp tunnels – often three or four to the kilometre – were narrow, the numerous bridges were windswept and so badly surfaced that at times the car jumped almost its own width from side to side. This might have been the richest country in the world, but we clearly weren't passing through a marginal seat.

To get the full idea of how the Cosmo handled on snow and ice you'd have to watch the scene in *Fantasia* in which the hippo is dancing in a tutu. On several occasions we hit black ice. At other times I experienced an almost total whiteout. Then, on that fateful hill outside Kisofukushima, the Cosmo decided – without consultation – to change its direction of travel. Touching the accelerator caused the rear wheels to spin freely and seemed to actually speed up our rearward progress. The brake pedal was no more effective in stopping our snow-ploughing. Everything was happening in slow motion. I looked at Carolyn, she at me. Her eyes were saying, 'Why aren't you doing something?' Mine were replying, 'Yeah, like what?'

I suddenly remembered something about this car having a handbrake that worked on all four wheels – twice as many as normal. I couldn't remember why it would have such a set-up, or why it would make any difference, considering I was already pushing the foot-brake through the floor. But I figured hoiking on the handbrake couldn't do any harm, and a short time later the car came to a halt as softly, slowly and unexpectedly as it had begun its rearward journey.

Carolyn and I clambered out to review the situation. We both slipped over. Then the empty car started slithering backwards. With only a little of the hill left, however, it stopped again before it built up too much speed. After four further attempts to make it up the hill (I found slightly more grip on the wrong side of the road), we eventually reached Takayama. But we were thoroughly demoralised and not even a therapeutic Mars Bar improved things. It was 8 pm and we were still 100 kilometres from our destination. Worse still, we had been averaging a mere 30 kilometres per hour despite near ten-tenths concentration.

I mentioned a modern tendency to pick up and drop countries almost like moods. I was ready to let Japan go crashing to the floor. It had let me down; it had thwarted my attempt to show to Carolyn what it was, and what it was capable of. My eyes were aching, my brain splitting and, anyway, driving was becoming far too dangerous. We arrived at a deserted Takayama intersection plastered with what looked like hundreds of signs. I stopped the car, climbed out and looked at them. I couldn't divine even the route out of town, let alone the correct road to Shirakawago.

Hunched up to keep out the cold, I walked around the car a few times trying to work out whether I had the energy to carry on. The conclusion was no. We had to find out where the people of Takayama were hiding, and ask them for somewhere to sleep. We could worry in the morning about historic Shiraka-bloody-wago. If there even was such a place.

It was then that a young woman walked up from nowhere and asked in a beautifully clear voice, 'Do you speak Japanese?' I must have visibly buckled. Here, finally, was someone – and someone who spoke English. Except, of course, the woman spoke only four words of English, which is why she had asked the question. Nonetheless, she appeared to be as keen to help as we were to be helped.

We started one of those conversations in which both sides are convinced if they speak slowly enough, clearly enough and loudly enough, the other party will somehow understand. Neither did. Carolyn had an idea. It should have been my idea. After all, it was my country, I had initiated the adventure and I was so far failing blatantly in my allotted portion of the hunter-gatherer-chauffeur duties. But I was lost and exhausted and despondent.

Carolyn walked across to a nearby phone box, pulled out a phone card and a diary and rang an Australian we knew who had a Japanese wife. She agreed to provide a remote translation service down the phone line. Our new best friend, it turned out, was happy to take us to the turnoff to Shirakawago. Furthermore, she assured us – via the phoneline – the road improved considerably and there were no trickily signposted sections. We followed the woman's tiny hatchback (fitted with steel studded snow tyres, I noticed) through a series of complex twists and turns which bore no relationship to any map, hand-drawn or professionally published. After about 20 minutes she stopped and pointed out the correct turn-off. We jumped back out into the cold, bowed and reverently said '*domo arigato gozaimasu*', which roughly translated as 'Thank you most grovellingly for saving Westerners with navigational hubris'.

I was revived and the road was indeed straighter, better marked and less icy, if no closer to the map. I suspected, however, this improvement was merely another element of the subterfuge, designed to give hoodwinked pilgrims a little extra false hope. With just 20 kilometres to go, my suspicions were confirmed. At the end of a long downhill section, we turned a corner to find the road blocked. At the mouth of a bridge was a cordon and a sign in Japanese. Two trucks were parked, engines running. A non-conversation with one of the drivers ended with him drawing a clock on a piece of paper with the big hand at 12 and the little hand on ten. Beside this he wrote '11.00 OK'. The truckie was another conspirator, without a doubt. I was now convinced Shirakawago had long since been turned into a chemical plant, powered by an on-site nuclear reactor, surrounded by characterless tower-block dormitories. These were built entirely with wood from old-growth Tasmanian forests. Nailed together with dolphin teeth . . .

Wedged between two mountains and settling down for an indeterminate wait, I could have cried. Except that would have set off another of the Cosmo's chimes or bells. There was a TV screen built into the instrument panel but we could get no reception, nor any radio except late night talkback. Which at least is more palatable in a language you don't understand.

Carolyn remained calm, sensible and a few other things I didn't. She refused to accept that Old Japan hadn't existed for decades or that the small number of people we met along the way, though outwardly friendly and helpful, were merely extras in an evil ruse to keep that fact hidden. Nor did she buy my explanation that we'd positively, definitely, be here until morning – or even something worse. Maybe under the cover of night the authorities collected all the duped travellers and threw them in Japan's special jail for people who dreamt of the old days. It was probably next to the one for driving offenders.

'Just have a short sleep,' she said. But I was too angry to sleep. And I was too tired. At 9.55 pm a dozen vehicles appeared at our rear, perhaps tipped off to the road closure by a sign in the previous village, a sign which had been deliberately and maliciously written in Japanese so that we couldn't read it. The road was suddenly opened. How, we never saw. No-one arrested us. We appeared to be free to continue.

At around 10.45 pm the Cosmo finally plodded and clumped into what looked like Shirakawago. Or perhaps a life-size mock-up, or a triumph of Japanese holograph technology. We turned right at the shrine – it looked like a real shrine – then passed through what appeared to be three-dimensional and solidly built intersections. Maybe it was all real but, like Brigadoon, appeared for just one day every 100 years. It would soon swallow Carolyn, the Cosmo and me.

There was only one other moving vehicle. It stopped and a short, dark-haired woman jumped out and yelled 'Dabises, Dabises'. All my unkind thoughts dissolved in a sigh that might have lasted a full minute.

Upon being led to our four-century old *ryokan*, taking off our shoes and banging our heads on the door frames, we found our hosts, the Yosobei family, had all stayed up to present us with an elaborate rural feast. We were revitalised enough to smile and bow several more times before shuffling in house slippers to our beautifully warmed, tatami-matted room. It was a long sleep.

When we awoke, Old Japan was under several centimetres of snow. For half an hour I looked at the snowflakes falling past a high window while I relaxed in a large wooden bath, the water lapping over the edges, the steam gently rising off the silvery surface. All around me were dark, heavily grained timber panels as old as the town itself. Everything was perfectly quiet. It could have been a million miles from Tokyo, or any other part of the modern world. It was an entirely different Japan and every bit as engaging. I had one of those traveller's moments: I never wanted to go home. I would stay here, I told myself. I would master the local language, absorb every Japanese tradition, divest myself of every Western foible. I would discover what makes these people tick and make lifelong friends in this rural paradise.

I returned to the large main room with its dark walls and central sandpit, where a huge cast-iron pot boiled over an open fire. Carolyn and I kneeled behind our individual, low, black-lacquered tables and used our chopsticks to eat a breakfast that Kellogg's had nothing whatsoever to do with. There was little to date the room except the rice thermos, the little plastic butane lighter next to the sandpit and the 100-or-so-centimetre colour television in the corner, which was, mercifully, turned off. We ate sweet-smelling rice and marinated plums and things we could scarcely identify but which tasted like an appropriate reward for those who had triumphed over adversity and finally made the summit. We could scarcely stop smiling.

The wind at Shirakawago is said to come straight off the plains of Siberia. Snow falls so heavily that, at a certain time of the season, most houses switch to a winter entrance on the second floor. It hadn't yet come to that, but we had to rug up tightly before walking out among the snow-coated fir trees, hedgerows and snap-frozen vegetable gardens. The whole town seemed to have come out to wave at the foreigners. Collar up and eyes wide open, Carolyn stood next to a monument made up of three huge slabs of rock pointing towards the sky. Framed by the cottages and barns, with their steeply pitched thatched roofs, she smiled broadly. She didn't have to say it: we should never go home.

For two whole days it made perfect sense. We shuffled around the town, explaining to each other how we really could live here. There'd be almost nothing stopping us, we could teach English, we simply needed to throw in our jobs and our daft hang-ups about status and security and family and work and have the guts to really live. We held hands while slipping and sliding around in the snow like schoolchildren and waved back at the locals. Carolyn was waving out of politeness, me in triumph. I had succeeded. My faith had been rewarded; Carolyn had been won over by my country. I was now prepared to absolve Japan of all crimes committed by its mapmakers. I could now applaud, too, the rotten roads that so successfully kept most tourists out of this perfect slice of the world.

Japan crashed shortly afterwards, bringing the rest of Asia with it. Or was it the other way around? Australia's economy somehow defied gravity. Overnight the Japanese weren't nearly as smart as everyone thought they were. And, just as suddenly, we were clever. Much, much too clever.

Carolyn and I never did move to rural Japan. We gave in to time and work and family obligations, and all the other things that too often hold people back. When we made close Japanese friends it was in Sydney. We changed jobs, moved somewhere less challenging than Tokyo or Shirakawago, started a family.

I didn't visit Japan again until recently. It was on another rushed work trip and I found myself staying in a characterless hotel at the edge of a massive car-park, next to a grey beach sloping into even greyer water. In the very early morning I walked across hundreds of metres of asphalt to a huge, empty baseball stadium with nothing but grey seagulls for company.

As I walked, I realised it wasn't only a bad choice of hotel that had brought me down. Japan had changed. You could sense a lack of confidence, a confusion about direction. The kids were suddenly fat on pizzas and Twinkies. There was even a little litter, graffiti and property crime. In my Japan!

I had changed too, but that wasn't the point. I had the sort of ridiculous idea that I suspect many tourists have: that foreign countries exist solely for our sake and – like retro-cars – they should stay not as they were, but as we choose to remember them.

I can't claim to have fallen in love with Japan before it was spoiled. But I fell in love with it when it was spoiled just the way I liked it. And although a small, selfish part of me curses them for not keeping it exactly like that, I will cling to the hope that consolation is to be found in a little village separated from the rest of Japan by bad roads and even worse maps. I may never get there again, but in my mind, the television in the corner of the main room is now widescreen and plasma. But it's still turned off, and everything else in Shirakawago is exactly as it always was.

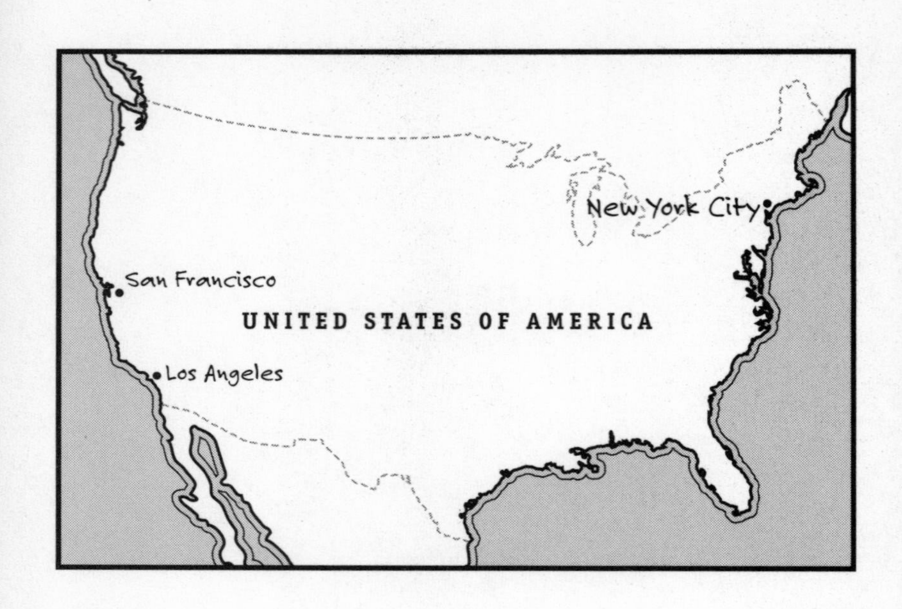
New York City
San Francisco
UNITED STATES OF AMERICA
Los Angeles

Be it Ever so Humble . . .

CAROLINE OVERINGTON

IT HAS been very cold in New York this winter, which means I start each day in a kind of agony. Should I get up early, and try to find the *New York Times* in the snow on my front doorstep before it freezes solid? Or should I wait until the snow melts a little, and then fish the newspaper out of an icy puddle, and read it wet?

Usually, I choose to get up early, and today was no exception, but I was still too late to find the *Times* before parts of it had frozen. I had to crack open the plastic bag and then shake the ice off the pages before I could start reading. But it was worth the effort: one of the stories on the front page was about me. Well, not literally about me, but about people like me and families like mine, who live underground in New York, in basements near the subway trains.

The headline on the story was 'Be it ever so low . . .' and, before I read it, I had assumed that my family's living arrangements were rare and special, but it seems that isn't the case.

The reporter said that around 100,000 people in New York live in basements, which are defined as being less than 50 per cent underground (as opposed to cellars which are more than 50 per cent underground and, strictly speaking, not fit for human habitation). It isn't always fun: the reporter said that some people have to put up with exposed pipes in their lounge-rooms, through which flows other people's sewage. We don't have that problem, but we do have challenges. A few times a week in winter, water comes up through the floor (which explains why large parts of the floor of our apartment are tiled, and so are some of the walls). If I want to go anywhere I have to lay down towels, and then squelch around, which is better than splashing from room to room, I suppose. The water is a health hazard: it attracts cockroaches, it causes mould and it rots through plasterboard. One of the walls in the main bedroom is like Swiss cheese: if you pressed hard enough, you would go through it. The water also creates a fire hazard: it gets into the power sockets and it means that you cannot leave any electrical cords lying on the floor. This is a bit of a problem in my office, but I think I have it solved: all the entrails from my computer are piled into a plastic wagon that is parked on a box under my desk.

Given that we live underground, we have very little natural light, which means that I have to keep all the lights on, almost all the time. I have learnt how to find the bathroom by running the back of my hand along the walls. I have also come to accept that every time I go to the supermarket, I will need to buy a jumbo pack of 100-watt bulbs, to replace those that are always blowing out. If I don't keep the stocks up, our home soon becomes a place of towering shadows. My children – Michael and Chloe, who are twins, now aged four – have developed deep rings around their eyes from fear and lack of sleep. Their pallor startles people: when we went home to Australia last Christmas, everybody noticed how small and white and tortured they seemed, compared to their sturdy cousins. But never mind, my children have an inner life, filled with goblins and other strange creatures that dwell in the gloomy corners of their bedroom, and now their minds. And my son has dreams: if you ask him what he wants to be when he grows up, he won't say a fireman, or a policeman, or even a doctor. He wants blue overalls and a tool belt with a torch tucked inside, 'like the guy who comes to our place'. He means the exterminator.

The reporter who wrote the article about basement living for the *Times* wondered how people could 'tolerate' such circumstances, which made me snort. One does not always have a choice, especially in a city where rents are steep and good places are hard to find.

Our wet basement has been home for two years, and we will probably live here for a while longer. My family – my husband, Martin, our two children and me – moved to New York from Sydney in February 2002, in part because I wanted a new life, even though there was nothing much wrong with the old one. On the contrary, until we moved, we had been very happy. That came out wrong: we are still very happy, it's just that our lives have changed so much. In March 2000, after eight years of IVF treatment, I gave birth to twins, which was exhilarating. The first decade of my marriage had been consumed by one question: will I be able to have children? It didn't seem likely, but it was the only thing Martin and I really wanted, so we ploughed all our effort and resources into it. Then, suddenly, in what seemed like a miracle of science, we had a son and a daughter.

When I brought my babies home from hospital, I expected to be overwhelmed by the responsibility, but the opposite was true: I suddenly felt very free. For the first time, I didn't have to think of creative ways to build a family. There were no more appointments at hospitals, no more clinics, no more blood to be drawn, no more embryos waiting to hatch, no more disappointments. These things had taken so much time and so much energy, and now, before I was 30, that part of my life was over. I couldn't help wondering how I would fill all this suddenly spare time? For Martin the answer was simple: we would settle down and live an ordinary life, filled with all the ordinary pleasures available to Australian families. We would go to the beach; renovate a house; drop in on the kids' cousins with our own children in tow.

I tried to do that for a while but, while nobody likes to admit it, I wasn't very good at staying home with my children when they were small and, when I tried to do it every day, I went kind of crazy.

My former neighbour can vouch for this. More than once, when I was home alone with my babies, she would peer through the vine that hung between our houses and say, 'Are you okay, love?' I was not okay. Usually, I would be sitting on my back step, smoking a cigar because I had given up cigarettes when I was pregnant and cigars were the only tobacco I could find in the house. The children would be inside, crying, and my T-shirt would be soaked, because I really should have been inside, breastfeeding them. The courtyard would be littered with dog poo because I never had the stomach to scoop it up. The garden would be hopelessly overgrown and the washing was never off the line, even when it was raining.

'You really need a break,' my neighbour would say, and she was right, but I had a problem familiar to millions of mothers: I had always worked, and I wanted to keep working, but not if it meant that somebody else would raise my children. For one thing, I'd fought too hard to have them. Besides, I truly adored almost everything about my kids: the heat of their bodies when they woke from afternoon naps; the smell of their bunny rugs; the way they made me feel that life was full and perfect. I wanted to be the one who lifted them out of their cots when they were still wet and warm from sleep. I wanted to be the one who ran the bath at night, and blew bubbles onto their faces. I wanted to be the one who struggled to get their socks over their chubby little feet, who wrapped their stinky nappies in plastic bags and ran them out to the wheelie bin. But, as much as I loved doing these things, I didn't want to do them *every single time* they had to be done. Caring for infants is exhausting. I keenly remember being shaken from sleep by the sound of a wailing baby and thinking, *oh please, oh please, oh please, just go back to sleep*. But my children never did, so I had to get up and rock and feed and change them and sometimes they kept screaming anyway. I won't say I resented them for that. As tough as it was, some of my best memories are of padding quietly through a dark house in the middle of the night, with one of my babies – usually my son, Michael – in my arms. I liked the quiet time we spent together, watching the milk bottle go around on the microwave plate. I liked the way he would get mesmerised with me, watching infomercials on TV.

My sister once worked in a crèche and, when my children were born, she assured me that mothers who work full-time when their children are infants miss important milestones.

'I feel sorry for them,' she said, with genuine compassion. 'They come in saying, "Oh, you'll never guess, little Joey walked yesterday!" And you think, little Joey has been walking for three days.' But then, my sister always worked, and my mother always worked, and so did my grandmother, and we all had a good excuse: we needed the money.

Mine is not a wealthy family. When I fell pregnant, Martin and I lived in a sweet little house in Bondi that was basically falling down. It had neither a laundry nor a bath, and I was about to have twins, so we thought, if we were going to bathe these children and wash their clothes, we'd better renovate. I envy those people who just rent another place while they get work done on their dream home, but we couldn't afford to do that. Instead, we got lucky. A friend was having a mid-life crisis and had decided to go into the priesthood. We asked him if we could take care of his worldly possessions – including a house in Woollahra – and he agreed. It was not a big house, but it was bigger than ours, and it was not a tidy house, but it was structurally more stable than ours, and so, after the children were born, we borrowed against our own place in Bondi so that we could extend it and we moved to Woollahra.

It was the first time I had lived amongst the rich and it bred in me the kind of envy I never want to feel again. The women, in particular, seemed so blessed: they were well-educated and well-travelled; they could cook; they had smart-looking kids in good schools and so much time on their hands. And they were kind. They would come over with casseroles for my husband and, sometimes, coffee and pastries for me, saying things like, 'Oh, I was just out in the neighbourhood and I thought you could do with a cuppa, so I bought you one. And here, I brought you something for dinner, too, and please, let me hold one of the babies!' I am sure they don't know how I cried when they left, because I was so pleased to see them, even though we were from totally different worlds.

I remember once I was standing on our verandah, rocking baby Chloe in my arms, when a neighbour came over to chat.

'Have you managed to get across the road, to see Tom Hughes's place?' she asked. The house she meant was a mansion owned by a Sydney barrister.

'No, I haven't,' I said. 'What's it like?'

She replied, 'Oh, it's just like your grandmother's house, stuffed with all these antiques!' In other words, it was nothing like my grandmother's brick-clad bungalow in working-class St Albans.

Another time I was strolling with my babies through the streets of Double Bay when a woman stopped me, peered underneath the pram hood and said, 'Oh, they're absolutely gorgeous! Whose are they?' I was taken aback. What did she mean?

'They're mine,' I said, which seemed to surprise her.

Later, I asked my friend about it. Did the woman think I had adopted them?

'Oh no,' my friend explained. 'She thought you were the nanny.'

I laughed at the time, but before long I *was* looking for some kind of help with the children. After four months at home with the children, I decided to try working part-time, since we still needed money. The only thing I am qualified to do is write for newspapers. My first job was as a cub reporter for a company called Fairfax, which publishes *The Age* and *The Sydney Morning Herald*, along with some free, suburban newspapers. By the time I got pregnant, I had been there almost 13 years. So, after my maternity leave ran out, I approached Fairfax and asked for a job that would enable me to spend some time at home and some time at the office. They were very good about it: they gave me all of the things that feminism has made possible. I got a new computer and a mobile telephone so I could work from home, and I had access to good-quality, subsidised childcare at the Fairfax crèche that I used two days each week when I went to the office. For a working woman with small children, I had a ridiculous amount of freedom. My days were mostly spent at my mothers' group, or on the beach at Bondi, or in the local toy library. I sewed costumes for the Christmas disco at the crèche. I shared recipes with other mums in the neighbourhood. I traded babysitting services with the couple across the street. I took my children to swimming lessons and I spent long afternoons, rocking my supermarket trolley back and forth in the aisle while I contemplated breakfast cereals. Then, in the evenings, I had my computer screen and a glass of wine, and freedom to write pretty much what I wanted, and I was happy.

Overall, life was good, and then, out of the blue, it promised to get better. Eighteen months after my children were born, the newspaper asked, via memo, did anybody want to be a foreign correspondent for *The Sydney Morning Herald* and *The Age*, based in either New York or Japan?

Well, yes. I did. For a long time, I had been talking to my

husband about wanting to live overseas. It was something he was already doing, since he was born in England and did not move to Australia until he was in his early twenties. During the nineties, we watched as many of our friends took postings in Bangkok, Singapore and Vietnam. Then, in 1997, one of my smart colleagues at *The Age*, Jason Koutsoukis, put a copy of *Scoop* – a classic satire about foreign correspondents – in my hands and I was sold. I wanted an assignment overseas. I'm not sure that Martin thought I was serious. After all, we could not really afford to move anywhere. I was simply not that senior: I had never earned enough to support a family of four in Bondi, let alone in New York (a fact that would become achingly clear, as we slowly went broke in Manhattan), and if we went overseas he would not be able to work. But I applied for both positions anyway.

Japan was announced first, and I didn't get it. I was upset, but another colleague at *The Age*, Antony Catalano, said, 'Don't fret, they'll give you New York.'

What made him think so?

'They don't want you to come back to the office,' he joked. 'And Japan is far, but not quite far enough. Sending you to New York will suit a lot of people.'

I hope it isn't true that I got posted to New York because Fairfax was keen to get rid of me, but Antony was right about one thing: I did get the job. In February 2002, we packed all our belongings into cardboard boxes and moved them into a storage shed. We palmed our dog off to Martin's parents, rented our place in Bondi to strangers, and caught a plane to New York.

Our first home in the Big Apple was a long-stay hotel called the Marmara Manhattan, which is about three blocks from Central Park on the Upper East Side of the island of

Manhattan. The finance manager at Fairfax had said I could stay in a hotel for four weeks while we searched for something permanent. I found the Marmara on the Internet. Its ad read: 'Perfect for people who are relocating, or between marriage and divorce.' This meant the bedroom was slightly larger than you'd find in a normal New York hotel, there was a little kitchen with a microwave, and a small lounge area, too. It cost $6500 for one month, which included cleaning, once a week.

When I booked the room, I told the receptionist I had young children and that we would like two cots. But Australians don't speak the same language as Americans. To an American, a 'cot' is a bed that a soldier sleeps on. A baby's bed is a 'crib'. I suppose the receptionist simply assumed I was crazy – not an uncommon thing in New York – because he just ignored the request. So, when we got to the Marmara that first night, after the long journey from Australia, there was just one double bed – and nowhere for the children to sleep.

I telephoned reception and said, 'I have young children with me. Do you by chance have cots?' At first the clerk was confused, but eventually he understood: I needed two cribs for the children to sleep in.

'No problem, ma'am,' he said. 'I'll have somebody bring them up.' I was grateful.

'Thank you,' I said. 'You're terrific.'

'No,' he replied, very earnestly. 'I'm not. But I am working on it, and I believe I'm on my way.'

I hope I never forget our first night in the Marmara. It was winter in New York, so the sun sank quickly. The view from all the windows was amazing: just rows and rows of skyscrapers like our own, each of them sparkling against the night sky. I could see people going about their business in their rooms, across the sky from us. Here, a man doing his ironing in his underpants. There, a woman doing some kind of yoga on a mat on her bedroom floor. Here, a couple making love. There, a man playing chess, apparently by phone, since there was nobody sitting opposite him and he never put down the receiver. I wondered whether to be shy about our own exposure to the world – some of our neighbours seemed so close I felt I could reach out through the window and tap on their glass – but I didn't want to draw the blinds on such a magnificent city so, before long, we were wandering around in our knickers and nappies for all the New World to see. I suppose we could have got dressed, but New York's hotels and apartments are very hot inside, and the heating systems are usually so old you cannot adjust the temperature. The result is peculiar: in winter, New Yorkers walk along the streets with their faces pointed down towards the pavement, with scarves wrapped tightly around their heads and with their fists jammed into their pockets. But when they get home they strip down to underpants, eat ice-cream straight from the freezer, and sleep under only their sheets.

It took just three days for me to fall in love with New York, and sometimes I wondered if I would ever leave the Marmara, because it was such a nice place. But really, we could not have stayed there for more than a month, even if the Fairfax budget had allowed for it. There was simply no room for the children to move around. Martin did his best: every morning, he would wrap the children in parkas, gloves, scarves and boots, and put them in a huge, double pram. He then wrapped the pram in protective plastic and headed out into the cold. But the children couldn't take it for long and soon they would be back in the hotel room. Within 15 minutes of being carried through the door they would have unravelled all the toilet paper and put the remote control into the toilet bowl.

They were bored, and I was frustrated because I couldn't work in such a small place. Every night at 7 o'clock – which was 9 am in Australia – I would put the children to sleep in the bedroom, and I would open my laptop and start to write. Martin would sit on the sofa next to me, with the television set turned down. From time to time, the children – who were then not yet two – would stir because the phone rang all the time, with editors from Australia, briefing me.

'Can you have a look at the Andrea Yates case, the woman who drowned all her babies in the bath in Texas?' they would say, while I juggled a baby from one hip to another. 'Are they going to execute her?'

After a while, the children would settle down with milk, and Martin would turn the sofa into a bed and fall asleep, while I tap-tap-tapped beside him by the light of my computer screen, sending stories back to Australia, which would appear in the *Herald* and *The Age* the next day.

Besides having nowhere to write, I also had no place to conduct interviews and so, when I wanted to speak to somebody, I had to arrange to meet them at a coffee shop. I am grateful to those people who made this arrangement easier than it could have been. Once, during that first month in New York, I telephoned Norman Rosenbaum – the brother of Yankel Rosenbaum, a Melbourne-born student who was stabbed to death during a riot in Brooklyn 10 years earlier – and asked him if we could meet to talk about the re-trial of the man who killed Yankel. He agreed, but it hardly seemed the thing to talk about in a restaurant and because Mr Rosenbaum is an Orthodox Jew I did not feel comfortable saying, 'Can I come to your hotel room to talk?'

So I said, 'Can you come to my hotel?' and he did, arriving after the children had been put to bed. My husband went and sat in the dark with them, forced to wait while Mr Rosenbaum and I sat on the sofa and talked about life and brutal death in New York.

To work as a foreign correspondent is to slowly acknowledge that your time is not your own and your home is not your haven. There is no such thing as a weekend: your antennae are always up, watching, listening, for any story that might be breaking across the United States. The telephone never stops ringing. It can happen at midnight, or on a Sunday afternoon:

'Did you see this? Is there anything you can write about that?' I knew I had to find a place to live, but I had to do it in whatever time I could find, and within a budget that quickly seemed inadequate. The company had given me a small fortune to spend on rent: three times as much as we were getting for our place in Bondi, in fact. So, even if the cost of living in Manhattan was twice or even three times as high as it was in Bondi, I should still get a good place, no?

Well, no. In fact, two of the first real estate 'brokers' (which is what they call agents in New York) said flatly that I would not get a three-bedroom apartment anywhere on the Upper West Side of Manhattan on our budget, and asked if I had considered living in New Jersey. Yes, I had considered living in New Jersey, which is just across the river from New York, but nevertheless, it's a different state. I was supposed to be the New York correspondent for the newspaper, and I would have felt like a fraud, writing, 'By Caroline Overington, correspondent in New York' if I actually lived in New Jersey. It would not have mattered so much, I suppose, if our company had an office in Manhattan, and I was going there every day on the train, like most of Wall Street's workers do, or if I had regularly been breathing the air around Central Park and Times Square. But to live and work in New Jersey would not, I felt, be properly doing my job. I needed to try to find a three-bedroom apartment – that is, with one room for Martin and me, one for the children to share and one that I could use as an office – in Manhattan. I wanted it to be on the Upper West Side, because there are two good museums for the children there and two parks – one of which is on a river and the other of which is the majestic Central Park, with its one-dollar carousel. I also wanted a garden for the children, which made brokers reel back, spluttering. After all, not even Madonna has a house with a garden in New York. People live in apartments. Their feet never touch earth.

Besides the shortage of cash, we had another problem.

Before moving to New York, Martin and I had not talked much about how things would work when we got there, because we weren't really sure. I'd figured I would be busy (which was good, because I was ready to be busier than I was in Sydney) and that he would be less busy (which was equally good, because he had been frantic for at least 20 years). But it was not until we started searching for a non-existent apartment that the reality of our new situation – the circumstances of our new marriage, as it were – became clear.

The brokers we consulted wanted to know how much we had to spend and how we earned it.

'I am a foreign correspondent,' I would say. 'I have just moved to Manhattan to take up a new job. I can supply you with references.' This, they liked.

Then they would turn to Martin and say, 'And what do you do?' For the first time in his life, Martin did not know what to say. He was no longer 'in advertising', which had been his answer for two decades. He was not yet a 'stay-at-home Dad' (and, in truth, neither of us would ever get comfortable with that description, which conjured up images, however unfairly, of a character in an apron with flour on his hands and children running rampant around his ankles). Still, for some reason – social conditioning, probably – it was hard for either of us to say, 'Martin is not working. We've come here for Caroline's job.' The words just sounded wrong.

I am embarrassed to admit that I felt less feminine when I had to explain to people what we had done and how we were living. It was as if, somewhere over the Pacific, we had segued into some other couple's life, one that we would not have chosen for ourselves and that did not suit us. But how do you explain that to an impatient real estate agent, with a ceaselessly-ringing cell-phone and a clipboard of bad ideas about where we should live? Mostly, Martin settled for saying, 'I was in advertising, but I'm not sure what I'm going to do here.'

But the brokers didn't like that. 'Not working?' they would

remark, for no matter how modern Manhattan is, it is still unusual for women – especially mothers – to be the sole income earners, and there is a fair (and correct) assumption that few women, regardless of skill and education, earn enough to support a family of four. In the end, I got my employers to fax me a copy of my rent allowance so I could show it to our prospective brokers and landlords, in the hope that they would not ask questions we had not yet answered for ourselves.

There was also the problem of what to do with our children while we looked for an apartment. We didn't know anybody in Manhattan, or at least, nobody we knew well enough to ask, 'Excuse me, do you mind looking after these squalling infants in their sagging nappies for half a day, while we go looking for somewhere to live?' At first, we tried to take them with us, but it's tough going in and out of buildings with a child on each hip, especially when the children immediately want to get down in their new surroundings and take things to pieces. The real estate market in New York is hot. There were usually seven couples ahead of us on any list, and all of them had more money and fewer children. They could also move more swiftly. Manhattan is a very fast city, and it is contemptuous of parents with children in tow. We did not have a car, because nobody in Manhattan has a car. You simply can't afford it and, even if you could, where would you park it? The skyscrapers do not come with undercover parking, the way they do in Sydney. The street parking is tightly patrolled (not that the rich care: they just park and pay the fines, or maybe don't pay the fines). Otherwise, everybody uses yellow taxis, which want only passengers who are heading to Wall Street, wearing a suit and not carrying a leaking baby bottle. Nobody has time for two people juggling children, child seats, nappy bags and squeak toys. Nobody wants to stop while you negotiate putting the child-seat on the back seat, then wrestle with the seat-belts, all the while holding a struggling infant who is trying to get out of your arms and play in the traffic. And even if the driver doesn't mind doing that, the other cars on the street won't let him. Cabs are allowed to stop only for long enough for a be-suited man or well-heeled woman to jump in and have their head snapped back as the car zooms into the career city.

So, after a few weekends of standing haplessly on street corners, with Martin waving madly at cabs that would not slow, we hired a babysitter. How do you do that, in a strange city? I didn't know, so I went to the front desk of the Marmara and asked, 'Do you have a babysitter service?'

The kind lady behind reception said, 'No.'

I think I must have looked like I was about to cry, because she paused, and added, 'But I have a cousin.' And that was our introduction into the way things work in New York. Every low-paid worker has 'a cousin' who will help you do your laundry, mop your floors or take care of your kids, while you pursue your career.

'Who is this cousin?' I asked.

The receptionist said, 'She's lovely. She's 22 years old and she works as a receptionist at a doctor's office, but she will mind children after hours.' For many people in New York there is no way to survive other than to mind children for the wealthier, after hours. The average wage for low-skilled workers like receptionists is $8 an hour, or $320 a week, in a city where a three-bedroom apartment on the Upper West Side costs $1000 a week, at least. Naturally, the working poor don't live there. They live in Morningside Heights, or Harlem, or the Bronx, or even in New Jersey.

We hired the cousin on the spot, which helped with the children, but not the apartment. For it seems that no matter how long you search, you cannot find what does not exist: a three-bedroom, two-bathroom New York apartment of the type featured in *Stuart Little*, or the one Jodie Foster rents in *The Panic Room*, or the one Charlotte got when she divorced

Trey in 'Sex and the City', or the one where Michael Douglas arranges to have his wife, Gwyneth Paltrow, killed in *A Perfect Murder*, for less than $50,000 a year. What you do get for that money is what the brokers showed us: *lovely* one-bedroom apartments that had been carved out of mansions; or two-bedroom apartments in ugly, modern skyscrapers, sometimes with a small 'maid's room' by the kitchen, which brokers like to call the third bedroom, even though it is usually smaller than a refrigerator.

I was in despair, in part because after a few of these searches, Martin was barely speaking to me. 'I will not live in these places,' he said, after yet another broker had opened the door on yet another horrible box in the sky, with a creaky elevator and a homeless person sleeping on cardboard in the foyer. I thought he meant: in this apartment. He actually meant: in this city, in this country, in these circumstances, especially not when I know I could be living beachside in Sydney, watching my children flip like brown seals in and out of swimming pools. Martin did not immediately see New York's charm. It would happen to him, but not as quickly as it happened to me.

In my first week I was already talking about staying forever, on streets that I physically loved, in a city that was already doing to my heart what my children had done: making it beat faster, with an ache in every pulse. I wanted my husband to feel what I felt, and I thought that might happen once we were properly unpacked and had a real place of our own. I became obsessed by real estate, so much so that one of my first stories for the newspaper, after I moved to New York, was about people who manage to make the city's rent laws work in their favour.

Riding in a cab through the city one day, I heard a reporter talking on the radio about how the mogul Donald Trump had purchased a lovely old building on Park Avenue. He wanted to renovate it and sell it for profit, but that is not easy to do in

New York because almost all of its old buildings have some 'rent-controlled' tenants who cannot be dislodged. The law is on their side: they have been living in one place long enough to demand the right to stay, and their landlords cannot increase their rent by more than a few dollars a year. The logic is simple: without such laws, some of Manhattan's more colourful (read: poor) residents, like the filmmakers and artists (but also people who simply think they can spend a taxpayer's dollar better than the person who earned it) would have to leave the city and that would make New York a culturally poorer place. In practice, this means that some people get to live on Park Avenue in colossal, seven-bedroom apartments with 18-foot ceilings for around $500 a month, because they have been there for ages, while others – like me – have to pay market rent for the dross that is left vacant.

As the market in New York rises – and oh, how it has risen – landlords have tried increasingly creative ways to rid themselves of their rent-controlled tenants, of whom there are about a million. Some have simply let their buildings go to ruin, so that tenants are forced out by rats and leaking sewage. Others have hired goons to prowl the halls, break the windows, and generally create a menace. Some have even set fire to apartment blocks that they want to raze, only to find themselves in court on charges of attempted murder. Such tactics never work, anyway. The rent-controlled tenants know their rights and the courts almost always decide in their favour. I was intrigued to know what Donald Trump was going to do about this, so I went home and researched his building and, before long, I found myself standing in an apartment occupied by Allyn Ehrman, chief thorn in Trump's side. Ehrman had lived forever in one of Trump's new apartments on Park Avenue and had no intention of shuffling on his way.

Now, rent-control is supposed to protect poor people from greed, but Ehrman did not look poor to me. In fact, he was keen to suggest that he was very well-connected.

'Do you know Kerry Packer?' he said, pretty soon after we first shook hands. I was startled.

'No,' I said. 'Do you?'

'I play polo with him,' Mr Ehrman said. 'Next time you see him, can you say hello?'

I promised to do so, since it will never happen. Then I took a seat on a big old leather lounge in Mr Ehrman's office, which had a marble floor and scarlet carpet. He sat behind a big desk, with polo mallets on racks behind his head.

'I came here in 1975,' Ehrman said, which is to say, he had been living in Trump's new apartment since before Trump's girlfriend was born. 'The rent when I came was $900 a month. It was the highest rent per square foot of any place in Manhattan. People said I was mad.'

But that was 1975. This was 2002. Trump's girlfriend was all – well, kind of – grown up, and Ehrman's apartment, if advertised on the open market, would have been worth tens of thousands of dollars a week. If you doubt that, think about this: the apartment that Hugh Jackman was living in while starring in 'The Boy from Oz' on Broadway, reportedly cost $18,000 a month. The apartment that Nicole Kidman rented, while she was in New York being romanced by Lenny Kravitz, was worth something like $22,000 a month. Neither of those places is on Park Avenue, which is still Manhattan's best address. But Ehrman's place was rent-controlled, which meant that the building's previous owner had only ever been able to increase the rent by a few per cent a year.

'Trump was on the phone immediately,' Ehrman said. 'He's got a very good personality. Very charming. He was, like, joking to me, saying, "Get the hell outta my goddamn building."'

And Ehrman's response? 'I said no.'

The two men were already acquainted, which was maybe why Ehrman felt so bold. At the height of his eighties celebrity, Trump asked Ehrman's company (among other things, it applies expensive wood panelling to office walls) to redecorate his extravagant headquarters overlooking Central Park.

'But I said no then, too,' Ehrman said, relishing the moment. 'He's not my type of customer. I cater to a finer customer, people who like something understated, classic.'

On buying the building, Trump paid Ehrman a visit, which Ehrman described as amusing. 'He travels with an entourage, you know. He was sitting right where you're sitting, but with eight or nine other people standing in the foyers, the hall, outside the building.'

Ehrman heard Trump out, then showed him out. After all, the law was on his side. He is a tenant and as long as he pays the rent he will remain a tenant, until he dies. Which is not to say that he doesn't have other places to lay his hat. Ehrman's company is very successful, and he's got a home in Paris and a 'summer home' on Long Island. I couldn't see how he – who was obviously a capitalist – thought that it was fair that he should live so cheaply in digs worth vast amounts, even though he was not poor. Besides, I didn't believe that he actually lived in the apartment on Park Avenue. I think he lived all over the place, and kept the apartment because it was cheap and the address was so good.

Of the relative pittance he was paying for the place, Ehrman said, 'Well, first of all, I don't consider it a small amount of money. Second of all, there are very, very few starving landlords in New York.' He was also offended by Trump's motivation in buying the building and then asking all its longtime residents to move. 'Park Avenue is an address for a certain type of person,' Ehrman said.

And that's true. You can't just move to Park Avenue. For one thing, there are virtually no rental properties, so you have to have enough money to buy. But that is the least of your problems, if the address has won your heart. Most of the buildings on Park Avenue are run by 'co-operatives', which means the people who are already domiciled there decide who can and can't move in. You have to prove you are a good person, that your money is legally made, and that you have some connections – some cachet, some bang with your buck. New Yorkers like Madonna have found themselves shut out of prestigious buildings by residents who simply don't accept that recent fame is evidence of good citizenship. Unlike any other city in the world, it doesn't matter if you come knocking with a great big bag of cash: if the 'co-op board' (which is code for 'people who already live in the building and who love nothing better than snooping through your personal papers') deems you to be crass or unfashionable, you have no hope of signing the contract.

'But anyone can live in a *Trump* building,' Mr Ehrman told me, with something like a sneer. 'You just show up with your cash. He won't care where it came from. He intends to let people get a Park Avenue address, where they'd never normally get one.' In other words, Ehrman saw himself as a gatekeeper, keeping rich riff-raff out of the city's best street. He could pull this off because he had a wonderful way with a blue blazer and a distinguished air about him, and all the little old ladies in the foyer, with their fading Chanel suits and their palm-sized dogs, seemed to love him so. Unhappily for Trump, Ehrman also had, well, the trump card. If he refused to move, the mogul would simply have to renovate around him which, Mr Erhman explained, 'is exactly what happened at Hudson'.

I had heard about Hudson but I couldn't really believe it existed. According to rumour, the hotel – which is on the Upper West Side and among Manhattan's chicest – has a floor full of batty tenants who are on rent-controlled contracts, and who therefore can never be evicted. Frustrated by my own search for a suitable apartment, I went one day to check out this rumour, and found that it was partly true: there is a floor full of rent-controlled tenants at Hudson, but they aren't batty. On the contrary, they've worked the system beautifully.

The first thing I saw when I approached the front of the

building, was a leather-clad model stepping out of a limousine. A white-gloved doorman was handling her luggage – Louis Vuitton, almost certainly not fake – while another was guiding her toward a mint-green glass door that slid open as she passed. I watched for a while, and then I went around the back of the building and searched until I found it: the unmarked door of Hudson legend. It did not slide; indeed, I could not see how it actually opened, so I stood on the street, waiting for somebody to come and enter it. Before long, an old man with a faded coat shuffled up and put out his hand.

'Hey, do you live here?' I asked, bouncing forward with my notebook in my hand. The poor man, whose name was Richard Altman, looked startled. But, when I explained that I was writing a story about rent control, he was soon waxing lyrical, and grinning at his good fortune through the gaps in his teeth.

'Been here for 20 years,' he said, with his white plastic shopping bag swinging by his side. 'When the developers bought the building, they offered me $20,000 to move, but I said no, I don't want to. After all these years, I've got too much stuff.' Mr Altman and his fellow tenants turned the money down, which forced the new owner of the building, Ian Schrager, to renovate around them.

'It was noisy, all the hammering,' Altman said of the multi-million-dollar transformation. 'But it looks good, I suppose.' He meant the outside of the hotel: he had never been into the foyer, or into any room other than his own. 'They don't let us use the front entrance,' Altman said. 'I mean, I've never tried, so this hasn't happened to me, but I heard if you try they've got security guards and they escort you round the back.'

Guests of the hotel would never know that Altman lives in the building: the hotel elevators cruise right past his floor without ever stopping. I wondered if anybody ever noticed that it seems to take a long time to get from the seventh to the eighth floor of Hudson. How many of them know that the eighth floor of the hotel is really the ninth floor of the building, that the real eighth floor is accessible only by a lift around the back, and that it is occupied by people who are paying just $101.70 a week for a room that would otherwise cost $275 a night? But I couldn't afford to dwell on the good fortune of these tenants, because doing so did not make a three-bedroom apartment on the Upper West Side – with a garden – cost less than my budget.

'It's a fantasy,' said one broker, when I told her about my family and how much we had to spend. And then it came true. Martin found the place, of course. He simply got sick of looking, so he rang a new broker and was blunt.

'What we want,' he said, 'is three bedrooms, two bathrooms and a garden, and this is how much we have to spend.' There was a pause while he listened to what the broker was saying, on the other end of the line, and then he said, 'And where is it?' There was another pause. 'We'll be there in a few minutes.'

We did not have a babysitter, so we bundled our children into a yellow taxi and let ourselves be flung about until we got to the address that Martin had scribbled on a pad. When the cab stopped, we found ourselves in front of a building with five chimneys. It was not a skyscraper; it was only five storeys tall. It did not have an entrance hall with a doorman. It had a stoop, or a set of stairs, leading up to a heavy front door, like you see on 'Sesame Street'.

The landlady, whose name was Jan, came out of a neighbouring building, smiled at the piles of scarves and parkas that were our children, and then used an old brass key to turn the lock. We walked down a long staircase into an apartment large enough to skate in. It had polished floorboards and a big kitchen, a garden out the back with brick paving, a single tree, and a couple of dead plants in pots.

'This place has been empty since September 12,' said Jan, who would soon become the person I was calling every day to ask where to find a dry cleaner, a newspaper, a stamp. 'There was a family here, and the wife didn't want to stay after the terrorist attacks. They got out the next day.' All around, there were signs of a place left in haste: the kettle was half-full, and there was something old in the fridge.

One flat minute after being put on the ground, my young son had found a wooden go-kart under the stairs and managed to get inside it. He then got both feet caught under the steering wheel and ended up face down on the floor, wailing. But it didn't matter: our new landlady is a mother, and she once loved an Australian man, and she was keen to get her big, empty space filled.

'This place used to be $5500 a month,' she said. 'But it's been empty for four months, so you can negotiate.' I told her how much I had to spend, and explained that spending any more would be taking food out of the children's mouths. She hesitated for just a minute and then said, 'Fine.' At which point, I hugged her.

Oh yes, there was a catch. The apartment was underground. Have you ever walked along the streets of an old city, and wondered who lives in those strange places below your knees? Well, we do. It isn't all bad: indeed, I am pleased that I don't live like other families we know, stacked one on top of the other in boxes in the sky, with windows for the children to tumble from. Instead, when people come to visit, I step out of our front door and yell up the staircase, 'We're down here, under your feet!' And Jan has made the place livable. All the floors are tiled or polished (which is much better when it floods) and you could fit a queen size bed in the fireplace in the front bedroom. We have a glass skylight out the back, which lets in some light from the garden, and we have a small window in the front room. It is near the ceiling but if I stand on tip-toes, I can see over the sill and up the trouser legs of people walking past.

There's something else about the apartment, too, something we didn't know about until after we had signed the lease and bolted all the new furniture together: the area outside our bedroom window is where other residents of our building dump their rubbish bags. They don't smell, but late at night tramps go sifting through them, looking for something to eat, or maybe something to sell. If our curtain is open, I can see their big brown hands picking stuff out of bins, tossing what they don't want (sometimes against our glass) and slipping what they do want into their coat pockets. I don't mind so much, but some of the people who live around me do.

A few months ago, I heard one of our neighbours shout out of his window, 'Hey you, down there, get out of the bins, you're making a mess!' The old hobo was indignant.

'I am not messy,' he said, drawing his hands out of the bags. 'I am very neat.'

Another time, the sound got too loud even for me, and it seemed to be going on forever, so I got out of bed, crept over to the open window and shouted upwards, 'Hey, shoo, get out of our bins!' But this time, there was nobody standing there. The bins were moving, but somehow from the inside.

'My God,' said Martin, who got up to stand beside me. 'That's not wind, you know. That's rats.'

He was right, but what could we do? I wasn't going to move out, only to have to start house-hunting again. So I did what most New Yorkers do: I became nonchalant. Two years on, to the horror of friends from Australia, I find I can sleep easily through the noise from rats and hobos in our bins, or the sound of water cascading down the walls. When the light bulbs blow out, I can find my way to the bathroom in the dark.

And so, this morning, I found myself chuckling as I sat on a kitchen stool – which was standing in a puddle – reading the article about basement living, in the *New York Times*. The journalist – who maybe has more money than we do – made living with such things sound like torture. To me, they are part of what makes a dirty basement home.

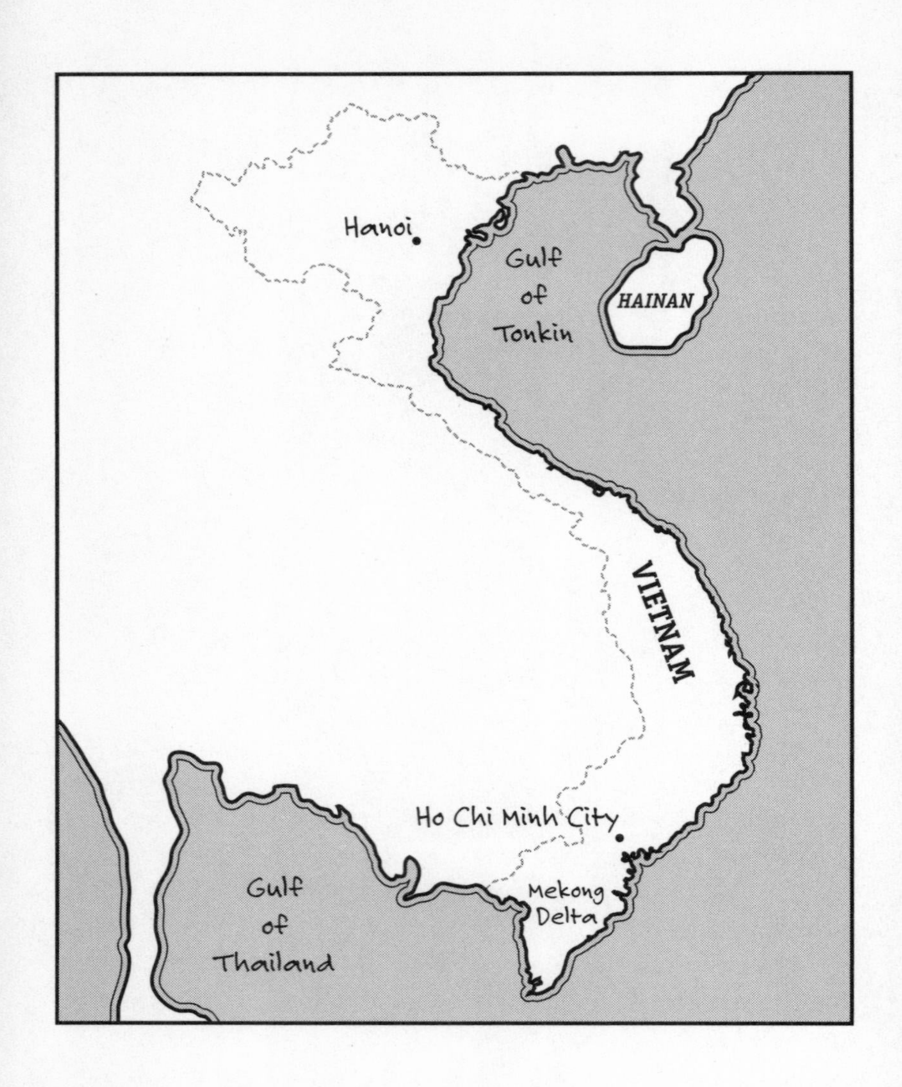
Hanoi
Gulf of Tonkin
HAINAN
VIETNAM
Ho Chi Minh City
Mekong Delta
Gulf of Thailand

Same Same but Different

PETER MOORE

I'M PROBABLY one of the few people in the world who can say that a surly taxi driver got his holiday off to the perfect start.

En route to a new life in London, I had arrived at Ho Chi Minh International Airport with nothing more than a notion of riding around the Mekong Delta on an old Vespa and permission from my long-suffering wife to spend a week doing it. And just moments after a long and unpleasant taxi ride in the company of a totally disagreeable taxi driver, I found myself with the keys to a beautifully restored old Vespa in my hand and carte blanche to do what I wanted with it for the next week.

The taxi driver didn't realise he was doing me such a huge favour. Indeed, after I refused to stay in a hotel his friend owned, he was in no mood to help me at all. On top of the voucher I'd bought from the special taxi counter at the airport to take me to the backpacker district at Pham Ngu Lao, he demanded I pay him another taxi fare. When I refused he got agitated and tried to dump me at each set of traffic lights we came to. He finally lost his temper at the edge of Pham Ngu Lao, stopping the taxi with a screech of brakes and dumping me and my bags unceremoniously on the pavement.

The first thing I noticed when I'd finished dusting myself off was the humidity. It hit me like a soggy blanket. The second thing I noticed was that he'd dumped me right outside the Zoom Café.

I'd like to say that I knew Zoom Café was Saigon's only Vespa-themed bar and that it was top of my list of places to visit. Or that I knew that its American owner, Steve Mueller, restored Vespas immaculately and sold them all around the world. But, in truth, the whole basis of my trip to Vietnam was rather vague. I knew Vespas were exported to Vietnam in the sixties. And I knew that I'd like to ride around the Mekong Delta on one. Whether that was possible, whether there were even any roadworthy Vespas left, I wasn't sure. My research hadn't progressed beyond an impulse.

The café was evocatively Vespa-themed, with a mural above the bar painted in the style of old French Vespa ads from the fifties. The front half of a Vespa VBB was bolted to the wall, giving the impression that it was in the process of magically passing through. And astonishingly, within minutes of walking into the café I had met and befriended Steve and he had handed me the keys to a 1968 150cc Vespa. It was painted a very fetching shade of bronze and had chrome protector bars that sparkled in the sun. I think Steve may have had a touch of heatstroke because he not only said I could ride around the Delta on it, but he wouldn't let me pay him anything, either. The scooter was one of his runabouts, he told me, and he wasn't using it anyway.

After a quick tour of the bike's idiosyncrasies – a dodgy front brake and a clutch cable with a tendency to work loose – I ventured out onto the roads of Ho Chi Minh City. You know that scene late in *Apocalypse Now* when Marlon Brando mumbles 'The horror! The horror!'? I used to think he was talking about the futility of war, but after half an hour riding in the traffic in HCMC I realised he was probably just shaken up after a quick trip to the big smoke for supplies. The motorcycle riders of old Saigon make the VC look like pussies.

There are over three million motor scooters in HCMC and I reckon most of them were in the centre of town that morning. They buzzed about like flies around a cow pat, each intent on forcing me off the road and into a noodle stall. Into the mix were thrown wobbling cyclists wearing conical hats, pedal-powered, three-wheeled cyclos with terrified passengers getting a ringside view from the seat in front, and pedestrians forced to scamper along the road by all the hawkers, motorcycles and small businesses that cluttered the footpath. Riding a motor scooter here wasn't just a way to get between Point A and Point B. It was an extreme sport.

I was the only person on the road riding alone and without encumbrance. Every scooter bore at least four passengers and some sort livestock as well. One family of three – small by Vietnamese standards – had a dozen ducks, still alive, hanging from the handle bar. Others carried less animate objects: one chap had a double mattress strapped precariously to his back as he wove through the traffic. And another brave pillion passenger held a pane of glass across his legs, seemingly oblivious to what an accident would do to his ability to father children. Every single vehicle on the road broke any number of traffic codes, but they were all allowed to continue, chaotic and unhindered.

The traffic lights offered no respite. Some bright spark in City Hall had decided to liven the traffic up even more by installing traffic lights with a display that counts down the seconds before the light would turn green again. As the counter approached the final five seconds the scooter riders began revving their engines and jostling for the best position at the head of the queue, sending plumes of blue fumes skyward as they took off with tinny roars that would have made Michael Schumacher feel right at home.

I returned to the café in need of a good lie-down and with a new understanding of why Steve was lending me the Vespa. He wasn't being generous. He was just a very sick individual who got his kicks from watching others suffer.

'You'll get used to it,' he said with a laugh when he saw me. I wasn't so sure.

My plan was to head south to the Delta as soon as possible, but when I woke the next morning I was still a little shell-shocked and instead decided to spend the day browsing the pirate CD shops on Bui Vien and De Tham streets. I wanted to have a closer look at the titles offered by the pirate book-seller girls, too. They walked around with 60 books at a time: photocopied, colour-covered and piled one on top of the other, a thin white ribbon holding them together. An English guy had emailed me from Vietnam once to tell me that he'd just bought a pirate copy of my book *No Shitting in the Toilet*. I wanted to see if they still had any.

The first bookseller found me as I was tucking into my breakfast, the obligatory banana pancake. She stood before me, politely pulling the ribbon aside so I could see the titles on offer more clearly.

'Lone Plan-et . . . good books . . . you *buuuyyy!*' the girl whined.

I scoured the pile, hoping to find one of my books, but the closest I got was *Stupid White Men* by Michael Moore. I asked the girl if she had anything by *Peter* Moore and she stared at me blankly. I repeated the name, my name, more slowly this time, and again there wasn't a flicker of recognition. She asked me to write it down and then plonked her books beside my table. 'I ask my boss,' she said, scurrying off down the lane.

She was back within minutes with a trim, muscly woman in her thirties who had more than a touch of the Lucy Lius about her. She was not happy at all about being dragged away from the nerve centre of her pirate publishing enterprise.

'No Peter Moore!' she spat, giving me the sort of withering look Lucy has become famous for. '*Michael* Moore. It *same*!'

I could have suggested that a quick comparison of Michael's and my royalty cheques would clear up that little misunderstanding, but the iciness of her stare and the muscle that twitched in her neck suggested that it wouldn't have been a good idea. Already a proud owner of the entire Michael Moore oeuvre, I took the diplomatic option of buying a copy of the Lonely Planet *Vietnamese Phrasebook*. It cost the full four dollars even though it was a fraction of the size of all the other books, but I'm not ashamed to admit that, frankly, the woman scared me.

The incident, as terrifying as it was, did give me an idea, though. I decided to spend the rest of the day asking every girl selling books in HCMC if they had any books by Peter Moore. At first I let them approach me, in the streets around Pham Ngu Lao, pretending that something in their pile of wares had caught my eye. But by the afternoon I was seeking them out – at the War Remnants Museum, in the Internet cafés along De Tham and the restaurants and bars along Dong Khoi, the more affluent part of town. My hope was that when they returned to the warehouse their gang masters would notice a staggering number of requests for books by some bloke called Peter Moore, amongst the usual ones for the latest John Grisham and Joanna Trollope. An illusion that there was a demand for my books would be created and, by the time I got back from the Delta, one of them would be photocopied and have slipped into the Ho Chi Minh City Top 60 as a hot new title. Well, a man can dream.

Before I headed south to the Delta, Steve insisted I joined him for a night on the town with an English spray painter called Daniel. Daniel was in Vietnam to teach Steve's local spray painters how use the latest products and had become quite enamoured with the HCMC scene.

'He's still thinking with his Johnson,' said Steve, 'so we'll have to keep an eye on him.'

We set out along Duong Dong Khoi, the wide boulevard that runs the length of the Dong Khoi district from the river to the cathedral. It is both the commercial centre of HCMC and home to most of its bars and clubs, and that night it felt like a scene from a Vietnamese pirate copy of *La Dolce Vita*. The footpaths were bustling with people eating at outdoor cafés and the street itself was teeming with young Vietnamese cruising on motor scooters. Everyone was wearing their Sunday best; the more affluent rode Honda Dreams and wore designer gear with the labels showing. Those riding the cheaper Chinese Majestys and Victorys made up for a lack of financial liquidity with originality and creativity in their clothing, using army surplus left behind by the Americans in new and unusual ways. And it has to be said that Steve, Daniel and I cut a stylish swathe on our Vespas. We attracted more than a few admiring glances from the locals, but I suspect that most were directed at our bikes.

'Vespas used to be regarded as peasant bikes,' yelled Steve as we rode slowly along the boulevard. 'But now they see them in ads and magazines and they're becoming cool.'

Vespas were popular with expats, too, and it certainly didn't hurt Steve's cause that the Vespas they saw on the streets of HCMC nearly always had a pretty Vietnamese girl on the back.

'Now all of the local Vietnamese rich guys want them,' laughed Steve. 'They think it's going to help them pull Miss Vietnam.'

We weaved our way through the traffic on the roundabout in front of Than Binh markets and down an alley to Duong Thi Sach and the Apocalypse Now nightclub. The club is an institution in HCMC – it's the closest thing the city's got to the R&R clubs of the Vietnam War – and Daniel was fidgeting like a schoolboy to get in.

'You can't walk from the front door to the back without falling in love,' he said. 'The girls are gorgeous!'

The girls were indeed gorgeous, in a mini-skirted, tight-topped kind of way. But their taste in men was exceedingly poor. They leant against the fattest and ugliest of the patrons, flirting with them as if they were Brad Pitt. Indeed, there seemed to be some kind of bizarre inverse law at work: the more ugly the bloke, the more stunning the woman.

There are exceptions to every rule, of course. Daniel was a good looking guy who dressed and groomed himself like David Beckham and all the girls loved him. In the time it took to have our first drink at the bar, at least half a dozen very attractive girls came up and greeted him with a kiss. The last and most attractive girl dragged him onto the dance floor.

'He's playing a dangerous game,' said Steve, watching him dance with three different girls in the space of one song – appropriately, Britney Spear's 'Toxic'. 'He's either going to get burnt out or caught out.'

I bought a round of 333's, the local Vietnamese beer, and expressed my surprise that the Vietnamese girls put up with this kind of behaviour. Those who had come up to Daniel were as smart and funny as they were attractive. Daniel had claimed the girls weren't bothered by the way the Western men acted because Vietnamese guys treat them like dogs. When Daniel was out of earshot on the dance floor, Steve ventured another, more plausible theory. 'It's money,' he said. 'These girls are hanging out for the one guy who will take them away. And they're willing to go through all this to get him.'

I asked him if that's why his wife, Phuong, had married him.

'She's keeping me, man!' he laughed. Phuong had already owned the café and she'd turned it into a Vespa-themed establishment so Steve would have something to do.

At midnight the lights were switched on and everyone was asked to leave. The government was having one of its periodic campaigns against immorality and was cracking down on closing times. The men looked even sadder under the stark glare of the fluorescent lights. Their skin was clammy and greasy and the sweat marks under their arms ate up half their shirts. The girls looked just as pretty, but with the lights on you could see the dullness in their eyes.

The alley outside was gridlocked as everyone got back on their bikes and buzzed off into the night. I headed back to my hotel. The nightwatchman opened the security grille and let me park the bike in the foyer of the hotel, beside the reception desk. I would have to get up early to move it but I wasn't concerned. Tomorrow, at last, I was heading off to the Mekong Delta. And despite my earlier reservations about riding on Vietnamese roads, I was ready and raring to go. Of course, that could have just been the 333's speaking.

The Vietnamese call the Delta *Cuu Long*, 'Nine Dragons', after the nine tributaries of the Mekong that crawl across the alluvial plain here like spidery veins. It is the final leg of the Mekong's 4000-kilometre journey from the Tibetan Plateau, and the nutrient-rich flats it passes through produce 38 per cent of Vietnam's annual food crop, despite making up only 10 per cent of the country's land mass. During the American war, the Delta was a Viet Cong stronghold – they had many well-hidden cells here – and was constantly strafed with bombs and defoliants.

The Delta begins on the outskirts of HCMC, but there it is heavily industrialised. The main road south, Highway 1, is a snarled ribbon of asphalt, lined with makeshift mechanic shacks, shops selling truck parts and grimy factories belching smoke into the grey skies. Eighty-three per cent of Vietnamese enterprises are based in this area, from fish processing plants through to tractor factories and, charmingly, the Ben Luc

Taffeta Company. It's not pretty, but the industry here is the reason more Vietnamese are riding Honda Dreams and talking on Nokia mobile phones.

Highway 1 is also the domain of lumbering trucks and buses, in varying degrees of disintegration, with brakes that don't work but horns that do. They bore down mercilessly on hapless scooter riders who scattered like cockroaches whenever one came near. As I dodged and weaved my way south, it struck me that the chaos on the roads was a metaphor for modern Vietnam. Since the introduction in 1986 of a policy of economic liberalisation called *Doi Moi* (which translates to 'change and newness'), everyone has been rushing madly in different directions, seemingly with no idea of where they are going. Yet, like the traffic, most seem to be getting to their destinations, with plenty of near misses, to be sure, but generally in one piece.

But it wasn't all taffeta factories and maniacal truck drivers. The Delta of tourist brochures could be glimpsed too, usually from one of the many bridges that span the countless rivers, streams and canals that criss-cross the region. Here life hadn't changed much at all. The water's edge was lined with water palms and stilt houses and, out in the middle, hand-hewn wooden cargo boats ploughed along low in the water, loaded with produce from the farms. Small dugout canoes ferried people from one side to the other and occasional ducks floated by on the murky brown water, scattering when young boys jumped in to wash. It was idyllic, really. Well, it was up until the moment when I was shaken from my reverie by the blaring horn of an oncoming truck.

My destination that day was Vinh Long, a major regional centre in the Mekong Delta, 140 kilometres south of HCMC. A brochure produced by the local Cuu Long Tourist Company fancifully claimed that the multitude of rivers that surround the town make it look like a 'flower with many petals'. I'm not sure which angle the guy was looking at the town from when he wrote that copy, but from where I was sitting – on the back of the Vespa – it looked like just another scrappy town of stilt houses tumbling into a murky brown river.

I had decided on Vinh Long as my mandatory Mekong River Boat Tour town and I was impressed enough by the Cuu Long Tourist Company's whimsical vision of their town to promptly engage them to organise a tour for me. They suggested I visit An Binh, an island that was 'a living picture in miniature of the whole Delta', sliced by canals into tiny jigsaw pieces connected by slight bridges called *arroyos* and dotted with orchards and farms. For a paltry sum I would enjoy a leisurely afternoon boat tour of the canals, an overnight stay on one of the island's farms, and then a dawn tour of the floating markets at Cai Be. An English-speaking guide was also included in the price.

My guide's name was Phuc, which he assured me meant 'lucky' in Vietnamese but which sounded very much like a popular Western expletive to me. I was tempted to say, 'So you're a lucky Phuc', but his sad, soulful eyes and sincerity told me to keep my crass schoolboy humour to myself. Besides, he obviously took his job seriously – he'd even kindly organised parking for the Vespa in the exclusive Cuu Long Hotel, where it would be watched over by a guy in a white uniform with epaulets and a natty peaked cap while I was away.

My solo afternoon boat tour consisted of chugging up the main canal, which cut the island in two, in a slender vessel designed to seat 10, dodging hulking cargo ships and hiding from them in the tiny rivulets that ran off the canal. The canal was just as busy as the highway, and the rules of the river were the same as on the road. The smaller vessels gave way to the huge sampans loaded high with rice husks that bore down on them. The sampans all had a pair of eyes painted on the front, supposedly to keep an eye out for the evil spirits of the river, but they were painted at such an angle as to make the boats look like they were getting some kind of crazy pleasure from the distress their wake caused tinier craft.

On the rivulets, life continued as it always had. People threshed, wove, planted and picked, or simply sat on the verandas of their wooden huts and watched the world go by. Here the waterways were so narrow that the branches of the trees that lined them formed a natural canopy, shielding us from the harsh afternoon sun. Children returning from school walked along narrow paths on the banks and waved excitedly as we passed. A European couple wearing conical hats floated past in a rustic version of a gondola, looking sheepish as they were rowed by a woman standing at the back of the craft. It was exactly how I had imagined the Delta to be, and for the first time in Vietnam I felt calm and peaceful.

The Cuu Long Tourist Company had organised quite an action-packed itinerary of nursery, orchard and coconut-candy factory tours for me that afternoon, but Phuc soon realised that I wasn't the kind of tourist who enjoyed wandering around bonsai gardens and or sampling exotic tropical fruits. Instead, we hung back in a beautiful teak room overlooking the gardens and knocked back a selection of local moonshine brought to us by a guy with the kind of long grey beard you only see in Kung Fu movies. Most of the drinks were made from rice, some were allowed to ferment with a snake in the bottom of the jar and they all had a kick like a mule. I don't think Phuc had had so much fun on a Mekong River tour before and he wandered back to the boat whistling a jaunty little Vietnamese ditty.

My homestay for the night was a traditional farmhouse with a packed dirt floor and a shrine to family's ancestors above the entrance. The kitchen had a single open fire and my camp bed came with a tattered mosquito net that had more holes in it than the American line of defence at Da Nang. A family of three generations of farmers lived there, under the watchful eye of the patriarch, Dung, a name that Phuc was quick to point out meant 'heroic' in Vietnamese. Dung was a tiny man of indeterminate age with a wispy grey beard and sparkling eyes and he seemed inordinately pleased when I said I would eat with the family rather than dine alone in my room. Dining solo seemed against the spirit of staying with a family – if I was going to eat alone I may as well have stayed in a hotel. And besides, if I ate in my room I'd be depriving the family of a night of highly anticipated entertainment.

Don't be fooled into thinking that these people open their houses up just for the extra money. Foreigners are allowed in to their family homes for another very important reason: to entertain. Every fumble with a chopstick, every clumsy faux pas and every blundering insensitivity is better than a night out at the movies. The money is essential, but the amusement is priceless.

Each of the dishes presented to me that night were sculpted into a Mekong Delta scene. A cucumber man rowed a cucumber boat through a river of spring rolls. And another cucumber man carrying carrots strode across a mountain of rice. It was all very quaint, but in truth it was just an edible game of Ker-plunk. Instead of pulling out plastic straws and hoping all the trapped marbles didn't coming crashing down, I had to eat my food without toppling the cucumber men. I failed miserably, of course. And when one man came crashing down into a bowl of soup, splashing hot liquid over most of the family, I failed spectacularly. I knew I had fulfilled my duties as the foreign fall guy. The family left the table that evening giggling and wiping tears from their eyes.

I retired with Phuc and Dung to a room where a shrine to the family's ancestors was kept – the most important room in the house. We sat drinking tea at a beautifully polished teak table, and Dung pointed proudly to a framed certificate hanging on the wall. He had received it from the government for being a soldier.

'He fought bravely for 25 years,' Phuc explained. 'First against the French and then the Americans.'

Dung smiled broadly, his eyes sparkling. This was obviously

something he was very proud of. I asked if he had fought Australians. He shook his head.

'They tried to avoid the Australians,' interpreted Phuc. 'They preferred fighting Americans. They were easier.'

I must have looked perplexed because Phuc explained further. Apparently the Australians patrolled their areas with soldiers spread hundreds of metres apart. At best the Viet Cong would be able to pick off one or two men before the rest of the patrol became aware of their presence. The Americans wandered along drinking, smoking and laughing together. They were easy to ambush and regularly were. It made better sense, explained Phuc, to let the Aussies pass.

It was a sobering experience to be able to talk to someone who had fought in the war and was willing to talk about it. Seventy-five per cent of Vietnam's population has been born since the end of the conflict and has had no direct experience of the sacrifices that were made. And because Vietnam is such a verdant country, particularly the Delta, any scars left by bombing and defoliants were quickly hidden and the land was reclaimed by the lush growth. I asked Dung if he was proud of how Vietnam had turned out and whether it had all been worth fighting for. He nodded his head slowly.

'Very proud,' interpreted Phuc. 'If they hadn't won he would still be fighting and his farm would be in ruins.'

We drank a toast to Vietnam and to a quick end to the troubles in Iraq, which Dung saw as America's new Vietnam. Then I retired to my room where every mosquito in the Delta was waiting to gorge on my sweet Western flesh.

It was still dark when breakfast was served the next morning. The men of the household sat around a long wooden table lit by a hurricane lamp, eating rice and discussing what needed to be done in the orchard that day. The women had risen earlier still to prepare the meal, and after laying the food on the table they disappeared to a back room. They would wait there until the men had finished, Phuc explained, eating what the men had left and only after they were gone. The lot of women, it seemed, had not been served well by the communist victory. Their prowess as exceptional soldiers had been rewarded with lots more hard work and very few rights.

With the farmyard tasks planned, the men drained the last of the tea from their cups and set off for the orchards. Then, just as the orange streaks of dawn appeared in the sky, the boat arrived to take Phuc and I to the floating markets at Cai Be.

The floating markets were very disappointing. I'd been expecting a colourful spectacle of jostling canoes full of tropical fruit being artfully manoeuvred by locals wearing conical hats. What I got was a sad collection of faded sampans with a couple of sweet potatoes strung up a pole to indicate that was what they were selling.

'The harvest has passed,' explained Phuc, sensing my disappointment. 'Now is the time for planting.'

The obligatory tour of a rice pancake workshop and a rice crisp factory didn't do much to lift the excitement factor either, but luckily Phuc realised that I wasn't interested in watching girls sort and pack snackfoods and we only stayed for moments. The most entertaining moment came at the rice crisp factory where the female manager told Phuc the latest gossip. She'd given a particular guide everyone's commissions for the month to distribute and he'd run off with the money. Phuc pressed her for details, laughing at the audacity of the guy and saying that he'd never trusted him anyway, so it was lunchtime before we were back in Vinh Long.

The white-uniformed chap at the Cuu Long Hotel rolled out the Vespa, wiping off the chalk mark that proved it was mine. After shaking Phuc's hand I kick-started the bike and set off again on Highway 1. My plan was to head west to Chau Doc, a town close to the Cambodian border, but when I reached Cantho just over an hour later I found a hotel and decided to stop. It wasn't because I was tired from getting up so early; rather, I'd made a snap decision to visit a place 60 kilometres in the opposite direction.

That place was the Bat Pagoda, or Chua Doi as the locals call it, and it was near the sleepy town of Soc Trang. My guidebook described it as 'one of the Mekong Delta's most unusual sights', which was quite a rap considering the extraordinary things I'd seen so far. Not least of which was the calendar I'd just seen on the wall at the Hien Guesthouse, the establishment in Cantho where I was bedding down for the evening. It featured a photo of the manager's husband, bare-chested and superimposed next to a mobile missile launcher in a green field. The Bat Pagoda would be have to be pretty amazing to beat that.

Having grown up watching Adam West swanning about as the caped crusader in 'Batman', my imagination immediately constructed a Bat Cave within this pagoda, complete with Bat Buddha and other Bat-worshipping gear. Even though I told myself there could not possibly be a Batman theme park at Chua Doi, it still didn't cross my mind that I might just find a Pagoda with some bats hanging in a nearby tree.

The road east to Soc Trang is a secondary road, but that afternoon it seemed to be carrying as much traffic as Highway 1. It was badly potholed, with some of the holes so big that people had filled them with sandbags, and the sport here for truck drivers seemed to be herding motorcycles into them.

Once I got past the towns of Cai Rang and Phung Hiep, however, the road ran parallel with a river and the scenery became distinctly more rural. Barges meandered peacefully down canals and the road was lined on either side with woven mats covered in rice. The villagers were drying the rice in the sun, and in most places the mats encroached onto the road. Just outside one tiny village the farmers had gotten so audacious that the drivable part of the road had shrunk to a single, narrow lane, barely wide enough for a minivan to pass. The mats acted like a chicane, slowing the traffic considerably. The local constabulary took full advantage of this, sitting under a tree just south of the mats and nabbing motorcycle riders for not wearing their helmets, before they had the chance to speed up.

The Bat Pagoda wasn't actually in Soc Trang. It was four kilometres out of town and it didn't take long for me to get terribly lost. I ended up in a remote part of the Delta down near the South China Sea, with plenty of rice paddies and shrimp factories but very few pagodas. I spotted a restaurant ahead and decided to ask a bunch of Vietnamese guys sitting at a table getting drunk if they knew where Chua Doi was. Before I could ask, one of them spoke to me in English.

'*Noice* bike,' he said in a broad Aussie accent, nodding towards the Vespa. 'Where ya from?' When I answered Sydney, he said, 'Me too!'

I'm not sure exactly what kind of odds a bookmaker would put on meeting a fellow Aussie in this neck of the woods but I would suggest that they would be rather long. I was lost in the middle of a one-duck province in rural Vietnam and I had stumbled upon not only someone who could speak English but who was an Aussie to boot. His name was Phu, he ran the shrimp factory down the road and best of all, he knew the way to the Bat Pagoda.

Before sending me on my way, Phu insisted that I join him and his friends for a drink. Judging by the number of empty bottles on the table, they had quite a start on me, but he waved over the waitress and soon I had my own bottle of warm beer and a glass full of ice. As is customary in Vietnam, the waitress also gave me a refresher towel sealed in a plastic pouch. I scrunched it up, getting all the air down one end, and popped it, just as I'd seen the locals do. The sound echoed around the hall like a gun shot.

Phu laughed. 'You are becoming Vietnamese!' he said, pouring me a beer.

Over the next hour, Phu continually topped up my beer, telling me about his life between rowdy cries of 'Cheers!' and the boisterous clinking of glasses. When I finally staggered out of the restaurant I knew that Phu had grown up in Cabramatta, that his kids went to school in Australia and that I was feeling a bit under the weather. I couldn't tell how many beers I'd had in my bottomless glass, but I hoped I was in better shape than Phu. He staggered out onto the road, blinking in sun, and used a telegraph pole for support while he gave me directions.

'The sign for the Bat Pagoda faces this way, so you'll see it this time,' he said with an effort. 'Just turn left.' His mates managed to join him on the road and waved goodbye too. I set off down the road, a little gingerly at first, pleased that I was still in the middle of nowhere. Hopefully I'd be in better shape by the time I hit any traffic.

The Bat Pagoda wasn't very good. It looked like every other pagoda in Vietnam – gaudily painted and in need of a good scrub – except for a tree where maybe 20 bats were hanging. A young novice dressed in a bright orange gown was sweeping the path and when he noticed my disappointment he pointed to three graves at the back of the compound.

'Five-toenailed pigs!' he said.

Now that would have been something to see. A family of deformed pigs with one more toenail each than they should have had. But they were dead and all that was left were their portraits, painted on their headstones.

I left Cantho the next morning just after dawn. I hadn't planned to leave that early but when I'd asked the night before what time check-out was, the manager had told me 5.30 am. I realise now that she just wanted me to go on a floating market tour to Cai Rang and was probably hoping I would say, 'What the heck? I'm up now, I may as well go see some more of those excellent floating markets.' But at US$18 for a half-day tour – more than a lot of Vietnamese earn in a month – that wasn't likely. I decided instead to hit the road before it got too busy.

The ride to Chau Doc went largely without incident. A number of roadwork projects had been started and abandoned, causing the kind of traffic jams that induced Vietnamese truck drivers to become even more reckless. At one point a bus came careering directly towards me in what appeared to be an attempt to dunk me into the grubby canal beside the road. But it was my second day on Highway 1 now and I realised that this was all just par for the course. Just like the truck drivers who insisted on blowing their air horns when they drew level with my eardrum. For some reason it never dawned on them that I could sense their lumbering presence just millimetres over my shoulder.

Just after the town of Long Xuyen, a guy on a Chinese motor scooter decided that riding along a major highway at 80 kilometres per hour was as good a place as any to practise his English. He wore a black pork-pie hat in place of a helmet and spoke in measured tones, even as he yelled to be heard over the road noise. There were trucks and buses bearing down murderously on us, but it seemed churlish of me to refuse to talk to him.

The lesson did not start well. He asked where I was going but before I could answer he had to swerve out of the way of a minivan that pulled across in front of us to pick up a passenger. He pulled alongside me again and continued by asking me where I was from. I told him I was from Australia but he missed my answer when a truck passed in the opposite direction, blaring its horn and barely missing him. Unfazed by the fact he had nearly ended up on the front grille of a Mitsubishi Canter, he asked me my name before waving goodbye and powering ahead. The lesson was over before I learned his name.

Chau Doc is a town with big plans. Its approaches are lined with giant fish farms and shrimp factories geared for international trade with neighbouring Cambodia, and the direct river link with Phnom Penh makes it perfectly placed to take advantage of the increasing commerce between the two countries. The impressive Victoria Chau Doc Hotel sits grandly overlooking the river and offers all mod cons, including a business centre, fitness club and in-room massages. But the clearest indication of the town's ambitions is that it has plans to build a monorail.

I spotted the sign for the monorail on the outskirts of town on my way to the Delta Adventure Centre, a place my guidebook described as the best-value lodging in town. The sign was nailed to a tree and featured illustrations of the monorail winding its way up nearby Sam Mountain and pulling into stations that looked like Disney-esque palaces. Naturally, the sign was hand painted, as most are outside of HCMC.

I thought immediately of the episode of 'The Simpsons' where the good folk of Springfield are conned into building a monorail by the smooth-talking Lyle Lanley. I suspect that the *indochine* version of Mr Lanley had been in town recently, congratulating the folk of Chau Doc for embracing *Doi Moi* so successfully and talking them into not just the monorail but the awful giant fish sculpture down on the waterfront as well. The money would have been better spent on improving the roads, of course – the potholes in Chau Doc were the kind that swallowed cyclos whole. But the last laugh would have been on Vietnamese Lyle: there just aren't too many places on the planet where you can spend a briefcase full of dong.

The Delta Adventure Centre seemed to be expecting big things too. It was halfway along the road to Sam Mountain and featured thatch-roofed bungalows set around a manmade lake. It described itself as tourist complex but I was the only one staying there. After being shown to my room, a sterile box where every surface was tiled, I ate in the attached restaurant that my guidebook promised had the ambience of a harem. To my untrained eye it looked like just another Asian restaurant with battered chairs and peeling paint. I decided that the guidebook writer had probably meant 'Harlem' – the cockroaches scuttling up the wall certainly gave the place that sort of vibe – and retired to my room early.

The next day I rode along the border with Cambodia to the Bone Pagoda at Ba Chuc. The pagoda is a memorial to the thousands of villagers massacred there by the Khmer Rouge in April 1978. Historically, the Cambodians have always regarded the Delta as part of the Khmer empire and this province in particular had seen a number of nasty border clashes. None as nasty as this one, though – over 2000 people were slaughtered in three days – and many claim that the Vietnamese invasion of Cambodia at the end of that year came as a direct result of it.

It could have been my imagination, but as I rode along the road that formed the border between the two countries there seemed to be a real menace in the air. The area was drier than the rest of the Delta and the road was dotted with bamboo watchtowers and signs that warned passers-by in Vietnamese, Khmer and English that they were travelling through a frontier zone. The plains were now backed by hills and mountains that seemed to press in threateningly. The smoke haze from countless fires lit by farmers burning off rice stalks seemed to hang oppressively in the air, cloaking the area in a dull, muted sheen. When a soft-drink vendor saw me approaching, he ran out of his shack to make sure I didn't take the wrong turn at a fork in the road. The look of relief on his face suggested that he had just saved me from some terrible danger.

No one warned the villagers of Ba Chuc of danger back on 22 April 1978. A sizeable force of the Khmer Rouge army captured the commune, herded the villagers into groups of between 30 and 40 people, and then shot them. Some tried to escape into the surrounding fields or took refuge in pagodas, but they were hunted down and killed. Some hid under the raised dais that supported the Buddha in the Phi Lai Tu Pagoda, only to be killed by a grenade thrown amongst them.

There is a photographic display next to the main memorial at the Bone Pagoda that includes grisly black and white images of fields littered with twisted and butchered bodies. The pictures were so horrific that my mind, numbed by violent Hollywood movies, had trouble processing them as real. More affecting was the eight-sided memorial where the skulls of the victims were piled. They were grouped according to age and I was particularly moved by the pile of 15-year-olds. That's how old I was when this terrible massacre took place. At 15, my biggest concerns were the unlikelihood of St George being able to retain the premiership and whether Christine Bartho, the cute girl on the bus, liked me. That there were boys my age being brutally slaughtered in a foreign field did not even enter my mind.

My mood wasn't lightened by the community service announcement I saw on the TV in my room that night. It was designed to encourage motorcycle riders to wear helmets and was presented by a pretty girl with Eurasian features wearing an army uniform and a perky peaked cap that looked something out of Mao's China circa the Cultural Revolution.

The show was basically a half-hour 'Death in Asia' snuff movie about motorcycle traffic accidents on Vietnamese roads. It featured close-up footage of police attending collisions, drawing chalk outlines around bodies and mugging for the cameras as they pulled a flattened head off the road, the gooey brains stuck to the tarmac and stretched like chewing gum on the bottom of a shoe. The message being pushed, and a spurious one at that, was that wearing a helmet would have saved these poor souls' lives. By the time the show finished – lingering on a shot of a man who had been hit by a bus, his body still tangled and mutilated under the wheel arch – I was ready to abandon Steve's Vespa and find a safer way back to HCMC.

I woke the next morning with the brilliant idea of travelling the 270 kilometres back to HCMC on a cargo boat. I was certain it was possible – the waterfront in Chau Doc was teeming with them – and I asked the pretty girl on reception if she knew of any cargo companies with boats that would take the Vespa and me back to Ho Chi Minh City. She tried to sell me the Delta Adventure Company's two-day tour.

The tour was a Mekong extravaganza that included a boat ride to Long Xuyen and then travel by airconditioned bus the rest of the way to HCMC. I pointed to the Vespa parked just beside the reception desk and asked if I would be able to put that on a bus. She looked at me as if I were crazy.

'Oh no,' she said with alarm. 'I don't think you could even get it on the boat.' That she hadn't even considered what I was going to do with the Vespa – a Vespa she had admired the night before and asked where I'd got it from – astounded me. Perhaps she thought I was leaving it for her as a gift.

I didn't have much luck down at the docks either. Most of the boats were only going as far as Cantho and even then didn't have room for the Vespa. In the end I chanced 25 kilometres back towards Long Xuyen along the Highway 1 Road of Death, before taking a small car ferry across to the other, less developed side of the river. Through a combination of B-roads, rural lanes and car ferries I'd be able to get as far as Cai Lay, near Mytho, without riding on another main road.

The moment I rode off the car ferry and nearly skittled a chicken I knew I had found the Mekong Delta I'd been dreaming of. There were no trucks or buses here, just drays pulled by oxen and bicycles ridden by girls with incredible posture, dressed in blindingly white *Ao Dai,* the elegant silk pantsuits favoured by the women in Vietnam. Here the Delta was a labyrinth of tiny roads and lanes, cutting through rice paddies and small rural villages populated by smiling children and toothless old men.

Every turn in the road revealed another magical Mekong vista. Old women in conical hats and VC pyjamas bending in the fields to plant rice, stopping only to buy ceramic pots sold by a hawker from a cart. Duck wranglers herding their wayward charges along a path. Joss sticks looking like neon-coloured sea urchins, drying beside the road. A cyclo rider with a harvest of spring onions as his passenger, the smell strong and acrid as I passed him.

It was a complicated route I'd chosen and I had to rely on the locals to give me directions. My method was simple. I stopped at each crossroads and anunciated the name of the next town to the nearest local. Vietnamese is a tonal language, so pronunciation is the key. To get it right I used my old technique of using the accent of a character from a cartoon or movie. In Mexico I used Speedy Gonzales as my vocal guide. In Spain it was Manuel from 'Fawlty Towers'. When I asked for directions in Vietnam I adopted the 'love you long time' accent of the Vietnamese hookers in *Full Metal Jacket*. It seemed to work. Most of the locals smiled and pointed me in the right direction.

By the end of the day I was approaching Cai Lay, a small town 100 kilometres southwest of HCMC and, alarmingly, I was back on Highway 1. I think the Vespa was as apprehensive as I was about returning to the main road for, after barely skipping a beat throughout the languid backwaters of the Delta, it died with a *blurgghh* just outside the town.

I could see the town ahead so I got off the bike and started pushing. It was hot and humid and within seconds I was dripping sweat like a tap. Even worse, before I could reach the town and, hopefully, a skilled motorcycle mechanic, I had to negotiate the inevitable arched bridge that signalled the start of every town in the Delta. When I stopped at the bottom of the bridge to collect my thoughts and catch my a breath, a guy on a Honda pulled up behind me and beeped his horn. Through a series of charades it finally dawned on me that he was offering to use his bike – and his outstretched leg – to push me up and over the bridge.

It was a Vietnamese push-tow and quite simple to do. The guy rode along beside me, a little to the rear, with his right leg outstretched and his foot resting on the Vespa's rear cowl. All I had to do was steer. We powered across the bridge with ease and I spotted a few motorcycle mechanics' shops just on the other side. When I went to pull off the road and roll into one, the guy pushing me beeped his horn and indicated for me to keep going. For a moment I thought he was going to push me all the way to Mytho, a major town 30 kilometres away, but on the opposite side of town we came upon a repair shop proudly displaying the Vespa logo. My good Samaritan said something in Vietnamese to the mechanic and then jumped back on his bike. I offered to pay him for his help but he refused and rode off with a smile.

The first thing the mechanic did was shove a dirty big screwdriver up the Vespa's exhaust and rattle it around. Steve had warned me that mechanics here did that. It's meant to clear blockages and they prescribe it like doctors prescribe paracetamol. Next he pulled off the cowl and examined the spark plug, cleaning it and then kicking the kick-start to see if it emitted any spark. When that didn't work, he used the same screwdriver to physically force the piston to turn. He turned and gave me the kind of look a schoolteacher gives a naughty child. From his wagging finger and a series of animated gestures, I deduced that the piston had seized.

Now, I would have thought that was a pretty major problem, but in Vietnam it seemed to be no big deal. And because Vespa engines employ such simple technology, all it took was a bit more oil in the petrol and a few more wrenches with the screwdriver to get the bike going again. The mechanic wouldn't accept payment – the whole process only took five minutes – but he wouldn't let me go until I promised to put 5 per cent oil in the petrol instead of 3 per cent and to not go over 40 kilometres per hour. I decided not to press my luck too much and after safely reaching Mytho, I found a room for the night.

I left Mytho the next morning at seven, while the air was still fresh and clean. I took it slow and easy like the mechanic had suggested and reached the outskirts of HCMC without incident, dodging the baseball caps and scarves that Vietnamese riders always seemed to be losing. After the mayhem of Highway 1, the streets of the city now seemed strangely ordered and calm. Motorcycles were the vehicle of choice here and the vibe on the road was easier and less threatening. A prang with another bike would leave me bruised and scratched, not being scraped off the tarmac.

I scootered through the tangled streets of HCMC, past the flower district and the mobile phone shops, back to the backpacker enclave of Pham Ngu Lao. The Vespa was a bit grubby from my travels so I decided to get it cleaned before I gave it back to Steve. I found a place on the corner of Nguyen Thai Hoc where boys washed and detailed motorcycles for 8000 dong. At night it became a restaurant, but its tiled walls and floor were perfect for hosing down grimy bikes during the day. The tables and chairs were piled in a corner and, while their vehicles were being detailed, customers sat on upturned plastic crates watching the Vietnamese version of 'Wheel of Fortune' on a TV that hung from the ceiling.

It was a very low-tech version of the show. The three contestants squirmed in suits a number of sizes too big for them, supplied by the studio because they couldn't afford their own. Not that the production had much of a budget. The backdrop for the show was a screen with cherry blossoms on it and the letters were written on a whiteboard that could be wiped clean and used again. The grand prize was a giant Sony flat screen television, though, and Sunsilk gave every contestant a pack of the company's products, including shampoo *and* conditioner.

The contestants tested their answers by scribbling them down on a piece of paper, which I felt was against the spirit of the game. It didn't make a scrap of difference to the

Vietnamese watching the show with me, though. To them the point of the show was to laugh at the contestants who accumulated a large amount of money and prizes and were then cruelly robbed when the wheel stopped on 'Bankrupt'. It happened three times while I sat there, and the other customers thought it was hilarious, whooping and clapping with delight. Soon I did too and I got so caught up in the perverse fun of it all that I didn't realise the boys had finished with the Vespa. It sat outside, completely immaculate, the chrome sparkling in the afternoon sun. It looked beautiful and I realised that I would be sad to give it back.

Barely a week after arriving in Vietnam I was back in Vroom Café, sitting at an outside table and waiting for a taxi to take me to the airport. Life in Pham Ngu Lao continued around me as normal. The cyclo rider who knew everyone's business on the block waved as he pedalled by. The ice vendor crouched on her haunches to saw up a huge block of ice delivered to her on the back of a bike. The cool Vietnamese couple on their jet black Vespa buzzed up and down Duong De Tham just to be seen. Steve's brothers-in-law sat around doing nothing, waiting, they claimed, to move the tables and bikes off the footpath when the police came along.

It struck me how lucky I'd been on this journey. Not just because the taxi driver had dumped me outside the Zoom Café and Steve had lent me his Vespa. And not just because I'd just ridden 600 kilometres along some of the craziest roads in the world and survived. (I've since had it on good authority that the Australian consul in HCMC spends a good deal of her time assisting injured Aussies.) No, my luck had come in the people I'd met and the experiences I'd enjoyed – the big night out with Steve and Daniel, the night in the homestay on An Binh, drinking with Phu and his mates, the guy who gave me the leg tow and the mechanic who fixed the Vespa for free. Without them the trip would have been rather different.

A girl selling books approached me and with a start I remembered my plan. This was my final chance to see if it had had worked – I had asked at least 30 different girls if they had any books by Peter Moore before I left for the Delta. Surely word must have filtered back to the powers that be by now. I took heart when the girl recognised my name instantly and pulled out a book with a smile. It was *Dude, Where's My Country*.

'Michael Moore!' she said triumphantly. 'Same same but different.'

I slid across US$4 and bought the book. I already had a copy but I figured that if push came to shove I could give it to my taxi driver.

Beijing
CHINA
Xian
Yangtze
River
Shanghai
Chongqing
Guangzhou
Hong Kong

China Ghosts

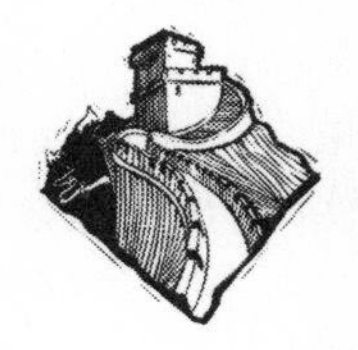

ANNETTE SHUN WAH

'THERE'S A ghost in our room. She looks very weak. You'd better come and talk to her to see if she's all right.'

We are cruising down the Yangtze, the river revered as the cradle of China's ancient civilisation, having inspired countless poems, myths and legends. Even so, I don't remember anything on my itinerary about having to tend to an ailing ghost. It isn't exactly my field of expertise. My new travelling companions seem genuinely concerned. A ghost. In their room. Hmm. Are they for real or is this a test, like the ones that David Carradine had to conquer in the TV series 'Kung Fu', before he could get out of the Shaolin monastery? I take a long hard look at their earnest faces and can't detect even a smudge of irony.

I call them my travelling companions, but in truth we've only just met. There are six of them. Like many tourists from Hong Kong I've seen, they're travelling in a pack, and their leader is *dai luo* – Big Brother. It is 1984 but he's not that kind of Big Brother. This scenario is more evocative of *Shaolin Kids*, the early Jet Li film in which a set of brothers practise kung fu on one riverbank, while on the opposite side a family of sisters perfect their secret Wu Tang style of swordplay. They are rivals, of course, until the hormones kick in. In my story, though, there are six brothers but only one girl – me – and the romance is one-sided. Three of my fellow travellers are siblings, two are cousins and one is their friend, but they're a close-knit bunch so I think of them as The Brothers. They defer to *dai luo* because he is the eldest. He holds all the cash, pays all the bills, and has the final word about where to go and how to get there.

I'm not quite sure why they've adopted me. Perhaps it's because they're curious about a woman who stands out from the crowd. Ironic really, because one of my reasons for coming to China was to see how it feels to be able to blend in. Would I feel lost, or would I feel like one of 'them'? This seems a simple enough question but it will take me years to figure it out. Coming to terms with China and the Chinese is a little like coming to terms with my appendix: it is part of me, yet has no apparent function in my everyday existence.

Twenty years on, China will have transformed remarkably from what I experience on this trip. So will I. This was the turning point, but I'm not altogether sure how that happened. Perhaps I need to re-trace a few steps to work it out. Don't worry, I'll come back to the ghost on the Yangtze. She's not the disappearing kind.

Until now my entire life has been lived in Australia. Born and educated there, I have no reason to think of myself as anything but a true-blue Aussie – unless I catch a glimpse of my reflection to remind me of my Chinese origins. My grandmother and father were born in Australia too. The family relocated to

Hong Kong in 1932, when my father was barely nine years old, because his parents wanted their children to experience the culture of their forebears. It took a war, a revolution and the victory of the communists they feared, to sour his family's affection for their homeland, and they reluctantly returned to the place where they had been born.

China as my father knew it lived on in his head, and that's the China he tried to instil in his three children. In the drought–ridden, fly-infested backblocks of Queensland where I grew up, his stories of craggy mountain landscapes, rivers too wide to cross and street markets alive with hawkers, muscle men, opera singers and freaks seemed no more real than fairy tales. But the images he conjured up were so vivid and so much more alluring than 1960s Queensland that they burned themselves into my imagination.

That's probably why I'm here – looking for the China that my father simply could not let go. The China that held him so strongly he could never feel at home in Australia, even after 30 years. Our home was a pool of Chineseness in a land baked hard by the dryness of the Australian character. But the pool grew stagnant. My brothers and I learnt to speak Cantonese before English. We were drilled on the obligations of a Confucian household, and taught that in all things – food, art, music, beliefs and the rearing of children – Chinese were superior. My parents would not socialise with non-Chinese, and eventually, with the growing workload of the family's poultry farm business, they didn't socialise at all.

I was drowning. They say it only takes three inches of water, and they're right. Outside the walls of my family home was another world, the one that I wanted to engage in, and the very moment I was able to escape, I plunged headlong into it. I had no use for Confucian obligation or Chinese loyalty. They were anachronisms in my world. This was my rebellion: a total rejection of all things Chinese because they represented the deep conservatism of my parents. But no matter how I felt inside, I couldn't peel away my Chinese skin.

It's as much a surprise to me as to anyone to find myself here, back at the source, the land of my ancestors, searching for the China that has made claims on me all my life. It seems I have a few ghosts of my own, and, consciously or not, this will be the time to decide whether to embrace them or to exorcise them.

I thought my father would be pleased that I wanted to undertake this journey – a kind of pilgrimage to the land of our ancestors. Surprisingly, when I told him of my plans, he was anything but. He conjured up another memory of China – the one he'd fled in the final days of the Second World War, as Mao Tse-tung's forces took over. 'Whatever you do,' he warned me, 'don't tell them your father was in the Chinese Army.' As if that is likely to come up in conversation. But I will admit to a slight flutter in the stomach when I landed at the half-built Shanghai airport. Red Guards seemed to be everywhere: searching luggage, interrogating passengers. What is the purpose of your travel? Do you have family here? Will you be visiting them? What will you take them as a gift? I tell them I have no family left in China, so I don't expect to be purchasing a refrigerator or a television to lug back to my ancestral village.

This China – Communist China – is confronting on a grand scale. Imagine, if you will, a nation of one billion control freaks. Well, not everyone can be in control. There are many who simply obey, which seems to eliminate the need for personal responsibility and initiative, not to mention originality and humour. There's a kind of dullness I encounter in the people behind the counters of hotel reception desks, travel bureaus and banks – in short, in anyone from whom you'd normally expect some service.

I'm sure they're completely different when they're off duty.

These are probably the very same young people I see at the nascent 'discos' in Shanghai. Drab rooms dressed up with coloured lights – consistently mauve and lime green for some reason – playing music at the officially-sanctioned volume. The songs are surreal. The tunes are faintly familiar, but even with my limited Chinese it's apparent the lyrics are not exact translations from the originals. At one disco I caught a snatch of Paul Simon's 'Me and Julio Down by the Schoolyard' but from what I could gather, the song now seemed to be about the thrills of having one's armpits tickled. The young disco dancers take to the floor in groups. Is everything done in groups in this country? They wait patiently for their favourite songs, then pile on to the tiny wooden surface to step, turn and clap in unison, executing set routines like an Eastern line dance. Synchronisation complete, they giggle themselves off the dance floor for a refreshing sip of locally-made cola with a name that sounds disturbingly like 'whore-lock'.

When they're at work, though, it's as if the thought police have wiped all traces of personality, spontaneity and joy from them, their faces no longer capable of smiling, the twinkle gone from their eyes. They limit themselves to operating by the rules and no amount of cajoling, pleading, yelling or piss-taking seems to have the slightest effect.

This is not the China I'd expected, and it is certainly not the country my father had described during my childhood. He'd painted a glorious picture, with all the brilliant hues that nostalgia affords, of a wondrous place where people were alive to possibility. That was the China he wanted me to embrace as my own.

Hong Kong was my introduction to China – a three-day stopover to get a visa and acclimatise before venturing to the mainland. There I'd found a street market that was a little like the ones in the stories my father had told. It had hawkers and opera singers and roadside dentists extracting teeth with hardware pliers and depositing the bloody fangs into used lychee tins. The place was called Poor Man's Market, a slice of 'old' Hong Kong preserved for tourists. Is this the only form in which my father's China survives?

I have a month to gather my own memories of China. After the thriving metropolis of Shanghai, I'll head to the official capital, Beijing, and travel to the Great Wall, then to Xian in central China for the archaeological wonder of the Terracotta Army, south to Chongqing to cruise down the Yangtze River and finally to Guangzhou, capital of Guangdong Province where my ancestors and many of the early Chinese settlers to Australia originated.

In Shanghai I scale a great wall of noise, courtesy of bus drivers on Nanjing Road mistaking their horns for accelerators and making the previously simple task of crossing a road seem almost impossible. There are few private cars, some faded green taxis and swarms of feral cyclists. I learn to trust in the power of the people and position myself in the middle of groups of pedestrians crossing en masse. Hit them, not me. I must be getting the knack of this socialist doctrine.

It takes almost a day of walking around Shanghai before I start to see past the drabness of the city. Beneath thick layers of black grime are the once-elegant banks and consulates built in the days when the city was divided into European concessions. Many have been gutted and pressed into service as bicycle or sewing-machine factories.

Even in the famous Peace Hotel, headquarters for the China International Travel Service (CITS), echoes of the past are drowned out by the dull thud of Chinese bureaucracy. In 1984 China is still coming to terms with the idea of independent travellers. Tour groups are fine. They have a tightly scheduled program and can be made to stick to it. Business travellers are easy too: just give them a guide or a driver to keep a close watch over their every move and file a report at the end of each day. But individuals with no set itinerary are anathema in a country that runs along strict lines of uniformity and predictability. Rather than helping individuals like me with our travel plans, which might allow them to keep track of what we are doing, the blank-faced folk at CITS have settled on a strategy of blocking every move: flights are always fully booked, train seats unobtainable, access to anywhere other than the 'authorised' destinations impossible to arrange. No one wants to risk assisting a rogue traveller. From the outset I suspect that nothing will be easy.

Still, I retreat to the lounge bar at the Peace Hotel more than once, taking respite from the oppressive summer humidity. Sipping something long and cool in the Art Deco surrounds, it's easier to conjure up the Shanghai of old, a thriving sea port that hungrily devoured the exotic and the forbidden. A place that became synonymous with greed, corruption, decadence and glamour. Money ruled and morality sank to its knees as gangsters shimmied alongside the respectable rich, all to the soundtrack of the Peace Hotel Jazz Band. Shanghai is also where great thinkers and writers congregated. This is where the Cultural Revolution began, where the feared Gang of Four, led by Madame Mao, had its power base, and where various uprisings and political betrayals were staged. Why is Shanghai so often the centre of things? Perhaps something of that daring, that taste for the dangerous and the allure of power still exists. I certainly won't find it here in the foyer of the Peace Hotel. Besides, I'm hungry.

I've mastered barely enough Mandarin to purchase a croissant from the bakery opposite the hotel on busy Nanjing Road. Only after I meet a local, Xi Feng, who offers to be my translator, can I return to the bakery to solve the mystery of how a Chinese baker can make such authentic French pastries. The owner is flabbergasted. The business and the recipes he uses have been passed down through his family, who've never been to France and have certainly never heard of a 'croissant'. Despite the horrors of the Cultural Revolution, which did its level best to obliterate all traces of foreign influence and anything deemed bourgeois, the legacy of the French endures on Nanjing Road in the form of a flaky pastry.

Xi Feng takes me along to his favourite Sunday morning rendezvous in People's Park. It's known as English Speaking Corner, and each Sunday locals gather to mob any foreign tourist who might indulge their attempts to get their hard tongues around English syllables. At first they skirt around me, eyeing my strange Western clothes with some suspicion. Then they scamper off in pursuit of a tall blond tourist. I can barely understand what he's saying through his thick German accent but the locals persist. 'Hallo. Can I plaktise my Ingriss wit you pliss?'

A group of five young men overcome their shyness and approach me. 'Hallo. Do you spik Ingriss pliss?' With only the slightest encouragement from me, they unload a barrage of questions, sucking up knowledge of the outside world like thirsty elephants. It's such a relief to talk to real people after dealing with hotel staff and rigid travel officials with their guarded responses. These people want to know everything about me. Having established it's my first time in China, they want to know not where I come from, but where I've come 'back' from. 'Oh Australia!' they nod eagerly. 'Yes, I know Australia. I think it is next to New Zealand.' Now there is a crowd of 30 or 40 people clamouring to hear me speak. The German is looking baffled about his sudden abandonment. He'll be sniffing his armpits next. The locals have learnt some English at school and picked up more from television and radio. Some attempt an American accent, preferring the Voice of America to the BBC World Service or Radio Australia. 'We feer vairy warm for you,' ventures the boldest, 'because you are Chinese.'

He is the only one articulate enough to say this to me, but I sense it everywhere I travel. It is why people happily follow me down the street just to watch what I do and where I go. It is what allows them to sit on the edge of my bunk when I later travel by boat or train, as if I were a friend or a sister, and take whatever I am holding out of my hands – a book, camera, cassette recorder – and examine it thoroughly before handing it back. I find their familiarity both comforting and intrusive. They interrogate me in Mandarin, and when I stare back dumbly they hold up a hand and draw the Chinese character on their palm, but I shrug and shake my head. I am illiterate. They feel sorry for me then, and maybe a little embarrassed that I am so ignorant of my own culture. But is it my culture? Why should I know any more than that tall German bloke they accosted in English Speaking Corner? The expectations of strangers start to get under my skin.

I take a plane to Beijing, the seat of government and the home of Peking Duck. It is very difficult to eat a Peking Duck all by yourself, so I'll need to hook up with one of those packs of Hong Kong travellers. I know enough Cantonese to communicate with them, and although some of them mistake me for being Japanese, I form a few friendships that will see me through what would otherwise be an unbearably lonely month of travel. I've been on the road for five months, through the United States and Europe, travelling part of the way with a friend and the rest on my own. It is only now that the loneliness sets in. Perhaps I've simply been away too long, feeling like a bystander as others get on with their lives.

In the meantime, without much effort at all, I lose myself amongst the countless rooms of the Forbidden City, imagining the Emperors sitting down daily to banquets of over a hundred dishes, waited on by thousands of servants and up to a hundred thousand eunuchs who, for some reason I cannot fathom, sacrificed their manhood for the privilege of Imperial service. The scale of it makes me sick. The City is silent and almost deserted now, with only sightseers like me to wonder if greatness can be counted in human lives. Outside the walls, through the Gate of Heavenly Peace in the massive Tiananmen Square, there is a present-day gathering of tens of thousands of young bodies. At least I'm told that's how many are there. Coming from Australia I don't really know what a gathering of tens of thousands looks like, unless it's Grand Final day at the footy. Even then, it doesn't compare to this. Martial music blares from loudspeakers placed throughout the square and the young people dance, march and chant in unison, waving flags and banners with all the joy of a man forced to flog his best friend. Screeching out orders over the top of all of this is a woman's voice that would not only peel paint but splinter the wood underneath. I flinch at every upward inflection. Only Chairman Mao, staring down placidly from his massive portrait overlooking the square, remains unmoved as the people rehearse for the annual commemoration of the founding of the republic.

I take a tour bus to the Great Wall. It's airconditioned but the locals like to hang out of open windows. On the bus I meet a young Hong Kong couple, lovely people but more inclined to browse souvenir stalls than to see the sights. The Great Wall suits them to a T. A T-shirt, that is – one with a garish depiction of the wall and an English slogan I translate for them as 'I climbed the Great Wall and survived.' It takes me a few attempts because I don't know the Cantonese word for 'survived'. I settle for a phrase that means 'didn't die'. I leave them to shop and take happy snaps, while I do the climb. The wall is incredibly steep, snaking over green mountains and down valleys as far as I can see, and every square millimetre of the section open to the public is etched with graffiti. I'd have recorded some of the entries in my diary if I could read Chinese. The wall truly is an astounding monument to Chinese ingenuity and perseverance, and I wonder if there is a modern-day equivalent.

On the long bus trip home, the fun-lovin' Hong Kong

couple decide to relieve the boredom by breaking into a jolly Cantonese song. The bus driver responds by turning his radio on full bore to drown them out. This reduces us to hysterical laughter, but once we manage to catch our breath, we decide to consolidate our friendship with dinner at the couple's glitzy five-star hotel, one of Beijing's newest. Besides, they'd like me to help translate a note in English that has been left by the housemaid. I'm hoping it doesn't involve the word 'survived'. As our taxi pulls into the hotel, the concierge greets us in English, 'Good evening madam, welcome to our hotel.' In the foyer the reception staff echo the sentiment. I feel immediately at home.

The note asks the couple to contact housekeeping. Unable to raise anyone on the in-house phone, I decide to follow it up in person with the friendly staff at reception. I'm looking forward to a little English chatter, no matter how mundane the topic. As I make my simple enquiry, the confident young woman behind the counter seems to crumple in front of me, like a wine cask bladder being sucked dry. I catch a glimpse of the fear in her eyes before she swiftly lowers her head. Is this a gesture of embarrassment or is she praying for help? Either way, there's no response to my question. Then I hear a faint flapping sound. I move closer and peek over the edge of the counter. Her fingers are feverishly flipping through the pages of a Chinese–English phrase book. Sensing she's been sprung, she shoots a look at me, then averts her gaze as a man walks through the foyer. 'Good evening sir, welcome to our hotel.' She does that bit so well.

I never did find out what the note was all about, but at dinner – the duck was fine, by the way – we were visited by the hotel manager, an impeccably suited young man, who switched effortlessly from English to Mandarin to Cantonese and immediately set my friends at ease. He was in charge of a team from Hong Kong who'd come to Beijing to train the locals in the art of Western hospitality. The staff had been selected largely on the basis of their language skills, but as they'd never experienced the kind of service they were meant to deliver, his job was turning out to be quite a challenge. So this is China: marching to the tune of progress, just as soon as they work out what key it is in.

My own accommodation is somewhat more basic. The Overseas Chinese Hotel accommodates China's prodigal sons and daughters – which, in a very generous and long-term view of history, appears to include even Japanese travellers – in single-sex dormitories. There seems to have been a mix up with the assignment of beds though, because there isn't one for me. I think this is payback from the front desk, because I refused to register in my Chinese name rather than the Western name that is on my passport and all official documentation. In fact, apart from my parents, hardly anyone knows my Chinese moniker, let alone uses it. No matter. The couch is vacant and it looks considerably cosier than the thin mattresses on the floor, placed out in regimented rows down the length of the room. Besides, I don't have the energy to deal with another blank-faced reception clerk.

Five nights on the couch is about all I can stand. Next stop is the ancient capital, Xian, a couple of hours' flight south-west of Beijing, where I opt for shared accommodation in the rather dilapidated People's Hotel. Much of what I've read about China stressed its strict moral standards, so I am bemused to walk into my room and find a young English couple cuddling up in a single bed in T-shirts and underpants. There are four beds lined up along one wall, and one bed on the opposite side of the room. That's where I dump my bag. When the English lovers move on the next day, my new roommates are three young Japanese lads from Yokohama. It could have been worse. I might have found myself bunked down next to the chain-smoking, whiskey-guzzling Japanese Buddhist monk I meet in the disco downstairs.

Once you get away from the main centres of Beijing,

Shanghai and Guangzhou, language becomes more of an issue. My sense of direction is pretty well non-existent and asking for help in Mandarin is still a challenge, but I'm pretty good with a map. Turning down the hotel clerk's offer to order me a taxi, I set off to find the local CITS office to book the next leg of my journey, to Chongqing. Within 15 minutes I'm standing on a street corner in torrential rain, clutching the only available tourist map of Xian, trying to match the symbols on the map with the ones on the street signs. I'm lost. I take a guess as to which way to go. I guess wrong. The footpath suddenly gives way to a huge muddy hole, and rather than risk life and limb on the road, I gingerly attempt to step around the edge. My slide to the bottom is quite elegant, really, but my three attempts to get out are less so. The only good thing about the unrelenting rain is that it washes off some of the mud before I get back to the hotel. I pass a group of Hong Kong girls in the corridor who ask, with some concern, what happened to me. Through gritted teeth I manage to approximate the Cantonese for 'I fell over.' They look at me for a bit, then shrug and walk off. Down the hall I hear one of them mutter, 'She must be Japanese.'

Pride severely dented, I spend the rest of the afternoon in the room watching my clothes dry. The room is reasonably comfortable, but drably furnished and run-down. It smells musty with age and too many human bodies. The paint's peeling and there are cracks in the walls. I assume it'll be ripe for the wrecker's ball before too long, but later I'm told the building is barely five years old. So much for Chinese workmanship.

Yet I'm here to see one of the great marvels of China's long history, the Terracotta Army – still standing after more than 2000 years. In a covered pavilion more expansive than the biggest hypermarket are 8000 life-sized clay soldiers. Some, only partly excavated, look as if they're climbing out of the earth. Each is realised in fine detail, clutching weapons, dressed in correct uniforms depicting rank and regiment, and every face is different. This is the army created to protect the first emperor of the Qin dynasty in the afterlife. It's an astonishing memorial to human endeavour, but equally a testament to one man's fear of death, and the ruthlessness of his power. Thousands of artisans and labourers must have worked on this tomb, and yet its location stayed secret for more than 2000 years. I have to wonder what fate those workers met, at the hands of an emperor who ordered the burning of all books other than practical manuals on agriculture and medicine, and buried 460 dissident scholars who dared defy him.

Every nation's history is marred by the atrocities of tyrants, but I am absolutely shocked by the barbarity that seems to underlie every great achievement here. I start to wonder if there is something in the Chinese character that makes them – us – more prone to ruthlessness. Every revelation hits me like a personal slight. What on earth is going on? I seem to have forgotten how to play the part of tourist. Why can't I just go 'ooh' and 'aah', like I did at the Acropolis or the Palace of Versailles, then walk away, content to have felt the breath of history?

Enough of monuments. I need to go back to the streets for something on a human scale.

The markets on the mainland don't have the nostalgic charm of Poor Man's Market in Hong Kong. Here, a few sad, wilted vegetables are laid out on an old bedspread, or scrawny cuts of meat dangle from wire coat hangers, of interest only to local flies. At first even the marketplaces seem infected by that same sense of torpor I've noticed behind every hotel desk, but eventually I notice something different, an undercurrent of change that is just seeping to the surface. For decades, people have been shoehorned into jobs assigned by schoolteachers and Party officials according to their aptitude at school, or the area in which they live, or the needs of the local commune, or the number of political Brownie points their family has accumulated by toeing the Party line. Now China's leaders have begun to loosen their grip on the economic levers, so people are finding moneymaking opportunities everywhere, and are playing with the possibility of determining their own destiny. The Chinese entrepreneurial spirit never went away in 35 years of communism: it just went underground. Given the faintest glimmer of daylight, it is sprouting up all over the place. The tiniest patch of bare soil is tilled to produce marketable produce or to house a pig that eventually will go to market, one joint at a time. Stallholders set up at every tourist destination to sell cheap souvenirs. City dwellers sit in their living areas – the footpaths outside their front doors – sewing, sawing, mending, painting and restoring anything that might feasibly return a buck.

It's an exciting time, but the grab for wealth seems a little crude in the shadow of China's great marvels. Xian's museum holds one of the country's finest collections of antiquities. Covered with dust and a few dead flies, ancient pieces of pottery and priceless dishes delicately inlaid with silver and gold are housed in flimsy cabinets that wouldn't look out of place displaying a range of spark plugs in a forgotten service station on a desert highway. Only tourists and scholars have time to contemplate China's great history. Everyone else is too busy moving forward to look back. At week's end, big shiny television sets are precariously ferried home on the backs of pushbikes. The footpaths are littered with packaging from refrigerators and washing machines. How can ancient culture compete with modern convenience? Still, the Great Wall and the Terracotta Army have withstood centuries of turmoil, so I suppose the onslaught of economic opportunism will be just another dust storm.

The concept of convenience hasn't quite filtered through to the management of the Xian People's Hotel. With an early flight to catch, I've paid my account the night before, and am packed and ready to leave by 5 am. I feel my way down the darkened corridor to the lift. Like the hallway lighting, the lift has been turned off. So I sling my bag over my shoulder and carefully make my way down seven flights of stairs to the deserted foyer. I'm not too concerned yet because I've allowed plenty of time to take a taxi to the airport. What I haven't allowed for are the bike chains and padlocks on the front doors of the hotel. I'm locked in. Yes, I think it's time to start panicking now. The door to the fire escape is locked too and I'm doubly glad I wasn't sharing with the chain-smoking monk. As I'm deciding whether or not to raise the panic level one more notch, I hear voices and movement. A couple of elderly Americans emerge from the gloom of the stairwell, complaining about the dead lifts. A few others follow. They're as alarmed as I was about the barricaded front doors, and as their panic levels rise, mine ease. Out the corner of my eye I notice a patch of sticking-up black hair bob up behind a wooden divider in the far corner, then disappear again. Rushing over, I find two of the staff sleeping on wooden benches. I try to wake them to unlock the doors. One stirs, takes a look at his watch, and turns towards the wall. The Americans aren't happy. They stand over the two dozing bodies and nag until finally one of the staff relents, gets up and walks off. The foyer is now full of Americans in their sixties and seventies. They're mumbling something about getting their luggage from their rooms, and how relieved they are to have made it down the stairs without suffering strokes. If this isn't God's waiting room, it's got to be his departure lounge.

Finally the dozy desk clerk returns with someone who looks only marginally more awake, but at least this man is clutching some keys. It has now been half an hour since I first contemplated smashing down the front doors. Bike chains and padlocks removed, I beg the desk clerk to call a taxi for me. He looks at me as if I've asked him to wipe my bum.

Having bonded with the Americans during our wait in God's departure lounge, I now beg a lift on God's tour bus. They drop me off at the airport right on departure time.

Fortunately the flight to Chongqing has been delayed 20 minutes. 'Don't worry,' the American tour leader assures me. 'They wouldn't have dared take off without you.'

Air travel in China is an exercise in hospitality – Eastern-style. On boarding, passengers are handed little gift packs, usually containing folded up vinyl carry bags and a Chinese fan shaped like a ping-pong bat, with a little lacquered wooden handle and tautly stretched nylon decorated with depictions of cherry blossoms or water reeds and goldfish. Today it is the Moon Festival, and our packs hold an extra treat: an individually wrapped mooncake. I have trouble locating my seat because the rows do not correspond to the letters and numbers on the luggage shelf. The seats have all been moved up to accommodate several extra rows, leaving just enough leg room between them for a praying mantis. Finally the passengers are settled, seatbelts fastened and cabin doors sealed shut. As we taxi down the runway there is a chorus of cellophane wrapping being ripped off as everyone dives into their gift packs to retrieve their fans. The airconditioning has been turned off so the aircraft has maximum power for take-off. I bet those extra rows of seats are to blame. Only when we're at cruising altitude does the flapping stop.

It's overcast so there isn't much to see, but the flight passes quickly and soon I hear the familiar sounds that indicate we're nearly there. The hum of the engine lowers as we descend, the undercarriage clunks into place and the 'fasten seatbelts' sign lights up. Strapped into her fold-down seat facing us, the stewardess goes through the routine instructions – tray tables stowed, seats upright. It's a little bumpy on the approach, with air draughts rising from the mountainous terrain. The pilot banks, then steadies the plane into position for the delicate job of landing. An excited passenger gabbles something on the other side of the plane. Then another joins in. Suddenly just about everyone on my side of the plane unbuckles their seat belts and rushes over to the other side to look out of the window. I don't know what's caught their attention because my eyes are tightly shut. The stewardess grabs her microphone and urgently shouts out orders to sit down. Her voice rises with each sentence and I'm wondering if she's related to the woman on the loudspeaker at Tiananmen Square. Now she's shrieking just one phrase over and over and although I don't understand the words, I think I recognise the meaning. It'll be something like: 'We are going to die. We are going to die.'

Reluctantly the passengers saunter back to their seats and buckle up. I'm shaking that fan like there's no tomorrow, trying to convince myself that the sweat trickling down my back and my shortness of breath have been caused by the lack of airconditioning. Two mildly terrifying bumps and we're safely on the runway. Thankfully, this is my last flight in China.

Chongqing is a hilly place – and the first Chinese town I've visited where there are no bicycles. I book myself in to the Great People's Guest Hall, a magnificent old wooden building with less-than-magnificent rooms. But it is cheap and, surprisingly, unbelievably, the staff are helpful and efficient. Even the CITS office is user-friendly and soon I have tickets on the Yangtze River cruise the next day. This must be the smoothest transaction I've experienced in all of China. Feeling like a tourist again, I stroll – or rather climb – the streets and alleyways, watching people separating raw wool with a strange contraption, and checking out the local markets. For a while I walk behind a man carrying two plastic shopping bags. One holds bottles of something that looks alcoholic. The other contains a black, amorphous mass. As I get closer the black mass seems to be moving. Closer still, I see them: tiny, brown snake-like creatures slithering over each other in the bag. The man steps up his pace. Looks like he's having sozzled eels for dinner.

The next morning is drizzly and overcast, and when the mini-bus drops me off at the ferry terminal, mist is rising from the river. I've enjoyed wandering around Chongqing on my own. The pace is slower, more contemplative, as life winds its way up and down the mountainside. Now I must join the throng making its way onto the boat. There is something about China, the close press of bodies and the uninvited familiarity of fellow Chinese travellers, that should make me feel accepted. Instead it makes me claustrophobic, frustrated and acutely aware of my aloneness.

This is the first time in my life that I haven't been in the minority, although it doesn't really feel like it right now. Let's face it – I do stand out. There are few other Chinese on the Yangtze boat cruise sporting spiky, tinted hair, designer jeans and runners. The locals dress in shapeless grey, khaki, white and navy blue. Some are commuters, crossing from one side of the great Yangtze to the other. Others are holidaying tourists like me, posing in front of clunky cameras that remind me of box brownies. When I pull my tiny, pocket-sized camera from my jacket, the snapshot-crazy locals gasp in awe. Before I know it a mob has gathered around me on the deck and the camera is being passed around for all to admire. Then it's gone. I've been in China long enough – three weeks – to know there's no point getting anxious just yet. Sure enough, the camera makes the rounds of just about everyone on the boat before making its way safely back to me. No-one's even dared to take a shot with it, which is a pity because their pictures might have been interesting.

The Brothers stand out too. They're hip dudes, clad in the latest designer knock-offs, lugging heavy backpacks and sporting fashionable haircuts. Their Hong Kong swagger is tempered with sweetness and childlike curiosity. They wouldn't look out of place on a Canto-pop album cover. *Dai luo* is a little different. Perhaps it's the responsibility of being the leader of the pack, but he seems more thoughtful and a little aloof. He's thickset while the others are slender. Close-cropped hair frames a round face usually concentrated into a serious frown, which makes the stubble on his upper lip stick out even more than usual. At least I think it's stubble. It could be a fully-fledged moustache. It's hard to tell with Chinese men, who are mostly follicly-challenged.

Dai luo acknowledges me with an almost imperceptible nod when I get to their fourth-class cabin to deal with the sick ghost. He motions me towards the bottom bunk.

My parents have always referred to people of European extraction as *faan gwai* – foreign ghosts. In fact, I have to think twice before I can remember what the proper term is. Being born in Australia, my entire Cantonese vocabulary has been gleaned from the conversations of my parents, aunts and uncles. Hence I'm pretty confident asking someone to pass the soy sauce, but rendered mute if the discussion turns to sex, politics or philosophy. My parent's short-sighted strategy irked me then, but I think it's hilarious now. They wanted so much for me to find a Chinese husband, but what on earth would we say to one another in our most intimate moments? Unless he had a soy sauce fetish, I guess. We naturally referred to our neighbours as *gwai luo* and *gwai por* – ghost men and ghost women – or to Aborigines as *hark gwai* – black ghosts – and it wasn't until my adulthood that I'd recognised the derogatory slurs imbedded in our everyday language. I tried to compensate by describing every one as *yun* – person – instead of ghost.

The Brothers bring me undone. They have a *gwai* in their midst and it's up to me to do something about it.

I crouch down by the bunk and see a thin, fair woman in her mid-twenties. I have to admit, she does look rather bloodless. Despite the mild weather, she's huddled underneath a coat. There are no blankets in fourth class. 'Excuse me,' I say in English. 'Are you all right?'

Having just spent four months in Europe I'm ready to try again in German, French or Italian if I don't get a response. But she slowly opens her eyes and looks at me, disoriented and confused.

I try again – apologising for disturbing her but explaining that my friends are worried that she might be ill. The fragile face eases into a weak smile, and in a broad Queensland accent she tells me that yes, she does feel a bit under the weather, but she's OK. Her name is Julie, and she's from my hometown, Brisbane. In fact, she studies in the very same faculty of the very same university I escaped from seven years earlier. She's been travelling through Asia for the past few months, most recently in the Philippines where she was caught up in a street riot and found herself on the wrong end of a tear gas canister. The poison is still working its way through her system. It probably doesn't help that she hasn't eaten for a day. (Later Julie tells me that when she heard my Aussie accent cutting through her stupor, she thought it was the voice of an angel and that she'd gone to the Other Side. Maybe The Brothers were right about her being a ghost after all.) Is that why The Brothers befriend me? Do they pity me, travelling on my own? Do they think there is something socially pathological about a person who chooses to travel on her own rather than with six or seven of her closest friends and relatives? We met when they helped me hoist my bags onto the mini-bus that brought us to the boat. In coming days *dai luo* will occasionally grab that bag from me and charge ahead so that I can keep up with them.

I am booked into third class – basically the same as fourth class but with fewer bunks – keeping close company with seven local men who wake at the crack of dawn with the most thorough and raucous session of throat clearing and phlegm expulsion imaginable, then fumigate the cabin with cheap and nasty locally-produced cancer sticks. Good morning to you, too. Then it's off to the bathroom to queue up behind hordes of women to take a turn splashing my face awake with the dribble of tepid water leaking out of the tap. Was this pumped up from the Yangtze? The colour looks right. I don't deal too well with the communal squat toilets, either. The motion of the boat is making stuff swill back and forth in the communal drain between my feet. I come to the conclusion that certain parts of my anatomy have a mind of their own. Some people say they have eyes in the back of their head. This trip to China has convinced me that my second pair of eyes is between my legs. Even though I turn my face away, my lower body is completely aware of what's happening down in the drain and it doesn't want anything to do with it. My system seizes up like a fused engine and no matter what orders the command centre in my brain is issuing, nothing budges.

If the toilet facilities are a challenge, the dining arrangements are impossible. There is such a long and chaotic queue that the only food I see is pre-masticated scraps on the floor. Even The Brothers are having trouble getting fed, and we are stuck on this boat for three days. I don't think my packet of vanilla wafer biscuits is going to do it for me. That's when *dai luo* works his magic. By lunchtime he has organised a table for us in the second-class dining room. The food is probably not very different from what is available downstairs, but here we can eat without being pressed in on all sides by shoving, shouting, hungry passengers. We make the most of the respite from the crowded deck, and the views are almost as good.

The Yangtze is China's longest river; so wide in places that you cannot see the banks. It couldn't be more different from my last voyage: a placid cruise down the Rhine past stately old castles and olde worlde vistas. Here the river is teeming with life. We pass watercraft of every size and description – diesel ferries, old junks, battered dinghies and rafts. Smoke rises from the chimneys of factories and occasionally houses on either side. The tiny distant specks on the landscape are villagers tending livestock, tilling farmland or fishing. Ancient pagodas and temples cling precariously to the cliffs that rise straight up from the water, the only access being via narrow steps carved into the rock and steep enough to give you a seizure just thinking about climbing them. The river itself is alive, too, the water churning into brown gravy.

As we approach the famous Yangtze Gorges, the river narrows dramatically. Here the current is so swift we see carcasses floating by: buffalo that didn't stand a chance, a dead dog or a horribly bloated pig. Then I catch my breath. Something in a whirlpool grips me in its gruesome spin. It's just a glimpse of what is unmistakably a human corpse – face down, black hair swirling, khaki shirt billowing loosely around the body. Then it disappears, sucked into the deep as if someone's pulled the plug in a bath. Several other passengers have seen it but no one raises the alarm and the crew makes no attempt to retrieve the body. As it happens, corpses are regularly seen from the Yangtze cruise boats. It is the mighty river reminding us that it holds the power of life and death.

I cannot imagine scenery more dramatic or spectacular. It's just like the ancient drawings my father so admired. Perhaps this is one part of his China that survives – for now. Everywhere you look – the vulnerable settlements on the riverbank, the lonely monasteries up high, the improbable shapes carved into mountainsides, like the wonderfully named Ox's Liver and Horse's Lung Gorge – is evidence of the unpredictable might of this river.

According to the ancient legends, the most powerful of mythic creatures, the dragons, live in waterways. Rivers, lakes and oceans reign supreme in the natural order of things. Yet here on the Yangtze, as on other great waterways, the Chinese are trying to invert that order to place man and his needs above nature. We're treated to a graphic illustration of this when we reach the Gezhouba Dam, the largest in China. As we enter the lock and the water drains away beneath us, my heart is pounding. Someone really has pulled the plug. The water level drops and I look at the concrete skin that holds back the mighty Yangtze and think how quickly and surely it would all be over if that skin gave way. Little did I realise that this is just the beginning of a much grander scheme. In a decade's time a modern engineering feat will be attempted here, damming the river to create the world's biggest hydro-electric scheme. Millions of people will be forced from the homes they have occupied for generations. Burial grounds, temples and shrines will be lost forever. The factories and settlements we see along the way will be submerged and the Three Gorges will never be the same. Some say it is environmental vandalism on a grand scale, but to the government, this is a monument to China's greatness. Perhaps this is intended to be the modern-day version of the Great Wall.

In the dining room, we discover there are other Australians aboard – a tour group travelling second class. They invite Julie and me to their lounge – a carpeted sitting room at the front of the boat, with big picture windows to take in the view, safe from the elements and the flying spittle, spent cigarette butts and other refuse tossed overboard by the locals on the upper deck. It's pure luxury. Not because of the quiet, expansive space, or the padded lounge chairs or the pots of tea on call, but because of that rare Western innovation – a flush toilet. Hallelujah!

Our three-day cruise ends in Wuhan, a drab industrial town as grey and bleak as the weather. *Dai luo* leads the way to a hotel, his enormous backpack carried as easily as an overcoat, my bag swung over one shoulder. Another of The Brothers lugs Julie's pack along with his own. We've both managed months of travel on our own, and now we're stringing along like children. The Brothers' chivalry is of the kind that cannot be turned down without causing offence. I've come to realise this over the last few days as we've gotten to know one another better. Several of the boys carry photographs of their girlfriends in their wallets: suitably pretty, sweet-looking girls. I wonder why they are not travelling too, but my questions are brushed aside. A couple of the boys don't have romantic partners, and eventually it dawns on me that this may be a factor in their seemingly insatiable curiosity about me and my life in Australia. But it's all good-natured, and they seem to be genuinely entertained by my somewhat inadequate language skills.

It's not my limited vocabulary that gets them chortling, it has something to do with the way I speak. I figure my pronunciation might leave something to be desired, or perhaps I have an Aussie accent. That'd be pretty funny. But no, that isn't what gets them. They think the way I speak is – get this – cute. Listen boys, you may carry my bags but don't try to patronise me! That's not what makes them laugh, either. They think I speak too quietly, too timidly. What a revelation. I've always thought Cantonese speakers in full flight sound like they're brawling even when they're just discussing the weather. That dynamism, though, is integral to the language. It's bred into native speakers. No wonder people in Hong Kong looked at me like a creature from outer space every time I opened my mouth. They understood the words that came out but were mystified by my namby-pamby delivery. Thanks to The Brothers, it begins to dawn on me. My language lacks the drama, energy and conviction of a 'real' Chinese speaker. They encourage me to say it one more time with FEELING. I take a deep breath, plant my feet apart, set my jaw, and work up a growl that comes right from the guts and let them have it. It works, all right. They're rolling around the floor in hysterics. So it isn't just the haircut and the clothing that sets me apart. It's my limp, timid tongue. How do I explain that, as a broadcaster back in Australia, I earn a living by talking, when here I couldn't impress a bus conductor?

If The Brothers need any further evidence of our helplessness it comes the next day when Julie and I try to make arrangements to leave Wuhan. We're both coming to the end of our journeys and we don't want to waste precious days in this dive of a town, but getting out isn't easy. Planes are fully booked for three days and the trains are packed. Besides, the prospect of standing for a 15-hour train trip to Guangzhou doesn't appeal, especially since neither of us slept last night. *Dai luo*'s choice of hotel left a bit to be desired. Paper-thin walls aren't much of a match for guests who choose to turn their televisions up to maximum volume so they can yell over the top of them. No problem with timid language there.

If we are to be stuck here for three days, I am moving to better accommodation. Julie agrees, and with deep sighs we brace ourselves for the farce ahead of us. It may be official policy, or just a complex Chinese puzzle that I will never figure out, but whenever an independent traveller fronts up to a hotel asking for a room the answer inevitably is '*mee-yiao*'. That's what it sounds like to me – just like the worst of feline arrogance and non-compliance. It means 'we have none'. The Great People's Guest Hall in Chongqing was an exception. The Jianghan Hotel in Wuhan is not. So we sit in the lobby and wait. Several of The Brothers keep us company while two of them go off on errands.

I've heard lots of stories about the trials and tribulations of securing accommodation in China, each more ludicrous than the last, and I believe them all. Everyone knows there are rooms available, and as you sit and wait this knowledge twists itself around in your head. Why on earth do we submit to this absurd waste of time? My favourite story concerns a Western traveller who when told that his chosen hotel had no rooms available, followed the well-worn ritual, found a seat in the foyer and waited. Resolving eventually not to play the game any longer, the traveller picked up his bags, walked through the hotel and found an empty room. He unpacked his luggage and lived there for three days before the staff politely knocked on his door to inform him: 'We have a room for you now.' Julie and I share this story with the boys as we wait in the foyer of the Jianghan Hotel, trying to keep the maniacal edge out of our laughter.

Eventually the two Brothers return with the news that they can get sleeper-class train tickets on the black market.

Intrigued, we follow their lead, making a big scene about taking our custom out of the hotel. As if anyone cares. The desk clerk stifles a yawn as he watches us go. That's not true. He doesn't stifle it at all.

At the appointed time, we make our way to Wuchang railway station. The Brothers take our bags and all we have to do is keep up as we leap aboard a crowded bus to the station. The tickets come courtesy of a station cleaner, warily checking us out as she pretends to sweep the platform. We must look a strange sight to her – the Canto-pop boy band with a Chinese punk and a blonde ghost.

Julie is worried about how much all this is going to cost. I'm worried about how authentic the tickets are and whether we'll find ourselves imprisoned and tortured for fare evasion, never to be released until my father comes all the way from Brisbane to rescue me by dropping to his knees in front of the Red Guards and confessing his role in the Chinese Army. Finally, the cleaner decides we're worthy of her trust. I guess she has far more to lose if this transaction is exposed than we do. My ticket costs precisely the same as one from the ticket office. Because I'm Chinese, she's decided not to charge me extra. This gives Julie the courage to ask for a student concession. The cleaner shakes her head, but she's decided not to add the usual foreigner surcharge. Julie can have the ticket for the same price I've paid, provided she pays with Foreign Exchange Certificates. There is a dual money system in China. Foreigners are issued with a different currency from the locals' *renminbi*. They have the same face value, but only Foreign Exchange Certificates (FEC) are accepted in hotels, airline ticket offices and the Friendship Stores which stock all sorts of desirable goodies unobtainable elsewhere in China. On street corners and down narrow alleyways, locals holding huge wads of *renminbi* offer them at very favourable exchange rates for the highly desirable FEC, and shrewd travellers eagerly negotiate. The catch is, you must spend all your *renminbi* in China because they cannot officially be exchanged for foreign cash. Julie relents and I think I see a thin strand of saliva dribbling out of the corner of the cleaner's mouth when she sees the crisp wad of FEC. I foresee a shopping spree in Guangzhou so each of us can use up our stash of local currency before leaving the country.

We saunter onto the station platform like a presidential entourage. *Dai luo* leads and the other Brothers flank us, our luggage in their hands. They clear a path through the scrum of scrambling, shoving, excitedly gabbling Chinese travellers, and see us safely onto the train. It's a fond farewell. The Brothers haven't eradicated my feeling of loneliness, but they've distracted me from it for a few days. We exchange addresses and they promise to keep in touch.

A few months later, the first of several letters arrives from the second youngest of The Brothers. He's the one who had eyes – all four of them – for me. The Brothers will eventually visit me in Sydney, we'll have our photograph taken together at the Opera House, and the bespectacled one will drape his arm around me like a lover. It's like being courted by Dennis the Menace. I would be pleased to see them, happy for the opportunity to repay their kindness and generosity, if it were not for what I realise is coming. I will turn down his marriage proposal as gently as I can. At this time my soft, timid delivery of the words will be just right. They will be my Brothers no more.

China has gotten under my skin in a way I never expected. She needles and prods and irritates me endlessly. I don't have a right to be annoyed by her but I can't help myself. This is not the China of my memory, or, more correctly, of my father's memory, because that China no longer exists. The landscapes that inspired great poetry and art have been bulldozed and flooded in the name of progress and engineering miracles. Ancient relics – the Great Wall, the Terracotta Warriors – defy the elements, while slipshod modern buildings crumble and lean. China welcomes me 'back' with open arms, then twists her grip into a clutch of obligation. Without realising it, I have come here with unrealistic expectations. I wanted China to answer my questions about who and what I was. I looked to her for something to admire, something to claim as my own, to anchor me in the swirl of a complicated identity. I leave feeling angry rather than proud; disappointed rather than inspired; taken advantage of rather than accepted. Only later, when I have settled back into the routine of my own life, when the souvenirs have been framed or mounted or gift-wrapped and distributed, and the holiday snaps have been put away to gather dust, will I realise what has happened.

By travelling to China I no longer see her in the mythical light of childhood stories. She has become too real and too flawed for that. I have been relating to her like a daughter relates to her mother, and a petulant misguided daughter at that. It's time to grow up. After all, it isn't China, but rather family, history and memory that make sense of my yellow skin – and that's what I must explore in order to oust the ghost burned into my imagination.

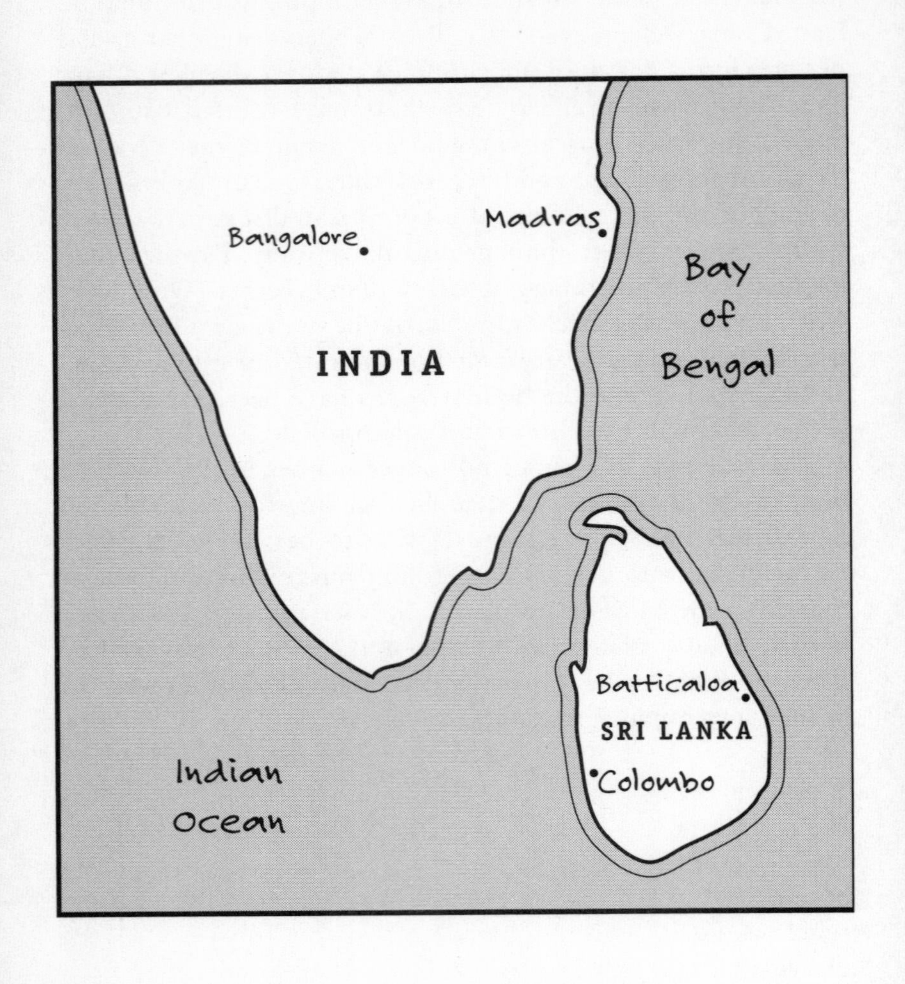
Madras
Bangalore
Bay
of
Bengal
INDIA
Batticaloa
SRI LANKA
Indian
Ocean
Colombo

Sri Lanka

TIM ELLIOTT

I'D BEEN in Sri Lanka two days when I witnessed the monks beat up the peaceniks. It was just after midday during the hottest part of the year, and the heat hung in the streets, pungent and dizzying. Colombo's canals, low from drought and choked with algae, glowed radioactive emerald, and the air danced with clouds of diesel and dust.

I'd come to Sri Lanka as a freelance journalist, to write about the war between the government and the Tamil Tiger rebels, a 10,000-strong guerrilla army that has for the past 20 years been fighting to establish an independent Tamil homeland, called Eelam, in the north-east of the island. I'd been anticipating plenty of death and destruction – this was a war, after all – but the last thing I expected was to find the monks doing the damage. As far as I knew, monks were peaceful. Monks were cool. Monks did not, under any circumstances, head-butt people.

The trouble started when the monks came face to face with

a group of peace demonstrators. The demonstrators wanted the government to re-enter talks with the Tigers. They weren't crazy about the Tigers per se, but they knew that the war against them was unwinnable. If peace meant giving them a slice of the island, then so be it.

The monks, however, believed in a united Sri Lanka, founded on Buddhist principles. For them, any reconciliation with the Tigers was unthinkable. Now a dozen or so monks milled about, brandishing little black umbrellas, their heads shaved to the scalp. They eyeballed the demonstrators, then began haranguing them for being Tamil-lovers and terrorists and traitors and several other things that monks shouldn't really call anybody. Then, almost without warning, the monks attacked, ploughing into the crowd like cannonballs, their hot orange robes billowing flame-like behind them. They punched and kicked and shrieked abuse as they tore up the protesters' placards, windmilling into the terrified demonstrators like so many bald-headed kamikazes. Some in the crowd fought back, but most were overwhelmed by the monks' ferocity. The fighting went on for 10 minutes or so, before a group of riot police finally restored order.

The peaceniks, however, were cowed. They huddled in shopfronts and peered around corners. Some were bleeding from the head and face. Nearby, a young monk stood quietly, hands clasped in prayer, his face a picture of serenity and repose.

'Typical really,' said Richard, an English expat I met later that day at my hotel. 'The war will never end at this rate.'

It was sunset, and we were sitting at the terrace bar of the Galle Face Hotel, a grand old Victorian building overlooking the Indian Ocean. Richard was tall and thin and pale. A micro-finance consultant, he had been in Sri Lanka for nine years and, like many expats, often popped into the Galle Face at the end of the day for his 'sunset G and T', served up by solemn waiters in starched white uniforms.

Richard expressed no surprise at the riot. 'You can't go round provoking the monks like that,' he said. 'They are very powerful. They have the government's ear.'

'But monks?' I asked. 'I thought monks were meant to be peaceful?'

'Peaceful?' said Richard, laughing. 'The monks are the worst of all.'

Suspended just 50 kilometres off the southern tip of India, Sri Lanka is one of the most densely populated countries in the world, with 20 million people squeezed onto an island the size of Tasmania. Colonised by the Portuguese, the Dutch and finally the British, it has long been peopled by two main groups: the Hindu Tamils of the north, and the Buddhist Sinhalese of the south. The Sinhalese make up about 74 per cent of the population and the Tamils about 18 per cent. There are also Muslims, Malays and Burghers, a trader class descended from the Portuguese and the Dutch. The island's original inhabitants are the forest dwelling Veddah, but these days their way of life is so precarious that many people consider them to be, for all intents and purposes, extinct.

Since the 1970s, Sri Lanka has been one of the world's premier holiday destinations, an Indian Ocean idyll where frostbitten Europeans could come and thaw their buttocks on clean white beaches, soaking up the tea, toddy and right-hand reef breaks. From surfers to Buddhists, Sri Lanka offered something for everyone: a one-stop holiday where you could stroll through a 17th-century Dutch fort in the morning, haggle for gems after lunch and go elephant spotting at sundown. So strong was Sri Lanka's appeal that the tourism industry even weathered the war, which by 2001 had killed some 62,000 Sri Lankans. Happily for the tourists, all the fighting took place in the north and east, hundreds of kilometres from the south-coast resorts, which were, in any case, never targeted by the Tigers. Basking like a sea lion under the palms of Hikkaduwa, you'd never have known a war was going on at all.

But, of course, it was. Some say the conflict is a continuation of the natural enmity that has always existed between the Sinhalese, descendants of people who migrated from north India around 500 BC, and the Tamils, who arrived from southern India some two centuries later. The two groups fought off and on for the best part of 2000 years, until the arrival of the British in 1796. Having conquered the island in 20 years, the Brits set about lathering the lush hills and coastal plateaus with coffee, coconuts and cinnamon, establishing industries that were for centuries to remain the cornerstone of the country's economy. (Killed by leaf blight, the coffee was later turned over to rubber and tea.) The British aimed to make Sri Lanka, or Ceylon, as it was then known, an agricultural powerhouse, with the locals doing all the heavy lifting. But the locals had other ideas. Unable to persuade them to work cheaply on the tea plantations, the British imported Tamil labourers from southern India, turfing out the Sinhalese peasants in the process. More importantly, they initiated a divisive and ultimately disastrous policy of installing local Tamils in plum administrative jobs, where they became fluent in English, by then the official language.

Before long, the Tamils had assumed a privileged position in Sri Lankan society. They were better paid and better educated. They had better jobs and a disproportionate number of university places. Together with the British, they formed an English-speaking elite, aloof to the concerns of the Sinhalese majority. But when independence came in 1948, the tables turned. Lacking the numbers in parliament, the Tamils found themselves on the wrong end of some nasty legislation – from the 'Sinhala only' law, which made Sinhala the country's sole official language, to 'standardisation', whereby university entry scores were set higher for Tamil students than for Sinhalese. At the same time, successive governments encouraged droves of poor Sinhalese from the south to colonise the traditionally Tamil-dominated north and east.

Not surprisingly, the Tamils soon saw themselves as a threatened minority. At first they tried *satyagrahas*, or peaceful protests, usually centred on the Tamil city of Jaffna, in the far north of the island. But when it became obvious that such resistance was useless, clandestine opposition began forming. First there was the PP (*Pulip Padai*, or Army of Tigers), 20 or so earnest young civil servants who had been inspired by Leon Uris's novel *Exodus*, about the foundation of Israel, whose struggle towards statehood they took as a template for Tamil independence. Then came a flood of other groups, each with their own Pythonesque acronym. There was the TLO (Tamil Liberation Organisation), the TNT (Tamil New Tigers), the TELO (Tamil Eelam Liberation Organisation), the TULF (Tamil United Liberation Front), and even EROS (Eelam Revolutionary Organisation of Students).

Many of these groups financed their activities by robbing banks in Jaffna. Each robbery would prompt a crackdown by security forces; Tamil militants would then respond by launching raids on Sri Lankan Army outposts, which in turn provoked anti-Tamil riots. These riots, which occurred in 1956, 1958, 1977, 1981 and 1983, killed thousands of Tamils, many of whom were beaten to death in the streets or burnt alive while police looked on. Gangs roamed Colombo, singling out Tamils for their *pottu* (Hindu forehead marking), or the way the women knotted their saris – Tamils at the front, Sinhalese at the side.

In 1976, however, another Tamil group emerged, calling itself the Liberation Tigers of Tamil Eelam (LTTE). The group was headed by 22-year-old Velupillai Prabhakaran, previously the leader of the TNT. Prabhakaran was wily and ruthless, prepared to kill not only Sinhalese but also any Tamils he considered insufficiently committed to the struggle: at 21 he assassinated the Tamil mayor of Jaffna. With guile, patience, treachery and charisma, Prabhakaran worked his way to the top of the Tamil nationalist movement. His fighters carried cyanide capsules into battle to avoid being captured alive; others became suicide bombers. A terrorist to some, freedom fighter to others, Prabhakaran became known to many Tamils simply as 'The Leader'.

When I first saw a photo of Prabhakaran on the Tamil Tigers' website, I felt a little disappointed: he was chubby and pop-eyed, like a Sri Lankan Rodney Dangerfield. Yet somehow he had moulded the Tigers into one of the most effective guerrilla armies in the world, one that had seen off the Indian Army, assorted mercenaries, and the Sri Lankan Armed Forces, which outnumbered them 30 to one.

I'd been to Sri Lanka twice on holiday, principally to go surfing. Now I began to wonder what the hell was actually going on there. And who, really, were the Tamil Tigers?

I'd just left a cushy job working on an in-flight magazine for an airline that had gone broke. I'd been in the job for three years and now that I'd left, I felt like I'd awoken from a coma. So, one day in June, I packed my camera and my notebooks, and bought a ticket to Sri Lanka, with a return date six weeks later. I told myself that I was searching for the Tigers; that I was going to write stories about the war, about the rebels and about the plight of a forgotten people. But, of course, I was also looking for something else. I was looking for adventure.

Colombo is a sprawling jumble of high rise towers and sweltering slums, a fantastically noisy and polluted city of almost one million souls on Sri Lanka's south-west coast. During the mid-1600s, the Dutch grew cinnamon here, but these days the environs are notably less fragrant. Flat and congested, the city sits swaddled in its own steamy juices: a blend of exhaust fumes, humidity, human odours and sea spray; a thick, sticky haze that wafts in off the Indian Ocean, day in, day out. This, together with the phenomenal heat, makes Colombo a difficult place to get anything done. When I first arrived I felt like I was under water. I waded through the air. My shirts stuck to me like shrink-wrap. My underwear clung to my thighs. My entire body, from toes to scalp and everything in between, felt as if it had been smeared in sump oil. God, I reflected, had designed Sri Lanka as a tropical retreat. I, however, had work to do.

My first job was to meet a man called Manoranjan Rajasingham, a prominent Tamil journalist who, I'd been told, had good contacts with the Tigers. I'd talked with Mano many times from Sydney. Apart from publishing a Tamil newspaper called *Thina Kkathir* (Tamil for 'daily ray of sunshine'), Mano worked as a 'fixer', helping to arrange interviews for foreign journalists. Mano certainly sounded the part: he spoke perfect Oxford-accented English, his voice as smooth and heavy as polished marble. When I asked him whether he could definitely get me to the Tigers, he said, 'Yes, of course. Just come,' his words rolling down the telephone line like boulders.

Mano lived in a large, white, two-storey house at the end of a narrow cul-de-sac in suburban Colombo. Separating the home from the street was a pair of tall metal gates. I'd only been standing at the gates for a moment or two when Mano appeared, as if from nowhere, looking almost exactly as I'd imagined. He had very dark skin, broad, high cheekbones, a hawkish nose and eyes the colour of peat. A thick mane of jet black hair swept back tight on his head, and he sported a moustache and beard ensemble that was both dapper and raffish. 'Good to see you,' he said, seizing my shoulders, his fingers like pliers in my upper arm. 'Come inside, come.'

His house was messy; the seats piled high with newspapers, the table smothered in magazines and mail. A tall, muscular boy – Mano's son, I later discovered – was lounging in the middle of the main room, watching SkyNews on a widescreen TV.

Taking a seat at the table, we quickly got down to business. Mano told me that there wouldn't be any problem meeting the Tigers. 'I have talked to them, and they have given their consent.' Mano was to escort me. 'We will travel to the east, to a town called Batticaloa. I have a place to stay there. A quiet place, out of the way. The authorities will know you are there, but we don't want them knowing what you're doing every moment of the day. Then, when the time is right, we will go across to meet the Tigers.'

'Go across?' I asked.

'Into uncleared territory.'

'What's uncleared territory?'

' "Uncleared" is a how these silly buggers in the Sri Lankan Army describe anything that the Tigers control. When the Sri Lankan Army controls it, it's "cleared"; when the Tigers win it back, it's "uncleared".'

The government controlled the town of Batticaloa itself, Mano explained, but some 70 per cent of the province it was in remained 'uncleared'. In other words, the Tigers had it surrounded. 'When you're in Batti you look straight across into uncleared territory,' said Mano. 'It's all very close.'

I asked him how he found life as a Tamil in Colombo. 'Oh, it's all right. Except for the fact that it's completely and utterly falling to pieces.' He shrugged. 'These fellows in the government are totally incompetent. There's a drought on at the moment, one of the worst we've had. The government was warned about it for years, yet they did nothing. Now all the dams and wells have dried up.' Some 75 per cent of Sri Lanka's power is hydroelectric, so the drought resulted in regular blackouts. Colombo's canals had become stagnant and malarial. 'This city is one huge swamp,' said Mano. 'All three of my kids have tested positive for dengue fever. And what does the government do?' He slid a newspaper across the table, pointing to an article about how water board officials had begun praying for rain. 'They do rain dances. Can you believe it? Honestly, one cannot live with these people. It is impossible.'

In order to go to the east of the island, I had to get permission from the army. I'd already dealt with Sri Lankan bureaucracy when obtaining my press card – a long and distressingly complex process involving several government departments – so the thought of further officialdom had me worried. Still, I had no choice. Calling the army, I was instructed to come for an interview with the media director, one Brigadier Sanath Karunaratne. Determined to impress, I donned a suit and tie.

Since the army headquarters were just around the corner from the Galle Face Hotel, where I was staying, I decided to walk, but this was easier said than done. No sooner had I stepped outside the lobby than I was set upon by a pack of tuk-tuk drivers, each of them jabbering at me and plucking at my suit. *'Please! Mister! Where you go? Cheap!'* In a country with an average daily wage of about 22 cents, a besuited foreigner emerging alone from an upscale hotel was like tossing a hunk of meat into a shark tank. What I should have done was hop in the nearest tuk-tuk, but like a fool I pushed on by foot, hot and harried, three-wheelers trailing behind me like a flock of gulls. In the end, the only way I could shake them was by making a halting, chicken-like dash across a busy four-lane highway.

By the time I found the army headquarters, I was deep-frying in my suit. The place was heavily guarded, with machine gun emplacements on either side of the entrance, in front of which lay a series of concrete bollards, spikes and chicanes, a precaution against ram-raids. (A 'Black Tiger' – a Tiger suicide bomber – had recently blown himself up near here.) After checking my papers, a young commando escorted me into the base, past rows of barracks and patches of scorched grass with 'No Walking' signs on them. Finally we entered a rickety wooden building. Wires dangled from the walls; paint peeled off in chunky, fist-sized scabs. After a short wait, I was shown into an office, where a chirpy looking man in a lime green uniform sat behind a large, empty desk.

'Mr Elliott,' he said, pouncing from his chair. 'My name is Sanath Karunaratne. Take a seat, please.'

Karunaratne had a politely trimmed moustache and a paunch that peeked, like Humpty Dumpty, above the edge of his desk. His hair was thin and meticulously parted.

I said I needed a pass to go into the east. Mano had told me to tell the army that I'd be writing about child soldiers, kids forcibly recruited by the Tigers. Karunaratne seemed satisfied by this. 'Do you want to wait or come back later to pick up the pass?' he asked.

'How long would it take?' I'd expected it to take several days.

'Ten minutes.'

I decided to wait. In the meantime, we got to talking. Karunaratne had been in the army for 26 years and had seen action many times. 'Once I was besieged for 26 days with my battalion at Elephant Pass, in the north. I lost my second-in-charge in the first 10 minutes; 39 of my men died. We cremated them inside the camp during the siege.' He shook his head wearily. 'But you know the worst part? My wife had just been diagnosed with diabetes in Colombo, and I couldn't get to see her.' Elephant Pass is near Jaffna, only an hour's flight north of the capital, but it may as well have been Antarctica. 'I was useless to her,' he said. There was an awkward silence that we both filled with solemn looks. I found the Brigadier's candidness unsettling; he was talking to me like I was his psychiatrist. I wasn't sure if I should comfort him or tell him to snap out of it. Suddenly he banged his palms on the table. 'Enough of that! I have something to show you.'

Ordering the sentry to dim the lights, he brought up a series of grisly images on his computer; 'just a sample of what the Tigers have done in this country.' There were headless bodies, disembowelled monks, brains, guts, blood. He tut-tutted after each shot, and shook his head.

'So, will the war ever end?' I asked.

'Some day. But morale in the army is poor. The desertion rate is 20 per cent. Many soldiers miss their homes. We haven't had a big victory in a while, so they get discouraged and run away.'

He paused. 'The Tamils set goals and achieve them. We Sinhalese are more easygoing. Maybe that's why we haven't beaten them yet.'

Shortly afterwards, my pass arrived and Karunaratne signed it. I could scarcely believe the man's efficiency. Leaning across the table, he said, 'Before this war, when you thought of the Tamils, you thought doctors, lawyers, lecturers. Now you think suicide bombers and terrorists. This is very sad, don't you think?'

That night I went to a dinner party at the house of Dr Marlene Jeyaraj, the Sinhalese aunt of a friend of mine from Sydney. The house was large and many-roomed, and had a familiar seventies feel – mirrored walls, orange couches, saloon-style swinging doors. Marlene and her husband were retired doctors. They ushered me inside and offered me a beer. Soon the other guests arrived: four couples in all, everyone filing into the living room. Most of them were, or had been, lawyers or architects or doctors. It was a sophisticated, upper-middle-class gathering, yet no sooner had we assembled than the women squared off to one side, the men to the other. I didn't know it then, but it was to stay that way for the entire night, as if there were an invisible wall through the middle of the room.

Being male, I sat with The Men. I asked about the 'Tamil question', but that didn't seem to interest them much; of more immediate concern was the President, Chandrika Kumaratunga, a Sinhalese woman who appeared incapable of, or unwilling to, rein in the island's almost endemic culture of corruption.

'I have to bribe my garbage man to collect my rubbish,' said a man called Ranjit. 'And these power cuts! They are being purposely prolonged! Today I read an article about how the water board has been bribed to drain the reservoirs, so they can sell more generators.'

Thanks to Kumaratunga's incompetence, the economy was headed 'nowhere'. 'Backvards.' 'Down de tubes.'

'If dare vaws a competition to throw de biggest rock at dees vooman,' said Laksman, a loping, heavy set man with beads of sweat on his forehead, 'I vood be de first in line.'

The men were drinking scotch, their hand gestures becoming more florid as the night wore on. On the other side of the room, the women had formed a conspiratorial huddle.

I glanced at my watch: 10.05 pm. When were these people going to eat? Marlene *had* said it was a dinner party . . .? I hadn't had so much as a bite since breakfast, 15 hours before. Drinking on an empty stomach was making my head spin. I needed food. I *prayed* for food. I scrutinised Marlene's every movement, trying to tell if she was preparing anything or whether I'd be left to expire on the living-room rug. I insisted on helping her, just so I could sneak a look at the kitchen, but she graciously declined.

Just when I thought I might topple face first out of my seat, Laksman leaned over. 'You are hungary, no?'

'Yes, I am, actually.'

'At Sri Lankan dinner parties, we don't eat at de beginning but at de bery end, when *aaaaall* de drinking is done.'

He shouted across the room: 'Marlene! Your Australian friend is starving! He did not know dat vee eet at de end of de party!'

A ripple of laughter washed around the room, after which everyone resumed their conversations.

I'm fucked, I thought.

Finally, after another two or three scotches – I lost count – dinner was served: great steaming curries and bowls of fluffy rice. The women helped themselves, then the men. When my turn came, I approached the spread with utmost caution, careful not to tip the entire lot onto the floor. Bent over the chicken, Laksman winked at me, his voice betraying a hint of pleasure. 'The Sri Lankan way is better, no?'

The day we were meant to leave for Batticaloa, Mano called to say that he'd been delayed. This didn't bother me, since I was beginning, in a masochistic kind of way, to actually enjoy Colombo. I'd been there 10 days and the city had grown on me. There was something about its sheer awesome ugliness that commanded a grudging respect and fascination. There was the noise, the heat, the beggars and the crowds. There were the military patrols and the roadblocks. Then there was the pollution, which was so strong as to have achieved a drug-like potency. You could get head-spins just standing on a street corner in Colombo. Most of the pollution came from the traffic: countless thousands of cars, trucks, buses and tuk-tuks, each farting out endless plumes of exhaust, toxic blue smoke that infested my nostrils and impregnated my hair. In the most congested parts of the city, like Pettah and Slave Island, it was so bad that my face and forearms would be dusted with a layer of fine, cindery particles. Stranded one day in a particularly claustrophobic downtown crowd, hemmed in by people and noise and cars and heat, I was suddenly overcome by an unmistakable sense of Armageddon. So *this* is how it all ends, I thought, *this* is what it all comes down to: the whole of human existence burning up in a cauldron of poverty and pollution and pestilence; everyone and everything vaporised in a gigantic pall of carbon monoxide.

The hotel became my sanctuary, a place of sanity, repose, and reflection. In other words, a Colombo-free zone. Here there existed a surreal parallel universe. Built in 1864, the Galle Face Hotel is still breezily elegant, with its football-field-sized marble foyer flanked by wraparound staircases. Everyone, from heads of state to famous authors, has stayed here. The foyer features a glassed-in bust of Arthur C. Clarke (who emigrated to Sri Lanka in 1956), and huge, carved stone urns filled with frangipani petals. The hotel is testament to a time when labourers in loincloths toiled by the hundreds to make the lives of the rich just that little bit more comfortable or aesthetically pleasing; up until the 1960s you could still see punkah wallahs fanning guests in the lobby.

These days, however, the hotel is falling apart. At night I would lie awake and listen as the sea winds tore shreds off the building, whole sections of roofing sent clattering to the ground. The ceiling in my room leaked. The bidet gurgled like a man on life-support. There were squirrels on the patio and cockroaches on the terrace. Yet the longer I stayed, the more I loved it. On my way to bed each night, I'd wander the hallways, lined with long ruby-coloured carpets and peopled by lugubrious, ghost-like attendants in cream tuxedos. As I passed they would bend their heads and say 'Goodnight, sir', their giant white moustaches curled up like tusks.

A couple of days later, Mano called again. He was still unable to leave, but he said I should go ahead and wait for him in Batticaloa. 'I have bought you two seats on the bus,' he said.

'You can fix me up for it later.' When I asked why he'd bought two seats, he said, 'So you can lie down. The trip takes 10 hours. You'll need to sleep.'

The bus left Colombo late at night. I took a sleeping pill and duly passed out. Just before dawn, I was awoken by the soothing sensation of my cranium ramming repeatedly against the wall of the bus. Hoping that it would pass, I lay there for some time, but the ramming continued, so I sat up, my skull throbbing, and gazed out the window. The landscape was scrubby, and the road was rough. The roads in Colombo aren't great, but this was horrendous – an endless series of apparently bottomless pits into which the driver was managing to place one or all of the vehicles' tyres. The passengers rocked from side to side, occasionally pitching forward violently, a savage whip-lashing movement that made us look like head bangers at a heavy metal concert.

We passed Sri Lankan Army checkpoints, one after the other. Most consisted of sandbagged gun emplacements, their roofs reinforced with railway sleepers. (This explained why the train no longer ran.) As we neared Batti, the emplacements became larger and more numerous. There were guard towers, too: tall, spindly timber turrets on top of which perched one-man pillboxes, precarious-looking shelters cobbled together like birds' nests with corrugated iron and palm fronds. A 200-metre buffer on either side of the road had been totally shaved of vegetation in an effort by the army to deny cover to the Tigers, who were always trying to get close enough to lay mines.

Suddenly the bus shuddered to a stop and two soldiers piled on board. One of them stayed up the front, his rifle at the ready, while the other passed down the aisle, checking everybody's papers. Then they ordered us out. Stepping from the bus, I approached a group of passengers who had gathered around what looked to be a crumpled blanket lying by the roadside. An officer stood by, staring nervously into the bush. Standing above the blanket, I saw a fine brown elbow poking out from underneath it and a slick of blood spreading from where the head must have been. Large flies, electric green and buzzing noisily, alighted daintily on the thick red liquid.

I asked the officer what had happened. 'He was a soldier on leave, going home to see his family,' I was told. He'd been on a bus that passed through just 20 minutes before we came along. The Tigers had stopped the vehicle to check everybody's papers, and when they'd discovered he was a Sri Lankan Army soldier, they'd hauled him off and shot him. He was 18 years old.

'Where are the Tigers now?' I asked.

'I don't know,' the officer replied.

We all stood staring at the body. One of the passengers turned to me and made a pistol with his hand. Placing it to his temple, he pulled the trigger, smiling. When they finished searching the bus, the soldiers herded us back on, and we took our seats in silence.

Soon we entered Batticaloa. It was early morning and people were going about their business before the heat of the day set in. Young men were establishing impromptu fish markets, laying out cane mats covered with seafood: squid, crab and silvery green garfish, translucent and dart-like. Women in brightly-coloured saris stood about, pointing at the produce and haggling.

I took a tuk-tuk to the hostel that Mano had recommended. Every hundred yards we came across an army checkpoint. The locals queued patiently while the soldiers rifled through their belongings, checking for contraband and explosives, but as soon as the soldiers saw I was white they waved us on, some of them smiling apologetically, which made me distinctly uncomfortable. My entire life had been one of privilege and opportunity, thanks to being born white and middle-class. But like a lot of white middle-class privileged people, it wasn't something I wanted to be reminded of, especially by people a lot less fortunate than me. Sitting in the back of the tuk-tuk, I allowed myself a little righteous indignation, mainly on behalf of the locals, whose race saw them having to stand in the hot sun like cattle, waiting to be inspected.

But indignation, I soon discovered, is a surprisingly cheap emotion: easy come, easy go. Within a day I was flogging my 'whiteness' for all it was worth, popping my head out of tuk-tuks like a jack-in-the-box whenever we approached a checkpoint. It saved a lot of time.

It was in Batti that I began to have serious doubts about what I was doing. I'd spent three weeks in Sri Lanka, long enough to know that patience was not so much a virtue as a life-support mechanism, but even so, Mano's absence set my mind to wondering. Would I ever meet the Tigers? And even if I did, would they give me any answers or simply more dogma?

Batti itself was a strange place; a dusty, one-storey town made of timber and corrugated iron; a hive of gold shops, call centres and dry-goods stores. It's small, but quite spread out, built around a system of murky lagoons that are criss-crossed with bridges and bunds. An informal curfew means no one goes out after dark, but during the day the streets are overrun with goats, cows and motorbikes. Batti could be quite beautiful: the first night I was there, the sunset on the lagoon turned the velvety waters a slow succession of hot pink, orange, mauve and lilac. But the town also had a nervous, teeth-grinding kind of energy, the signature feature being the clouds of crows that gathered, sleek, black and fat, to feast on the piles of rubbish by the roadside.

Moreover, Batti was under siege by the Tigers. An attack was expected any day. At least this was what Sivaram told me, and I believed him. Sivaram was a journalist friend of Mano's who worked in the Batticaloa office of *Thina Kkathir*. He also wrote columns for *The Island* newspaper, which was based in Colombo. Before becoming a journalist, Sivaram had been number three in a paramilitary organisation called PLOTE, a Tiger splinter group. (The government claimed he was now a Tiger spy, but Sivaram denied this.) Gruff and fatalistic, with a moustache like a furry black caterpillar, Sivaram gave the impression of having been around the block, so to speak, and of having inflicted more than his fair share of grievous bodily harm. He was also an alcoholic, his eyes heavy-lidded and permanently bloodshot. It didn't matter what time I saw him, he always appeared hung-over, and was forever scratching the back of his head in a ponderous, bear-like way that suggested he'd just crawled out of a cave somewhere.

Three days after my arrival, with Mano still delayed, Sivaram invited me on a trip he was taking to a beach called Passikudah, about 30 kilometres to the north. 'I think you will find it most illuminating,' he said. Hopping on the back of his motorbike, we set off, speeding out of town and through the bombed-out district of Eravur, the scene of heavy fighting in 1991, when the army had blasted its way into Batti. All that remained of entire streets were a few jagged walls. There were no roofs. No rooms. No nothing. 'No one's got the money to rebuild,' said Sivaram. 'So they just squat in the ruins.'

After 10 minutes on the open road we took a hard right and swooped into the bush. The road devolved into a sandy track. Chickens darted across our path; naked children lingered at the fringes. A rusty, broken-down fence held back the jungle on either side. The sand was deep and the track was narrow, but Sivaram maintained a solid speed, indifferent to tailspins and minor slide-outs. I could feel my adrenalin rising. If we take a spill here, I thought, I'll be impaled on a rotting picket in the middle of the jungle. Suddenly Sivaram turned his head and yelled: 'Fancy a beer?'

Pulling up before what looked like a tea-house, Sivaram strode into the front room, which was full of skinny men smoking cigarettes. Bidding them hello, he continued out back through a doorway covered with a dirty sheet and into a rambling garden. 'A secret pub,' he explained. 'This is where local Muslims come when they want to get shickered.'

Although I was happy that even here, in deepest, darkest Sri Lanka, Muslims could have their alcoholic exigencies attended to, I found myself more concerned with the Tigers, specifically, with rumours that they would shortly be blasting Batti and everything in it – including me – to pieces.

'Actually, the Tigers don't really *need* to attack,' said Sivaram. 'They already have the initiative. Batti's local garrison has 600 soldiers, surrounded by 2000 Tigers. All day the soldiers are at their checkpoints, watching, waiting. They're sitting ducks. Sometimes the Tigers slip into town at night and drop leaflets saying "The Tigers are coming to cut your throats!" They like to scare the soldiers.'

'So will the Tigers ever attack?' If I couldn't get to the Tigers, I thought, perhaps the Tigers would come to me.

'There's a rumour that they'll do it on the twenty-sixth – Thileepan's anniversary.' Thileepan is a legendary Tamil martyr who died during a hunger strike in the early stages of the insurgency.

'But why would they attack then?' I asked. 'Wouldn't the army be expecting it?'

'The place you come from works on logic,' he told me. 'Here we leave all that behind.'

We got back on the bike. Sivaram seemed calmer. Shafts of musty sunlight smouldered through the foliage. Fingers of wind ran through my hair. Soon the track petered out, the jungle ended and we arrived at a broad, clean, sun-bleached beach.

'Welcome to Passikudah,' said Sivaram, collapsing on the sand, arms outstretched.

The beach was a perfect half-moon, what I estimated to be roughly two kilometres from end to end, and totally deserted. The water winked and glinted like crushed sapphires.

'What's that?' I asked, spotting a building shimmering in the heat halfway up the sand.

'The old hotel,' said Sivaram. 'It used to be a luxury resort, before it was destroyed in the fighting.'

I set off to take a look. 'Watch out for ordnance!' he yelled.

It took me 15 minutes to reach the building, but when I got there I couldn't believe my eyes. It was like Club Med after the apocalypse. All the walls were charred and bullet pocked. A thin wind whistled down the corridors. Small trees had sprouted in the bedrooms. Beautifully tiled bathrooms were lathered in rubble and burnt wallpaper. Abandoned, the hotel had been set upon by all manner of vines and creepers; colonised by a rapacious wave of vegetation that shoved its tendrils, worm-like, into every nook and cranny, swallowing whole rooms at a time. Standing in what must have been the foyer, I found a large water-feature strangled with weeds, like a bug embalmed in a spider's web.

Most of the stairwells were blown out, but somehow I clambered up to the second floor, plaster shards and glass crunching underfoot. From up here, the view of the bay was even more impressive; flawless and mesmerisingly bright. For some time I stood staring out over the water, imagining myself eating bacon and eggs on the balcony. Then, strolling down the sand, I stripped naked and walked into the water, feeling like the last person on earth.

The next day, at Sivaram's suggestion, I visited the local hospital in Batticaloa. Sivaram told me to speak to Dr Garnesha, the chief psychiatrist. The hospital was full of government soldiers who'd been injured in the recent fighting. The wards were dirty and airless, the beds set close together. I saw a soldier with a freshly dressed stump for a leg, another with his arm twisted at a freakish angle. One man was racked with fever, bound to the bed to stop him rolling off. His young wife watched over him, rigid with fear, looking for all the world as if she'd just been put out on an ice floe. Further down I found a girl, her body burned pink as raw sausage. Her father bent over her, tucking in her mosquito net to keep away the flies. I didn't see a nurse or doctor, or a single piece of what might pass for even rudimentary medical equipment. As for the white stranger wandering around with a notebook in his hand, I was all but invisible, so alone was each person in their grief and pain.

The main wards were bad enough, but the psychiatric unit, tucked out of sight at the back of the grounds, was worse. Patients lay on clammy mattresses, ranting in Tamil, scouring each others' scalps for lice or sleeping, buried in the subterranean slumber of the heavily medicated. A tangy, zoological odour permeated the corridors: a mix of urea, sweat, dirty linen and cheap cleaning agents. An orderly sloshed out a room with a bucket of soapy water, cleaning it like you would a pub after closing time.

Dr Garnesha bustled down the corridor, as if trying to outrun a nervous breakdown. 'The psych unit only opened two years ago,' he explained. 'Before that there was no care for the mentally ill here. People did what they had always done: seek a native remedy.'

Native remedies usually involve a *palisari*, or traditional healer. The most common treatment for someone suffering a psychotic episode is to strip them to the waist, tie them to a tree and beat them with sticks.

'I see it all the time. People come in here with fractures and whip marks all over their bodies. The problem is that people here don't see the mentally ill as victims. They think they're possessed, and that they must have done something to deserve it. They think that beating them will purge the evil spirits.'

'But what about those affected by the war?' I asked.

'What about them? Everybody here is affected by the war. The child soldiers, the displaced, the torture victims. Do you know what the police here do with suspected guerrillas? They put their testicles in a drawer and slam it! They shove chilli powder down the eye of their penis. This is very common. But I can't help them. I don't have the resources. You must understand, I'm the only psychiatrist for 180 kilometres. I have no psychologist, no patient therapist, no social workers. I don't even have the time to treat all the patients with so-called normally occurring mental illnesses. So the last thing I want to do is encourage thousands of people with Post Traumatic Stress Disorder. We'd be overrun.'

The next afternoon, much to my relief, Mano arrived. Until then I'd been the only guest at the 'hostel', which was in fact just a very simple, poured-concrete home, converted to take boarders. It was a nice enough place, with a front yard that rambled down to the banks of the lagoon. But every night for the past week I'd eaten alone, watched incomprehensible Sinhalese game shows on television until the power cut out, then shuffled into my room with a hurricane lamp and a book, offering my sweat-lathered body like a human sacrifice to the local mosquito population. I was anxious and lonely, and my skin had erupted with a tropical rash that kept me awake at night, scratching till I bled. Now, with Mano here, I finally had a fellow traveller. Now, at least, I felt a little less marooned.

Besides, I liked Mano. I liked being around him. I tried to find out more about him, but he was evasive, the kind of person about whom you only ever discover things indirectly. I knew he'd been educated in England, sent abroad in the 1970s when standardisation barred him from study at home. In 1983, he was almost killed by rioters in Colombo. (In the end, he was sheltered by a Sinhalese friend.) Mano regarded his countrymen – Sinhalese and Tamil alike – with cool fascination, like a lab technician observing bacteria in a Petri dish. A certain part of him had remained an expat, a connoisseur of the country's essential weirdness. He told me about a two-year-old boy who had recently been identified as the reincarnation of Ranasinghe Premadasa, a former president of Sri Lanka who had been murdered in 1993 by a Tiger suicide bomber. Apparently the boy could recount details from the late president's life, like his old address and the names of his wife and children. 'He is supposed to have pointed to a coin with Premadasa's head on it and said, "This is me,"' said Mano, with relish. 'Isn't that fantastic?'

He seemed larger than life, and had stories to prove it. He recounted how, years before, he'd taken part in a meeting with several Tamil resistance groups in Madras. 'Prabhakaran was there as leader of the Tigers, and we were all sitting around a table, talking, when suddenly the lights went out. It couldn't have been dark for more than 10 seconds, but when the lights came back on we were all still in our seats – except for Prabhakaran, who was standing at the door with a gun in his hand. They will never catch that man. He's way too smart.'

Mano denied being a Tiger, though he described Prabhakaran as 'a sweet man'. He admitted to being a one-time member of a Tamil militant group called the Eelam People's Revolutionary Liberation Front, but said he'd 'never had the stomach for violence'. He was calm, urbane, aloof. Though he was actually some inches shorter than me, I always had it in my head that he was taller. Mano was that kind of guy.

Only once did I see him lose his temper. It was the night before we met the Tigers. We were eating dinner when I suggested that a Tamil homeland might be too small to be viable. 'Of course it would be viable!' he said. 'Look at Singapore! Look at Luxembourg! All we have to do is be left alone, to do our own thing. This is all we are asking.' Mano looked wounded, and sat chewing his food with uncharacteristic inelegance. I never mentioned the topic again.

At eight the following morning, we set off to meet the Tigers. Well, *a* Tiger. Mano had arranged an interview with a man called Karikalan, the Tigers' political number three and head of their eastern division. 'The only problem,' said Mano, 'will be finding him.' Despite organising the interview over a period of months, Karikalan (whose name means 'Black Foot' in Tamil), was difficult to pin down. The army had recently tried to kill him and his bodyguard with a remote-detonated Claymore mine. Now he liked to keep on the move.

Doubling on Mano's motorbike, we rode out of town in high spirits. But we struck trouble at the final checkpoint, a rickety wooden bridge spanning a dried-up river. As soon as the guards realised we intended to cross into uncleared territory, they embarked on a forensic examination of my paperwork, picking over my passport, press card and Special Access Slip – a ludicrous document I'd obtained from the Ministry of Defence absolving the government of any legal responsibility should I have my head blown off or anything. 'They're looking for a reason to send us back,' Mano whispered. 'They don't want journalists talking to the Tigers.' Eventually, with a queue of biblical proportions banking up behind us, the soldiers relented, and we rumbled over the bridge, the loose slats banging like crackers beneath our tyres.

I'd initially been nervous about 'crossing over', but the minute we did so I somehow felt much safer. For one thing, there were no more checkpoints and no more soldiers. There were no fortified bunkers and no heavy machine guns. There were no cars, either, and very few motorbikes. Most people got around on bicycles. Women carried baskets of food on their heads. By the side of the road, water buffalo wallowed in mud-filled craters. It was like stepping back in time. Years of privation and government embargoes had reduced life here to a pre-industrial subsistence. Accustomed to Batti's insistent noise, everything seemed implausibly tranquil; a world with the sound turned down.

We continued for some time past paddy fields and mud-pack villages, stopping at a 'martyrs' graveyard', a military-style cemetery for Tigers killed in action. Each grave was marked by a small tin plate, modest and austere. A painted sign – of a fist clutching a Kalashnikov bursting from the earth – adorned the entrance.

Mano had been pulling into houses all along the way, consulting people about Karikalan's whereabouts. The houses were simple, with thatched roofs and dirt floors; toilets were a hole in the ground. One of the houses had a framed photo on the wall of a Black Tiger surrounded by a border of roses. Mano told me it was one of the family's sons, who had blown himself up in Colombo. Beside the photo was a poster of a mountain scene from Switzerland, pasted with photos of the son's face, plus a few shots of Prabhakaran. Together the Tiger leader and the boy floated, disembodied, above green fields full of large-uddered cows. It was so surreal as to be almost artistic, and I couldn't help feeling that some contemporary curator in London would pay thousands of pounds for it.

'What's this about?' I asked Mano.

He appraised the poster for some time, nodding sagely. Then he turned to me. 'I have absolutely no idea.'

It took us another couple of hours of hard, hot riding to find Karikalan. By the time we pulled into his dusty compound, my kidneys felt swollen and pulpy, like mangoes that had been in a tumble drier for a day or two.

The compound consisted of two open-sided bungalows and a thatched pagoda. Palm trees had been placed at discreet intervals and were bordered with decorative circles of clay tiling. Three boys lingered about in the shade, machine guns by their side. One of them showed Mano and me to the pagoda, where we were served tea and cupcakes.

Ten minutes later, Karikalan rode in on his motorbike, his bodyguard riding pillion. Karikalan looked pretty harmless – a plump man with a pear-shaped face and square glasses. It was his bodyguard I was worried about. A young guy dressed in black baggy pants and a golf shirt, he was packing a personal arsenal that included an M16 automatic rifle, two grenades, a knife, a walkie-talkie, several ammo packs and a very unhappy expression. He eyed me curtly, slinging his gun around like my nephew with an old GameBoy. From a cord around his neck dangled a small white vial – 'the *kuppi*,' Mano explained, or cyanide capsule.

Karikalan took a seat in the pagoda. He was polite and spoke in a small, high voice. I started by asking him about the Black Tigers, those involved in suicide missions. All of them, men and women, said Karikalan, were volunteers. 'And we have more volunteers than we can cope with.'

'To become Black Tigers,' he explained, 'cadre must apply in writing to our leader, Mr Velupillai Prabhakaran. He then goes through the applications, looking at the applicant's particular skills, the kinds of missions he or she has been on, their motivations, and their family situation. Are they an only son or daughter? Do they have dependents? All these things are considered, after which the applicant is told whether he or she can become a Black Tiger.

'The kind of people who apply are extremely motivated, the kind of people who want to create maximum damage to the Sri Lankan state.'

I asked Karikalan why he had joined the movement and he frowned, as if it were something he hadn't considered for a while. 'It was many years ago. I grew up in the country. Right from the start, there were little things that made me aware that we couldn't live with the Sinhalese. For example, our Sinhalese neighbours thought they had a right to stop water getting through to our fields. In the end, I had to go at night and open the sluices to let the water reach our land. I used to get beaten for this. But to me, the choice was clear.'

'Unfortunately,' he added, 'the only thing the Sinhalese understand is violence.'

We talked for almost two hours. But the more Karikalan spoke, the more I found myself lulled by his gentle delivery, his narcotising tone. His answers started sounding rehearsed, so I tried to spike him with accusations of extorting 'war tax', whereby local farmers had to surrender a portion of their rice harvest. I asked him how he felt about child recruitment. I even invoked Osama bin Laden, asking whether the Tigers had any links to al Qaeda. Yet he remained obliging throughout; measured, calm and oddly ambivalent.

Suddenly he rose, without warning. 'I must leave now.' He took my hand in his and nodded toward the cupcakes. 'But please, stay and finish your tea.'

Driving back to Batti, I was overwhelmed by a sense of anti-climax. I'd been hoping for some insights from Karikalan, or some passion, at the least. Instead I got a bureaucrat. Deep down, what I really wanted was to be convinced. In my naïveté, I'd wanted to *believe* in the Tigers. I was looking for a cause, some inspiration, an easy answer, perhaps. But what I'd found was just more hatred, prepackaged and stale. And there's nothing inspiring about that.

On the way back to Batti, we stopped so I could buy a bottle of toddy, a potent drink made from fermented coconut sap. Back at the hotel, while Mano ran errands in town, I took the toddy onto the landing overlooking the lagoon, and quietly and methodically got smashed out of my brain.

Later that night I was woken by a strange noise. At first I

thought it was thunder. How pleasant, I thought, to have some rain to wash away this heat. But then the windowpane above my bed began tinkling – faintly at first, like a chandelier, and then more insistently, until I realised that the thunder wasn't thunder at all but heavy artillery.

Walking out onto the verandah, I stood listening as the barrage intensified. Gut-deep, rolling volleys – *boom-boom, boom-boom, boom-boom* – soon became one long *boomboom-BOOOOOOM*. It was a furious, infantile sound, like some demented child banging an enormous drum just over the horizon. I marvelled at the power of it, swooned even, before realising, almost as an afterthought, that somewhere out there in the thick wet jungle – *right that very moment* – people were probably dying.

I spent a few more days in Batti, tying up some interviews. I talked to human rights workers and community leaders. There was some interesting stuff, but most of it confirmed what little I already knew. The country was a mess. People were unhappy. The situation was complex. What could one do?

The night before I was due to return to Colombo, Batti was attacked again. And again, I watched it unfold from the verandah, tracers looping over the water like fireworks. There was lots of machine-gun fire, so much that I thought the town was being overrun. But I was wrong. 'Sounds much worse than it is,' Mano explained the next morning. 'Whenever the Tigers attack, the soldiers hop in their trucks and race out to where the action is, making sure to shoot off as much ammo as they can, hoping that by the time they arrive the Tigers would have heard them coming and taken off. It's a joke, really.'

When it came time to leave, Mano and I hired a mini-van to take us to Colombo. Sivaram came too; he wanted to visit an editor. The van was more expensive than the bus, but quicker and more comfortable, and we could stop whenever we wanted.

For much of the trip I sat by the window, gazing dumbly at the landscape. Everything passed in a blur. I felt numb, vacant, deflated. What had I learnt about Sri Lanka? What had I learnt about the Tigers? I'd spent six weeks here, and though I'd talked to lots of people, and discovered lots of interesting things, I felt I knew less than when I'd arrived. The complexity and illogic of the place had put a spell on me. Or perhaps I'd been searching for a meaning that didn't exist. I wasn't sure anymore.

Suddenly the van pulled over. 'Look,' said Mano, 'it's an elephant!' Sure enough, there across the plain a big bull elephant was emerging from the jungle fringe, loping through the tall grass about 200 metres away.

I got out to take a photo. Scrambling down the embankment, I slunk toward the creature, hunching in the grass, slowly moving closer. The sun bore down on my back. I moved in 10, 20, then 30 metres. I could see the animal's ears, leathery and wrinkled; his trunk like a pendulum, feet like anvils. My heart was pounding; my breath grew heavy.

'Stay where you are. Don't go any closer!' It was Mano. Looking back, I realised I'd come much further than I thought. 'They're fast. It's dangerous.'

But I wasn't listening anymore. I turned back toward the elephant, and kept on moving closer. I wanted to get every detail. Just for once, I wanted to see things clearly. Taking another step through the hot, dry grass, I stood up, trembling, and raised the camera to my eye.

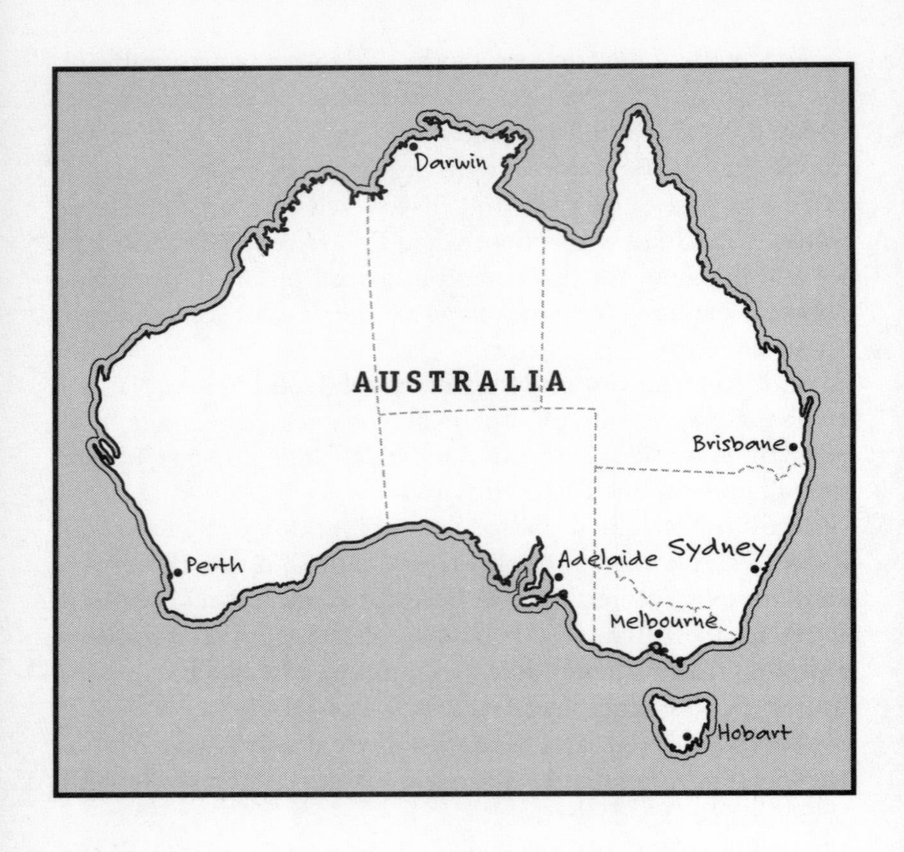
Darwin
AUSTRALIA
Brisbane
Perth
Adelaide
Sydney
Melbourne
Hobart

Country of Love

SARAH MACDONALD

INDIA HAS always exhausted me but now I've lost refuge in the peace of the night. I've begun to take vast journeys in my sleep – trips that take me out of my New Delhi suburb of clanging cowbells and cricket games, beyond this city of bedlam and dust and far from the barrage of a country where one billion lives are lived close. In the first dreams I travelled old haunts; waking sun-tickled from picnics on Italian hillsides or with the bitter-sweet taste of Sri Lankan curd on my lips. Then I began to travel beyond my own being: I dreamed I was a French child crying in frustration during a school exam; I was a tingling teenager squealing down a Disneyland water-slide; I was the lover of Mad King Ludwig, watching as he jumped into the ravines of Liechtenstein. In the last few weeks I've travelled to different dimensions and times; one night I became a vampire and the next I escaped from a futuristic cult where fanatics were lengthening their sex organs with gene technology.

Last night I dreamt I was a flying ET being chased by a zombie alien who could sense me by smell (I escaped by throwing my socks and undies at my pursuer who followed them while I dived into the sea). I woke up today naked, shivering, entirely exhausted and doubtful of my sanity. I dread the thought of an Indian psychiatric hospital but have one hope that the dreams may contain a positive prognosis. I skip breakfast to drudge up the road to the local shopping centre where roadside vendors call from rickety barrows stacked high with boxes. I know I'll quickly find what I need, for the chemist/haberdashery vendor sells everything from anti-dandruff shampoo to zippers (I swear if you asked for a smuggled pack of Viagra he could produce it with little fanfare). I stumble and whisper as I talk to the bloke in the tight black jeans and spotless lab coat. He beams, claps his hands, grabs a small box covered in American flags and hands it to me with a yell that the entire suburb can hear.

'This American best! And madam, please allow me to say best of luck for positive yeses.'

The Indian-made 'American best' packet instructs me to 'wait for the first morning passing'. So the next day, after waking from a gruelling battle against intergalactic worms, I stumble to the bathroom to test my urine. But, while waiting the required five minutes for the results, I fall asleep on the toilet and knock the strip into the sink where the clogged plughole ensures the results of my efforts are washed away. I revisit the stallholder, who seems even more enthusiastic than yesterday. I scurry away from his yells of 'good lucks' with the little box wrapped up in my shawl.

The next morning I try again. This time I manage to stay awake as a faint pink stain forms on the litmus paper. I hold my breath and lean on the sink, for I can sense that this little line divides my life in two. As confirmation of my pregnancy seeps into my consciousness I feel all the water within surge and wash me in a wave of desire. I suddenly ache to breathe

the air of my childhood, to be surrounded by the familiarity of family and friends and to be in a place that I understand.

I want to go home.

As the desire to leave India grows, I shrink from the farewell parties and sink further and further into my world of dreams. Not just because I feel a daily exhaustion akin to being run over by a truck, not just because sleep is suddenly more attractive than food, but also because I sense my nightly journeys are helping to liberate me from the desire to travel physically. Perhaps they are kindly preparing me for a very different journey of vastly different parameters.

This was planned. I feel ready to embrace parenthood. I'm 35, I've found the right guy, and after two and a half years travelling throughout the subcontinent I'm ready to stand still. My journeys around India's spiritual supermarket have cured me of restlessness and reduced my ambition for career success. By coming close to death and disease, by witnessing lives of both terrible loss and outrageous wealth and by becoming infected with the country's irrepressible enthusiasm, I have a new appreciation for the sanctity of life. And I feel the country itself has been the perfect training ground for motherhood. Here I have learnt to cede control to a power greater than myself. I have learnt to submit to fate. I have learnt to embrace the simple things that make life worth living. Isn't that what mothers do? What's more, in India children are adored as mini-gods and while this means a great number of the richer ones turn out to be brats, I sense that such a basic and emotional form of worship is one that may be easy to embrace.

A month later, my husband Jonathan, my foetus and I fly into an Australia washed clean with our hopes for a new life. It's as if the landscape rises to greet us; the grass seems so green, the sky so large and blue, the light so strong. My country looks fertile and fecund and I dig in deep to let it enrich me. I sleep in my childhood bed; its small lumpy mattress contoured to my essential being; I walk around the parks I roamed freely in my youth and I let the laziness powered by familiarity and sleepy hormones soften my ways. Not even the bizarre first sighting of my child on the ultrasound can dent my new sense of wellbeing (it's a small space prawn that looks like the alien that had chased me across the skies in my dream).

After the morning sickness subsides I become hyperactive with energy. We move to a rented flat by the sea and I prowl along paths that bend around headlands, dip deeply into beaches and clamber up cliffs. I spend hours in the local graveyard, strolling between white angels outlined starkly against the blue sky. Here, the new life within me twists and turns, as if responding to forces emanating from the old life littered below. With limitless power I mark the territory where my child will grow up.

The last three months are more difficult. I feel I am about to burst, the acid of my stomach sits in my throat and Sydney loses some of its initial shine as its obsessions come to feel strangely alienating. In India we felt blessed, wealthy and lucky, but here we feel as if we have been left behind in the great race for real estate. Most agents treat us with contempt and, as my stomach expands and our desperation grows, they seem to thrive on our vulnerability. We cannot find anything we can afford, yet feel powerless to walk away from the disgusting scene as we are both full of desire to build a nest for our child. Jonathan takes the endless rejections and auction losses more acutely than I; as the man, he feels it is his job to provide the home. I would laugh at his sudden traditional bent, but I am softened by his desire to be part of the baby-growing process. There are times when we wonder how we can so quickly have forgotten what's most important.

The month before I am due we find a little semi that's liveable and buy it more out of a desire to stop shopping than a total love for its look. But we are happy with it; it's in a neighbourhood we like, there is a good local school up the road and we can walk to the sea that we missed so much in desert-locked New Delhi. We cannot afford to live in it so we rent it out and put all our energy into preparing to become parents. I am gripped with a desire to clean, yet because I can hardly move I force Jonathan up ladders, into the back corners of cupboards and down drains.

Then, I give birth to a book. *Holy Cow!* is a travel book and a personal memoir about modern India's many paths of enlightenment, from Bollywood to Buddhism and beyond. It's not a guidebook; the India depicted can only be my own and I therefore feel bound to reveal myself as a storyteller. While I'm willing to share my stories and my vulnerabilities, the audacity in presuming people will want to hear them fills me with a desire to disappear into a dark hole. Thankfully, most readers respond with affection, warmth and love. With a part of myself circulating through such a welcome society I find permission for a joyful retreat from the world. I even make the first sacrifice of parenthood without too much bitter complaint – turning down an appearance on 'Good Morning Australia' with Bert Newton that's too close to my due date to make flying to Melbourne safe. I lie in shallow pools of water and wait for my life to change. I sleep and I sleep and I sleep.

And then the dreams stop.

At five one perfect Sydney summer morning, green parrots with chests of fire-red dance in a tree outside our window. They sing me awake to the feeling of a dull ache. Faced with the moment I have anticipated for so long, I feel suddenly unwilling to take the leap ahead, I have a cup of tea and toast and try to go back to sleep. For three hours I live in total denial. After every contraction finishes, I pretend it never happened. Even when they are coming in crashing waves that wrench me up into the air and then throw me onto my face, dumping again just as I manage to pull myself onto my knees, I turn to Jonathan and say, 'Let's go out for lunch'.

When the hospital firmly suggests we come in, I insist on washing my hair. It's only when I am in the back of the car, up on all fours, panting like a panther and I see the shock and fear on the face of the man driving behind us do I realise I really am in labour. I'll spare you the gory details of the next few hours except to say that there is a warm bath, lemonade icy-poles, ear-splitting screams and a hysterical request for an epidural as the baby's head emerges. Later, of course, I insist I was only joking.

A few hours on, I have stopped shaking and marvelling at the miracle, my baby and I are clean and Jonathan, the midwives and my family have left. I pick up my child and sit and stare at her for a long time. Perhaps it's the hormones, perhaps it's a trick of the light, but the puffy, squashed and slightly battered face of the half-alien, half-angel is undoubtedly the most glorious and exquisite thing I have ever seen. She opens her eyes and stares back at me, alert and calm. And in that look, I sense that this tiny new being knows me, she knows the past and she knows the future. She knows the secrets of creation. A wave of fear and a convulsion of thrill sweep my body, mixing with a heady cocktail of adrenalin and hormones. I feel myself utterly surrender to the tiny world I hold crooked within my elbow.

As a summer heatwave bakes and buckles the streets outside, I trudge down hospital corridors feeling sore and stretched, yet elated with achievement. I wheel before me sleeping perfection, tied tight with cotton wraps, held down with blankets and enclosed in a plastic capsule. We attend classes about sleep, about back pain, about breastfeeding and about preserving the pelvic floor, but all the talk washes over me as do the gasps of visitors, the tears of mothers suffering from cracked nipples and the constant phone calls. All I can see is her. I can't take my eyes off her sweet swollen head and red pursed lips and I can't tune to any sound that doesn't emanate from her helpless little body.

As Sydney becomes brutalised by bushfires, I, too, undergo a plundering of sorts. Yet I remain detached even from the most intimate intrusions; watching unblinking as a midwife prods my stomach (which has settled into the consistency of unrisen bread dough), as another inspects my stitches and a third pinches my breast into the shape of a hamburger. It's as if my body, long possessed in pregnancy, is now utterly claimed. I as a single entity no longer exist. I am she. And she is me. And, as the Beatles sing, 'we are altogether'. For she may be out of my body, but I know she is still a part of me. And will be for life. My every moment belongs to her. I am a slave to her mastery. Days ago, this realisation would have terrified me, but now I feel an almost catatonic contentment. I am utterly changed.

After three nights the hospital puts on a farewell dinner. As the babies sleep in the nursery, the fathers drink champagne and we mothers sit on cushions (even those who had to have caesareans or were too posh to push). A mother at the next table tells us she's demanded to stay another night.

'It's outrageous! They keep telling me different things to do. I'm not ready to go,' she rants and we laugh quietly at her neurosis. But the next morning we feel just like she does.

'How can they let us just take her?' Jonathan whispers to me as the nurses wave us goodbye.

'God knows, but hurry up before they change their minds,' I whisper back, pushing him down the hall. I too feel manifestly unprepared for life with a tiny newborn baby; I just don't want anyone to know about my ignorance. Breastfeeding is an entirely new skill that requires training, supervision and intense practice, I have no idea what her strange rattling breathing means and I have yet to learn the language of her different squawks. The midwives confidently handle my baby like she is a football, burp her like she's a set of bagpipes and can tell at 50 paces whether the look on her face means tiredness or wind. While I'd once assumed motherhood came naturally, the stay in hospital has made me feel less confident about the journey ahead. Perhaps motherhood is, in some ways, a profession that needs to be taught, learned and practised, and yet there is no guidebook, no trainers and no performance pay. Besides, I'm in no state to learn all there is to know in three days. Perhaps that's because I've never liked being packaged into an organised tour of anywhere, perhaps because I want to set my own path in mapping my child's needs, but mostly because my brain has turned to absolute mush.

If I were Indian I would be returning to a house filled with family. I would be forced into a room, pushed onto a bed and the baby would be brought to me for feedings and sleeps. Mothers, sisters, mother-in-law and aunts would take over everything else. But we are about to return to a little flat on the other side of the city and the country from our families. In our society, we will be cocooned in privacy but isolated. We will have to take this trip alone.

The short trip home seems like a momentous journey; Jonathan drives like a nervous L-plater, and I sit stiff with excitement and trepidation. Suddenly the safe city I love seems full of danger, with its gleaming fast cars, glass shards of the skyscrapers and unpredictable people. Once safely inside our flat I breath a sigh that ends only with a sagging possession of the couch. I refuse to budge until nightfall.

The next day my adventures entail a trip to the window to look at the street below and a journey to sit on a chair for a spell before waddling back to bed. This is all done without ever letting her go. All I want to do is fill up with food and feast on the impossibly endless fascination of her. Days turn to weeks of doing nothing but holding her in my arms, nestling her under my neck, rocking her, kissing her, feeding her, breathing her, consuming her. Jonathan makes endless cups of tea for visitors and in those short moments when our baby is awake we bang heads to share each jerky, staccato movement of limbs. At night I wake to touch her soft skin, to watch her breathing, to kiss her soft downy hair and to feed her every whim. Within weeks she has joined us in the bed, our bond not broken by anything, not even air.

She is three weeks old when I first journey out into the other world.

'Go for a walk! Get out!' Jonathan urges me, on a sparkling Sydney Sunday.

'In India and China they stay in bed for 40 days,' I plead.

'Sarah, come on, move,' he begs, his voice rising to betray increasing fear that I may never return from the land of baby. I relent to keep him happy, craning to peek over his shoulder and catch a last glimpse at her, wrapped tight like a mummy, her little pink face fluttering with sleeping mysteries, or, more likely, wind. I let him push me out the door, drag me down the stairs and release me back into the wild.

I walk in much the same way that an astronaut would take his or her first steps on a never-touched planet. Each foot placed meticulously, each step a triumph, each breath a bonus. I set myself on a course for the beach and arrive with a small sense of triumph. I sink my bare soft feet into the wet sand and stand facing the sea, watching the pounding pull of the waves and letting the salt spray settle on my skin. I see the cigarette-butt-scattered sand and the cliff face's swirl of caramel coloured sandstone. I see the brazen beach umbrellas and the tanned bodies of my neighbours. It all looks reassuringly familiar. But at the same time it all seems so different. It's as if the atoms of everything have been rearranged; as if I have left the planet and returned to a world that now travels on a different trajectory.

And when I turn to walk past the people on the beach it shocks me to find that they are chatting and laughing, swimming and playing volleyball as if nothing has happened. Don't they know that the world has changed? Don't they know my part in it? Why are they ignoring me? Why aren't they approaching me to exclaim, to congratulate or even to worship? For I am mother! I have created! I have given birth! I am a god! I am amazed how estranged I feel from a world I inhabited so comfortably only a month ago. My baby calls me home; my breasts spray milk through my T-shirt and onto the sand and I turn and stumble to the safety and security of her world. Back in the flat, I reclaim my island of bliss.

I refuse to acknowledge the outside world again until my daughter, at five weeks, decides she is ready to join me in it. On New Year's Eve she smiles, acknowledging her father with a wide gummy pink grin that suggests a mischievous spirit. We take this as an indication she is ready to be shown off and we take her to a party. There she lies on a friend's bed, kicking her spindly legs, jerking her little hands and moving her head side to side like Stevie Wonder. I race up and down the stairs to check on her every 10 minutes or so, lingering to be with her, rather than in the company of those gathered below, for I feel awkward amongst the groups of drinking and dancing revellers and I cannot remember how to join in. We are in bed by midnight, oblivious to the fireworks and the start of the New Year.

Fortunately we get a decent sleep, because the next day demands all our energy. Our baby wakes listless and discontent. She cries as she feeds. By night she is dozy and floppy and not responding to me at all. She wakes at midnight and tries to suckle but is too weak and lapses back into a sleep that seems too deep. I begin to hyperventilate with concern. We ring the hospital and a nurse suggests we come immediately.

We drive fast, the air in the car heavy with silent pleadings. I am suddenly keenly aware that I am vulnerable to a degree I never imagined possible. While I spent much of my time in India trying not to be scared of that which I could not control, our child has made me more furiously fearful of disease, disorder and death than I ever imagined possible. The instinct to protect her surges through my veins in violent intensity.

Jonathan's face is set in a grimace that shows he is trying to be brave, but I know he is feeling the same pain. As we pull up to Emergency I lose the will and the ability to hold in my feelings. I cry at reception, I cry for three hours in the waiting room and when they prick her heel for a blood test and she comes alive, screaming in fury, I cry again to mourn her first encounter with cruelty. And when the doctor finally comes and she gives him her second smile ever – the smile I had reserved for myself – I weep. Thankfully, she then shits all over him, which cheers me up no end.

Our baby has a virus from which she quickly recovers, but from that moment she begins to let the imperfect world intrude into her sleepy bliss. She becomes almost too alert, as if life at large is too much to cope with and it overloads her pristine soul. She starts to cry in large patches. One day she begins to grizzle at 10 am and refuses to respond to hugs, feedings or rocking. As lunchtime approaches, Jonathan and I look at each other in increasing panic.

'Is she hungry?' he pleads.

'No, I've just fed her'

'Is she tired?'

'She just slept.'

'Is she scared?'

'How the hell would I know?' I snap at him, infuriated that I can not read my baby's mind.

I rock her, whispering at her in increasing desperation. 'Tell me what's wrong, baby? God I wish you could tell me!'

She's still crying at midday and as the afternoon wears on, the cracked little wail of a lost lamb rises to a bleat like a nanny goat, transforms to a howling hyena and eventually settles in at the decibel of a wailing banshee. I ring a parent help-line, I ring mothers, I ring nurses, I ring doctors and I ring chemists, and they all suggest remedies with a confidence and cheer that makes me want to kill them. We put her in the pram and rock it over a coat hanger (babies are meant to feel soothed by bumps), we put a warm nappy over her stomach, we rub her back; we wheel her in the crib, we sing, we smile, we bath, we rock and eventually we lie down and weep with her. We feel marooned in a sea of tears and too helpless to hope for rescue.

By 5 pm I feel I could die. All I want is for my baby to be happy and all I can achieve is a red-faced fury. Never has a sound cut me so deep. Her cry sounds worse to me than fingernails down a blackboard; more excruciating than talk of real estate at a dinner party; more spine-curling than a late night infomercial. It's a sound that jiggers and cuts me, a noise I would almost kill to silence. And yet I can't walk away from it. As the sun sets and the horizon turns pink, Jonathan turns his red eyes to me and clicks his fingers.

'The sling!' he exclaims, remembering a friend has given us a cotton sling that loops over the head and one arm. I run, wrench the sling from the cupboard, lift it over my head and almost throw her in. The instant her body bends into the cotton she stops screaming. And moving.

'I think I've broken her neck,' I choke. We peer down to a smiling deep sleep and grunting piglet-like sounds of contentment. It's the most beautiful thing.

With equilibrium restored, Jonathan, our baby and I slowly expand our travels; at three months of age she has now seen the shops, the park and even the beach. But we take the days slowly, as if to savour every second. We spend delicious mornings on the island of our bed, making faces, blowing bubbles, singing songs and competing to make her laugh. In the afternoons we stride our suburb with increasing confidence; Jonathan proudly carrying her in the sling; me toddling beside, endlessly checking that her bald head is covered, she peeking over the lip in the cotton to laugh at a change in the traffic lights, stare in wide-eyed wonder at the boys on skateboards and blink in bliss at flickers of a neon sign. Her delight triggers giggles in us that we share like a secret language. We stop to eat gelato, kiss the dimples on her star-like hands and make ourselves dizzy with devotion at the smell of her head. Drunk on her wonder, we together criss-cross the terrain of a new land of love.

I still feel like a traveller unsure of her new surrounds. While the planet no longer feels tilted on its axis, it is undoubtedly changed and I already sense this shift is permanent. For I now see the world through her eyes. Everything seems washed in newness – the blue of the sea seems deeper, the play of light on the waves more sparkly and I see the dizzying majesty of the stars as if for the first time. And yet, in those brief moments when I am apart from my baby, those things that once gave me infinite pleasure are now slightly dulled. The freedom of swimming in the water is marred by an absence of her form and walks along steep cliffs reveal hidden threats. At a snatched dinner, people treat me as the same person I once was, but I feel limbless without her and I have little to say that is not about my baby.

And then Jonathan returns to work as a producer and reporter on the ABC's 'Lateline' show. Like a child facing its first day at school, I am excited by the prospect of independence, yet I feel overwhelmed by the strangeness and the challenge. I sense this marks the end of the idyllic holiday of babyhood and the beginning of a more challenging journey. He delays his departure with a sweet longing to stay in the nest but after he shuts the door, it's me who gulps back the tears. I look at my baby and my tiny world and I again fantasise, for just a moment, about having a map and a guide to the journey of parenthood. I mourn the days of large families; when people had parents who lived next door and non-working siblings. I have never felt so alone and a day ahead has never felt so empty. I am a housewife! And I have no idea what they do. I fill the day with little things; we walk, we eat, we sleep. But at four o'clock disaster strikes: my baby does the most massive poo I've ever seen. Her clothes are covered and a brown smear extends down her legs, up her back and all over her stomach. I stand above her, frozen, for its Jonathan's job to bathe her. It's a job he guards jealously and lovingly as his special time with her and I've never wanted to challenge his joy. But now, as ridiculous as it sounds, I am totally at sea. I ring him to tell him to come home and he patiently reminds me of what I have watched so many times, explaining how to hold her head with my forearm and loop her shoulder between my thumb and middle finger. I hold my breath as I put her in the bath. She laughs and swims – her legs bent like a frog and her body liquid in motion.

With the world of daytime reduced to just she and I, the boundaries of my existence blur further. I become so relaxed about my obsession, and about my new role in the world, that it takes me some time to realise that I have become one of those people that I used to look right through. People who look worn and weary, who sport a ridiculous look of soppy sentimentality and adoration on their faces, and who have soft eyes unfocused on a distant point. New mothers. Yet I am not shocked or challenged by this realisation; for I now know the secret code that mothers live by and the bliss they endure. My body is further unravelling – piling on weight, broadening under the happiness – and I begin to go out with daggy pants, bare of lipstick and in splattered old shirts. I pull my bra open to feed my baby in front of friends and strangers who have never before seen my breasts. I am proud to be a mass of cells that exists to serve her. I am willingly conquered territory, still pliable to my invader. And I feel liberated by my submission and free from the desire to impress anyone but her.

Yet the world of other mothers seems a difficult one to inhabit. I attend a mothers' group run by the local baby health care centre. Twenty women sit in a circle and introduce our babies before we introduce ourselves. Then, as if aware that they are our only bond, we struggle to say anything that is not about our new children. It is a circle of stories that validates, verifies and vanquishes fears, and yet I want more. I am dripping with desire to discuss the universals of motherhood, rather than compare poo times, mothers' wind and husbands' fears, yet I also feel shy about sharing. We are strangers united by coincidence, forced into familiarities and sometimes partial to comparing our children and we soon drift apart. I meet up with other friends who I knew before baby, perhaps subconsciously hoping to preserve a miniscule part of myself that continues to exist.

But as the role of mother continues to claim me, I shrink further from the intrusion of most of the outside world. The former news junkie in me is surprised the first time I turn off the TV news. But the new me does it without thinking. The images of death, disease and disharmony, the rawness of violence and discord, threaten to slice my plastic bubble of optimism. My baby represents my belief in hope over despair and a desire for a future better than the past. Letting the brutality of humanity into our home challenges the foundation of my existence. What's more, I have become overly emotive. I weep at the sight of a child hurt, I shed tears in soap opera dramas, wipe my eyes at nappy ads featuring babies and swell with emotion at Weet-Bix promotions for 'Aussie Kids'. One day when I find myself sobbing in front of 'The Bold and the Beautiful' I begin to fear I may never be able to operate in the other world again.

Friends email from overseas to say they have spotted my book in Switzerland, Germany, America and London. I find it comforting to know that *Holy Cow!* is travelling places I cannot and is living the life that I have lost. And with a part of me still travelling I find greater permission to revel in the triumphs of my new world. I celebrate my baby lifting her head up and smiling at herself in the mirror as major thrills. And I whoop with delight when she discovers her own hand, circling the dimpled star over her face with infinite fascination and then punching herself strongly between the eyes. Days later I am thrilled beyond belief when she manages to plunge her fist into her mouth and ram it so far down her throat that she vomits.

When she is four months old I can no longer keep the other world at bay. The U.S. invades Iraq and the ripples of violence, displacement and destruction wash up on our sheltered shore when Jonathan is sent off to cover the war. He is assigned to the Coalition Central Command in Qatar; a place he tells me is so distant from the fighting that its greatest danger is death by buffet at the hotel. Yet when he tells me he is going I am dumfounded at his betrayal.

'Why on earth do you want to go?' I ask, incredulous.

'I'm interested. It's a war. Someone has to tell us what's happening,' he explains perfectly reasonably, yet I look at him aghast, as if I am not sure who he is and what he is talking about. Our attitudes to the war bring the difference in our lives into sharp relief. Jonathan is still a member of the workforce and a participant in life, while I am lost in the private universe of baby. Not only can I not come close to understanding his desire to engage with the war, I simply cannot fathom how he could leave our beautiful baby to do so. In fact, I can't understand how he could leave her for anything at all. I can't be away from her for more than an hour without feeling the pull of her soft face, without my breasts weeping milk, without picturing her hands, without my ears ringing with the echo of her cry. As Jonathan pulls away in the taxi I shake my head at the new differences between us.

For the next month my baby becomes my everything; my 24-hours-a-day, seven-days-a-week, constant companion. Our emotions become further linked; if she is fractious I feel cranky; if she is tired I sleep; if she gets a fright my heart leaps; if she gurgles I giggle and when she laughs we enter our own universe of mirth. She begins to hold my finger in her hand as she feeds from me, forming a circle of connection safe from the interference of others.

Yet after a few weeks, the constancy of her demands, the lack of air between us and the smallness of our journeys begins to yoke me. I long for Jonathan's other perspective and presence; I feel shut in and weighed down with her demands. She decides that this is the perfect time for a clingy phase and cries if I leave the room. One day I leave her with my mother to go to the supermarket and I rush through the aisles driven by the fear that she will wake up before I return. I ring home from the cash register to hear her screams in the background of my Mum's reassurance that all is well.

'It's not like I'm having fun or getting a massage or doing anything for myself,' I wail to the check-out chick.

'Sweetie,' she says patting me on the hand as she gives me my change, 'when you do something fun they scream even harder.'

The next week I am scheduled to appear in a public debate that will be broadcast on the radio. This is a worry. I have not been in front of an audience for months; the expanding body I now occupy is one that I feel more comfortable in at home and my brain does not feel equipped to engage in the world of ideas, discourse and judgment. Yet I am more nervous about her performance than my own. To avoid a night of hell for my mother (who I have been treating rather better since I realised with heinous embarrassment all she did for me when I was a baby), I take my child with me. I put her to sleep in the pram and a friend who adores her stays with her in a quiet room downstairs from the debating stage. But halfway through my address I sense she is awake. I can feel her distress rise through the concrete ceiling and seep into my feet, climbing up to my hands and face. I begin to shake as I read my notes. When I finish I jump from the stage and run down the stairs to find my daughter, screaming and kicking, her fury beyond belief. I pick her up and hold her to my chest whispering, pleading and begging her forgiveness.

'Shh, shhh, I'm so sorry, I'm sorry, it's all right, it'll be all right. Mummy's here, I'll never leave you. I'll never leave you.'

As she falls asleep I begin to sob out of sympathy, guilt and shame. I feel heavy with the responsibility of being the only one she wants and it occurs to me that I have lost all my independence. I can no longer act selfishly and spontaneously. I cannot learn to sky-dive, take a trip to Mozambique or join a religious cult. And, despite the fact that I've never wanted to do those things, the knowledge that she restricts me seems oppressive for the first time. For I know I will never act with a total freedom and abandonment to my self ever again.

I grow desperate for some personal space. As if sensing this, desiring to prove her power, my baby reduces her daytime sleeps to 45-minute snatches. I only have time for a cup of tea and one load of the endless washing before she wakes. The only way she sleeps longer is if I take her for a drive. A week before Jonathan returns I become so desperate for an hour to myself that I drive to Wollongong. She sleeps deep and long. I am in bliss. I listen to the radio, sing along to a CD and have animated conversations with myself. As I re-enter Sydney, the traffic slows and she stirs. I am not ready for company. I run three orange lights to avoid stopping and when I am forced to stop at a red light I roll the car back and forth to keep it in motion. A police car pulls up beside me.

'What are you doing love?' a young cop yells from his window on the passenger side.

'Shhhhhhhhhhhhhh,' I snap at him, holding my finger to my lips. 'I'm trying to keep my baby asleep and if you wake her I'll bloody kill you.'

It takes the policeman a moment to close his mouth before he reaches for the door to get out and charge me. His partner in the driver's seat grabs his arm.

'Leave her,' he says. 'Mine's the same, love,' he yells across his confused colleague. 'It's bloody killing us.'

They drive off. I mouth silent thanks to the god of small babies. If they had pulled me over I think I would have driven off and let them give chase rather than let her wake up.

When Jonathan returns I reclaim sleep and they take long walks on the winter beach. She strides forward from his chest, bundled in a blue bear suit facing the ocean, letting him steer her hands around the world. They come home to wake me with cold noses and cackles. We celebrate her achievements as our own; screaming with glee when she sucks her toes, rolls over, walks while holding onto the furniture and kisses her reflection in a mirror. I feel my face settle back into that of a besotted new parent – doughy with love and pride.

For a couple of months our life is again complete. Then, when she is seven months old, we strike one of the icebergs of babyhood, a disaster that threatens to sink all enjoyment of our adventure. The horrors begin, innocuously enough, with the discovery of the letter p.

One day our baby wakes at two to lie in the dark reciting: 'p, p, P P P P P.'

We are initially thrilled, but after half an hour not so enchanted. The next night we wake to the letter b. And stay awake to the letter b for two hours. On the third night she produces a pterodactyl-like scream which she finds so deliciously funny she insists on working to perfect it until daylight. The next night we lie awake moaning as she claps her hands over and over and over again and the night after that grimace through her display of thigh-slapping. The night after that she recites 'dada' until her Dada demands we move her out of our room. And then on the seventh night, the one that we pray will be the night of rest, she wakes and demands her audience. When I pull her into the bed and try to quieten her she yanks my hair, tries to dance on my chest and climbs up on my shoulders. Jonathan and I clutch each other in horror. We take turns with endless hours of patting, rocking, singing. I feed her endlessly. To no avail. She continues to party on. We even try playing dead – pretending to be asleep while she jumps on our heads. Friends that knew the old me laugh when I tell them our child peaks at 3 am, but we have lost our sense of humour. We begin a battle of wills and a parents' journey into exhaustion, frustration, fury and desperation. Together we enter the world of the sleep-obsessed.

My baby has become my India. A place, an experience and a journey that pushes me to my limits of endurance and that strips me bare to expose my most essential being. For she and India share a maddening raft of complexities, mysteries and contradictions and they both speak an entirely different language than mine. Until now this has brought out the best in me, but now, as she stops sleeping, she begins to bring out the worst. After three weeks of days that begin at 2 am, my left eye develops a permanent pulsating tick. I become so tired all I can talk about is sleep, so tired I dread going to bed at night, knowing that she will pull me from my slumber and rip into my passionate embrace of the pillow, so tired I wander in a jet-lag-like haze, unsure of what I am doing, what day it is and where I am going. I begin to dream again – but only when I'm awake – and then I dream I'm asleep. In the pre-dawn winter hours I find my beloved baby increasingly infuriating. After a month of sleep deprivation I understand why it's such an effective torture method. I want to give in to my interrogator but she just wants to play. And so, one night, I hear my voice, thick with exhaustion, whisper threats and then veiled screams. I watch her laugh in my worn, withered face. And suddenly, I am seized by an infinite fury.

'Go to sleep you little shit!' I bellow, raising my hand to slap her.

In the half-light I can see my child looking at me, astonished. She begins to laugh but I am shattered by my betrayal. Eventually she crashes out, but the guilt consumes me until dawn. Self-hatred seizes my heart. I am a bad mother.

As I reach out for help I discover that in our society, the journey of motherhood has two distinct paths. There is a vast chasm between these paths and I search endlessly for a bridge. The rift represents the difference between the parent-centred and the child-centred parents: the control-criers versus the attachment babies. Attachment parents continue to wear their babies in a sling in the day, demand feed, let their babies suckle to slumber, encourage them to sleep in the parental bed and comfort them when they are distressed. Controlled crying advocates believe a baby can and should sleep through the night from six months. They put the baby in a cot in its own room and leave it to cry, returning at set times to comfort by patting but never picking up. These parents and the baby health care experts inform me that I am an attachment parent and my style is failing. They assure me that two to three nights of one-to-two-hour blocks of crying will cure my child's sleep problems and reward me with 12-hour sleep sessions. I am indecisive and nervous about choosing a path; torn between the need to set boundaries and the desire to let my baby live a perfect existence with all her needs met as long as possible. I am aware that in India they would think controlled crying barbaric.

So I struggle on. I try homeopathic sleep drops, I run her ragged in a baby gym (which gives her more nocturnal moves to practice on my head); I put her on solids, I take her off solids, I try magic, I consider voodoo. My baby continues to behave like a Duracell toy that will not give up. I become a fraught, fat zombie – exposing my parlous state to others by unwittingly posing for a newspaper photo wearing my pyjama pants. The public humiliation just further highlights my feelings of low self-esteem and my isolation, for this year, babies are the new black. Everyone who is anyone is having or buying a baby: Madonna has Rocco, Sarah Jessica Parker is glowing about her bundle of joy, Angelina Jolie has a little Cambodian boy with a mohawk and Reese Witherspoon has given birth to her second. I begin to hate these glowing, spunky women with their full-time nannies, their gym instructors, their plastic surgeons, their fashion stylists and their ability to go out at night. It is obvious that their babies sleep, or if they don't, that these glamour mothers rarely get up to them.

Yet it isn't the burning of my *Who Weekly* magazines that makes me finally call in the cavalry. It isn't the fact that I am incapable of appearing lucid and engaged with the world and cancel the few outside activities I've maintained in my life. (Although I am bitterly disappointed that I have to can an appearance at a writers' festival and some other book projects that would have given me some sense of self, some well-needed contact with the outside world and some engagement with others.) It's not even the embarrassing incident where I burst into a flood of tears and fall into the arms of a strange man when I'm too tired and brain-dead to fold my pram in the park. It's the night I attend my school reunion. I have not been out at night for many months and my desire to have a drink, to talk to people who live outside my suburb and to travel to the city burns like the wish of a 17-year-old to have sex, or a 20-year-old saving hard to go overseas. As the sun sets I make increasingly frantic calls in the style of a party-animal searching for a fix.

'Have you got anything I can use tonight?' I whisper furtively onto the answering machines of friend after friend. Finally, at six, a mate opens her door with a conspiratorial smile. She is a doctor and a parent and she knows what I need. She presses a vial into my hand and recommends a dose. I back out of her house, giggling hysterically, glancing over my shoulder. Dangerous thoughts and excitement course through my veins.

'I can't believe I'm doing this!' I squeal.

She bundles me into my car, laughing at my innocence. 'Don't worry. Everyone does it sooner or later. Everyone. Believe me, I know. I'm a doctor.'

I drug my child to sleep with a dose of baby cough medicine and I travel into the other world for a visit.

The next morning I realise this behaviour is ridiculous. I also remember that all I talked about all night long was my baby's inability to sleep. I suspect my old school buddies thought I was stark, raving mad. What's worse, I am boring all my current friends to death with minute details of my night waking; I even begin boring myself. Soon after, several friends ambush me in the park. It's an intervention. Six women stand in a circle that I cannot escape and they recite the magic chant.

'Karitane!'

The word flies from their lips and echoes around the park. As it fades away on the wind, women across the suburb prick up their ears and cross their hearts and bow their heads in silent reverie. For Karitane is the blessed organisation that assists parents and babies with everything from sleeping and feeding difficulties to pattern-setting to beating bewilderment.

'It's the mothers' saviour and you have to go,' states one friend.

'It's for her good. You are going crazy,' recites the next.

'To get in, you will have to say you are even worse than you are,' warns the third.

'Ramp it up or it's a six-week waiting list,' demands the fourth.

'Listen, motherhood is 90 per cent drudgery and 10 per cent pure unadulterated bliss. You're not even getting that,' points out the fifth.

'Do it or we'll bloody kill you,' blurts out the bluntest.

So I ring the local health nurse and make an appointment at the baby health care clinic. But I am so tired and emotional I overdo the pathos and am sent for a test for post-natal depression. I visit a young, single male psychiatric intern and tell him about the last month of my life. He looks at me wide-eyed and obviously terrified at the prospect of ever having a child.

'God, you don't need drugs, you need to sleep,' he says, as he dismisses my case and dials a number. After booking himself a vasectomy he rings Karitane to see if I can be referred fast, but I am only one of many desperate, tired women and I can not escape the waiting list.

Six weeks later, my body racked with chronic exhaustion, my mind in a fugue-like state of fatigue, my baby and I enter baby boot camp.

In India I survived an extreme meditation camp. For 10 days I did not talk, write, interact with others, or do anything at all except sit and meditate. Karitane is the absolute opposite to Vipassana. For seven days I am to endure anything but silence and inner peace. I have to embrace a camp of concentrated screams, corridors of crying and internal turmoil. At Karitane I am taught how to let my baby cry. I am supervised as I put her in the cot and leave the room and then watched so I don't return to her before a certain interval. As a mothercraft nurse stands beside me, I wait for one minute, three minutes and then five before going into comfort my baby. I cannot wait for 10 and none of them are strong enough to make me. Standing outside the door of my child's room and listening to her cry is the hardest thing I've ever done. It goes against every fibre of my being. My body strains to be with her. The blood beats loudly in my head. I cry for the shame, I cry for her pain, and I cry for her broken spirit. I mourn the fact that I am teaching her that there will be times where I cannot help her and that life is not perfect. The guilt is palpable.

I awake every morning with a sore throat, body punched and exhausted by grief.

The other mothers smile at my sadness. They clearly enjoy the sense of control sleep gives them and their babies learn fast. Of course mine proves the most stubborn. After a week at baby boot camp the other babies are sleeping soundly from seven at night until seven in the morning. My baby still wakes a few times but she does learn to go back to sleep until 5 am

She is eating better and less grumpy during the day. I sense success. I drive home shamefully elated. She has a pattern! A routine! I am in control! I am once again a master of my life's journey!

She must have heard me.

She sleeps at home for one night and then begins to wake again. I ring the Karitane help-line and the nurse tells me to keep going. The next night, she repeats the message. On the third night she sternly warns me that their methods don't always work. On the fourth night of yelling I am beyond all consolation. I am so frustrated and confused I began to hit myself in punishment. Jonathan and I fight in whispers.

'It's not working.'

'Give it time.'

'We're torturing her.'

'We're not.'

'The neighbours!'

'Don't worry about them.'

Finally I yell, 'Enough!' I pick my baby up and carry her into our bed. She tucks herself into my neck, hiccups snot all over my chest and falls fast asleep. When she wakes a few hours later, she sighs, pats me and returns to slumber. I feel pinned, trapped and tied down by her desire to be near or on me all night, but as I look at her sleeping form I melt with bliss. For when she is asleep I will forgive her anything. The stunning sight of her bottom in the air, her soft cheeks flushed pink, her lips pursed in a bow, her warm breath on my neck and her fluttering eyelid on my cheek is nothing short of perfection in pyjamas.

And now she is two. Thanks to pregnancy dreams, pregnancy bladder and the fact she still wakes every few hours for a comforting pat it's been nearly three years since I've slept all night. Still, I swell with love as I watch her draw 'Mummy', see the curl at the back of her neck bob as she jumps into a puddle and have her welcome me home with a lisping 'hello ttthweetie-pie'. I am full of pride at the way she blows kisses to the moon, waves to strangers and gives other children toys. I spend hours watching her skip with a lurch and trot that is reminiscent of a cross between an angel and a drunk. I am still endlessly seized by convulsions of adoration and passion for her.

She is undoubtedly my greatest achievement; although I know that in most ways I had little to do with what she is and what she will become. She has taken me on an endless journey to worlds of possibility and joy. She has reduced my life to a tiny circle of infinite love and responsibility and pushed me to my outer limits of pain, endurance, patience and passion. And just recently, I have started to travel again. Not by day – unless you include a radius of playgroup, park, the shopping centre and casual work shifts at the ABC. But by night. The strange dreams have come back. I am again leaving my body and my life to roam far and wide around the universe of the subconscious. For I am soon to take another journey with another baby. To take another expedition that will confine me to a small nest; that will narrow my mind but broaden my heart; that will send me on a passionate trip to unrecognisable galaxies of existence. To embark on another journey that will never end.

About the Authors

TONY DAVIS

Tony Davis works at *The Sydney Morning Herald*. He is the author of *Lemon! Sixty Heroic Failures of Motoring* and he is presently working on an idiosyncratic memoir about writing a novel in Paris.

NICK EARLS

Nick Earls is the author of two collections of short stories and eight novels, including *Zigzag Street*, *Bachelor Kisses* and *Perfect Skin*. His latest novel is *The Thompson Gunner*. His work has been adapted successfully for theatre, and film and TV adaptations are underway. He lives in Brisbane and is published internationally in English and in translation.

TIM ELLIOTT

Tim Elliott is a journalist and author whose work has appeared in London's *The Financial Times*, *The Sunday Times*, *The Sydney Morning Herald*, *The Australian Financial Review* and *The South China Morning Post*. His first book, *The Bolivian Times*, is an account of six months he spent working on an English-language paper in South America. He is currently writing a book about Spain.

NIKKI GEMMELL

Nikki Gemmell has written four novels: *Shiver*, *Cleave*, *Lovesong* and *The Bride Stripped Bare*. Her work has been internationally critically acclaimed and translated into many languages. Born in Wollongong, Australia, she now lives in London.

CHRISTOPHER KREMMER

Christopher Kremmer is the author of *The Carpet Wars: A Journey Across the Islamic Heartlands* and *Bamboo Palace: Discovering the Lost Dynasty of Laos*. His story is a fictional memoir.

SARAH MACDONALD

Sarah Macdonald is a radio broadcaster, television presenter, journalist and commentator best known for her work at the ABC's Triple J radio station where she hosted the Morning Show, Arts Program and covered political events in Canberra. Sarah also appeared on 'Recovery', 'Race Around the World' and 'Two Shot' on ABC Television. She wrote *Holy Cow! An Indian Adventure* in 2002. Sarah now works as a casual presenter at ABC Radio's 702 and Radio National.

IRRIS MAKLER

Irris Makler is the author of *Our Woman in Kabul* and a foreign correspondent currently based in Jerusalem, where she covers the Israel–Palestine conflict, as well as the conflict in Iraq, for broadcasters all over the world. Previously she was based in Russia, including as the ABC's Moscow correspondent. That's where she had the experiences described in this book.

PETER MOORE

Peter Moore is an author from Sydney who has been described as 'the Australian Bill Bryson'. His books include *The Wrong Way Home*, which saw him travelling overland from London to Sydney, *Swahili for the Broken-hearted*, an account of a journey from Cape Town to Cairo, and *Vroom with a View*, where he went in search of Italy's *dolce vita* on a 1961 Vespa. At last count he had visited 93 countries and written six books. When he is not travelling he can be found in either Sydney or London watching 'Neighbours'. For more information about Peter – and pictures from all his trips – visit his website at www.petermoore.net.

CAROLINE OVERINGTON

Caroline Overington has been the New York correspondent for *The Sydney Morning Herald* and *The Age* since March 2002. Prior to that, she was a sports writer. Prior to that, she waited tables, picked avocados, and once had a job on an assembly line in a plastics factory, trimming sharp edges from drinking cups. She lives in Manhattan with her husband, Martin, and two children, Michael and Chloe.

ANNETTE SHUN WAH

Annette Shun Wah is an author, actor and television and radio producer and presenter. Her extensive career credits include SBS TV programs 'Imagine', 'The Noise' and 'Eat Carpet', and a range of documentaries, live telecasts and weekly series for ABC TV including 'The Big Picture', 'Studio 22' and 'Media Dimensions'. She is a regular contributor to *The Sydney Morning Herald*, and she serves on the advisory panels of both the Sydney Asia Pacific Film Festival and Theatre 4A. Annette is the co-author of *Banquet – Ten Courses to Harmony*.